THE GAY RIGHTS QUESTION IN CONTEMPORARY AMERICAN LAW

ANDREW KOPPELMAN

THE GAY RIGHTS QUESTION IN CONTEMPORARY AMERICAN LAW

THE UNIVERSITY OF CHICAGO PRESS • CHICAGO AND LONDON

ANDREW KOPPELMAN is associate professor of law and
political science at Northwestern University. He is the author
of *Antidiscrimination Law and Social Equality* (1996).

The University of Chicago Press, Chicago 60637
The University of Chicago Press, Ltd., London
© 2002 by The University of Chicago
All rights reserved. Published 2002
Printed in the United States of America
11 10 09 08 07 06 05 04 03 02   1 2 3 4 5

ISBN: 0-226-45100-3 (cloth)
ISBN: 0-226-45101-1 (paper)

Library of Congress Cataloging-in-Publication Data

Koppelman, Andrew.
  The gay rights question in contemporary American law /
Andrew Koppelman.
      p.   cm.
  Includes bibliographical references and index.
    ISBN 0-226-45100-3 (cloth : alk. paper)—
  ISBN 0-226-45101-1 (pbk. : alk. paper)
      1. Gays—Legal status, laws, etc.—United States. I. Title.

KF4754.5 .K67 2002
346.7301'3—dc21   2001057454

For Kitty and Melvin, who made it personal

CONTENTS

ACKNOWLEDGMENTS

More friends than I can name have helped me with this book over the past decade and a half. Many of them have already been thanked in the articles (enumerated below) from which portions of this book are drawn, and I incorporate those acknowledgements by reference. A complete enumeration would be much longer.

During the preparation of this manuscript, the assistance of Chris Cedillo, Mark Hamill, and Michael Hasday was invaluable, as were the indispensable skills of Marcia Lehr, reference librarian at Northwestern University School of Law. My secretary, Jane Brock, provided extensive help. The entire manuscript was read by William Eskridge, Jr., Arthur Leonard, and John Tryneski, all of whom made very helpful suggestions.

Chapter 2 received valuable comments at a workshop at the University of Chicago, especially those of Douglas Baird, Eric Posner, and Adrian Vermeule. Thanks also to Henry Cohen for his assistance.

Chapter 3 benefited from the comments of Mary Anne Case, Robert Wintemute, and Iris Marion Young, and from conversations with John Gardner, Richard Posner, and Jim Speta. Earlier versions were presented at the American Philosophical Association Eastern Division meeting, Washington, D.C., December, 1998, and the Freedom to Marry conference, Harvard Law School, February, 1999. Special thanks to Edward Stein, whose paper at the American Philosophical Association provoked me to write the first draft.

The discussion of the new natural law theory in chapter 4 was read with care by Robert P. George, who rescued me from numerous errors. Carlos Ball and Janice Nadler also provided valuable assistance.

A disclosure: during the trial in *Romer v. Evans*, a case that I discuss extensively in chapter 1, I advised the plaintiffs' attorneys and agreed to be listed as a potential expert witness on the plaintiffs' side, but was never called to testify.

Research on this book began while I was a graduate student at Yale University. The work has, at various times, received support from Princeton University, the Harvard Program in Ethics and the Professions, the University of Texas School of Law, and Northwestern University. A research leave and numerous research grants from

Northwestern University School of Law made it possible to complete the manuscript. I owe special thanks to Northwestern and its dean, David Van Zandt, for unstinting research support.

Valerie, Miles, and Gina not only provided constant support but, more importantly, helped keep this work in perspective.

The entire book has benefited from the enormous outpouring of scholarship on the gay rights issue that has emerged in the past two decades. The articles from which this book is drawn contain extensive citations to that scholarship, which are largely omitted here. Specialists interested in my engagement with the literature should consult those articles.

Some chapters in this book are revised (in one case, entirely rewritten) versions of previously published articles, and I am grateful to the publishers for permission to use that material in this volume. An earlier version of chapter 1 appeared as *Romer v. Evans* and Invidious Intent, 6 Wm. & Mary Bill of Rights J. 89 (1997); reprinted by permission of the William & Mary Bill of Rights Journal. Portions of chapter 2 appeared in Why Gay Legal History Matters, 113 Harv. L. Rev. 2035 (2000); copyright © 2000 by the Harvard Law Review Association, reprinted by permission of the Harvard Law Review. Portions of chapter 4 appeared in Is Marriage Inherently Heterosexual?, 42 Am. J. Juris. 51 (1997); reprinted by permission of the American Journal of Jurisprudence. An earlier version of chapter 5 appeared as Same-Sex Marriage, Choice of Law, and Public Policy, 76 Tex. L. Rev. 921 (1998); copyright © 1998 by Texas Law Review, reprinted by permission of the Texas Law Review. An earlier version of chapter 6 appeared as Dumb and DOMA: Why the Defense of Marriage Act Is Unconstitutional, 83 Iowa L. Rev. 1 (1997); reprinted by permission of the Iowa Law Review.

INTRODUCTION

It used to be worse. Law no longer strives to hound gays to the margins of society, as it did in the 1950s. Still, gays endure many legal disabilities. Eighteen states criminalize sodomy between consenting adults, and six of them target same-sex sodomy. Several have created express presumptions against custody for gay parents, and three officially prohibit gays from adopting. The armed forces officially exclude gays, and some states formally or informally exclude them from employment as teachers, police officers, or even firefighters. Several states require schools to teach that same-sex intimacy is unacceptable. Antidiscrimination laws that prohibit gender stereotyping and sexual harassment have been interpreted to give no protection to gays. And, of course, gays are everywhere forbidden to marry each other.[1]

The gay rights question is whether this state of affairs should be changed.

Particularly with respect to sexual mores, we live in a radically pluralistic society, in which large groups of citizens disagree about moral fundamentals. This situation gives rise to the question in political theory that has been put so well by John Rawls: "[H]ow is it possible for there to exist over time a just and stable society of free and equal citizens, who remain profoundly divided by reasonable religious, philosophical, and moral doctrines?"[2] This moral plurality also gives rise to a corresponding problem for law, since the citizens, with their manifold moral views, must all live under a single legal regime.

Three approaches to this kind of deep disagreement have long pedigrees in American law. The first, the *constitutional rights* approach, asks, are there constitutional constraints upon the range of acceptable political outcomes, so that one of the sides in this controversy is legally entitled to what it seeks? The second, the *moral* approach, asks, is there one and only one morally acceptable resolution to the controversy? The third, the *conflict of laws* approach, assumes that political decision making is not constrained by any legal or moral claim of right and that different resolutions can legitimately be reached in different parts of the country. It then asks, how can these various legitimate policies be harmonized into a coherent federal system, so that no state's law unnecessarily impairs the operation of the others?

The three approaches are not consistent. The first two, each in its own way, demand national uniformity, while the third accommodates plurality (while tolerating local options that may be quite repressive within their own spheres). Although I am quite confident that the first two approaches are the appropriate ones to follow and that they demand legal equality for gay people, I consider all three approaches here because I am equally confident that such equality is not possible in the present political climate. While gays have a powerful legal and moral claim for equal treatment as a matter of principle, these claims must be moderated when they are refracted through the political resistance that they engender.

This book will begin by establishing the strength of gays' abstract claims and then explore how these claims should be altered, but not extinguished, in the face of contemporary political reality. I thus offer a perspective on the gay rights question that is distinct from the two opposing views that dominate contemporary discussions: that the courts should impose equality as a national mandate or that gays' equality claims are without merit.

All three of these approaches are reflected in the recent outpouring of legal scholarship on gay rights.[3] In each area, something of a consensus has emerged. Each consensus, however, rests on false assumptions and weak reasoning.

The present scholarly consensus is quite favorable to the cause of gay rights. As Justice Scalia has observed, the legal academy has become an extraordinarily friendly place for gay rights claims.[4] Not only are contemporary scholars certain that gays are constitutionally entitled to better legal treatment than they now get, they also largely agree on the arguments. Most think that the strongest argument relies on the unenumerated right to privacy, which the United States Supreme Court has held protects, among other things, contraception and abortion.[5] Less important than the privacy argument, but still significant, is the equal protection argument: gays are relevantly like blacks and entitled to protection for the same reason that blacks are. Finally, there is a third argument that relies on sex discrimination doctrine. This is commonly thought to be the weakest argument of the three, and somewhat beside the point as well.

With respect to the moral arguments concerning homosexuality,[6] it is generally supposed that "morality" can refer only to the rules that prevent persons from physically harming other persons. In light of this premise, claims that homosexual conduct is immoral are generally agreed to be not only mistaken but incomprehensible. The invocation of morality, then, is understood to be nothing more than a fig leaf for bigotry.

Finally, with respect to the question whether same-sex marriages can be exported to other states, it is widely thought that other states are constitutionally required to recognize such marriages by the Full Faith and Credit Clause of the Constitution. Here, however, more than with the other arguments, a substantial counterliterature has been developed by conservative scholars. The body of work that has emerged on this question has converged around two opposing views. The first, typically presented by gay rights advocates, is that courts everywhere must recognize such marriages, under all circumstances. The second, typically presented by defenders of traditional sexual mores, is that other states need never recognize such marriages for any purpose.

This is the present consensus. It is almost entirely wrong.

The Constitution indeed forbids official discrimination against gays, but not for the reasons generally believed. The privacy argument is vulnerable because it has no textual basis; it inappropriately requires judges to decide what is important in life; and it excessively disables the state from legislating on the basis of morality. Moreover, privacy is a poor characterization of what is at stake in the gay rights debate. The contemporary gay rights movement seeks public status—not seclusion and noninterference. The equal protection argument is stronger than the privacy argument, but turns on the disputed and probably unanswerable question of what motives underlie laws that discriminate against gays.

The sex discrimination argument avoids these pitfalls. Discrimination against gays is a simple case of sex discrimination, in which persons are penalized for acting in ways that would be permissible for members of the other sex. Moreover, the homosexuality taboo, entangled as it is with notions of sex-appropriate behavior, has always been deeply implicated in the subordination of women. It thus operates, both formally and functionally, in a way that resembles the prohibition of interracial sex—a prohibition that classified on the basis of race and maintained the subordination of blacks.

This is not to deny the practical strengths of the other arguments. The privacy argument, for example, has been used by a number of state courts and by courts outside the United States to invalidate laws prohibiting homosexual sex. My claim is not that advocates are wrong to use these arguments. It is rather that these arguments are weak, and that courts should rely on other, stronger arguments. In law, it is not enough for the good guys to win. They must win for the right reasons.

If courts rely on bad arguments, the rule of law is compromised. The rule of law is a very great value, and it does not compete with, but supports, the equality of gay people.

Even if the arguments for constitutional protection of gays are persuasive, however, the political reality is that these arguments are not likely soon to prevail in the federal courts (although they have persuaded some state courts). Thus, the law is likely to vary from one state to another for the foreseeable future. Legal theory addressing the rights of gays must confront that fact and take it into account.

Because the gay rights question is one that will be primarily resolved by legislatures rather than courts, it is important to identify and address the strongest arguments in *favor* of discrimination against gays. The most powerful such arguments have not received the attention that they deserve. Only the Catholic natural law theorists have understood the task that a defense of the status quo must face. They alone understand that empirical generalizations about the poor quality of homosexual relationships are not sustainable and that their task is to defend heterosexuality as such, by identifying some valuable characteristic that is present in all (even infertile) heterosexual couples but in no gay couples. Because even their arguments ultimately fail, I conclude that discrimination against gays is never justified.

That conclusion is not likely to be shared by any American legislature in the near future. Although Americans are more receptive to gay rights claims than they once were, powerful reservations remain, and the likelihood is nearly zero that any state legislature will soon recognize same-sex marriage.[7] On the other hand, Vermont has already extended to same-sex relationships all the *benefits* of marriage except the name, and it seems almost certain that eventually, in some state, the name will follow. And what happens to that legal status when one of the parties travels into another state? I conclude, on the basis of ordinary choice-of-law principles, that such relationships must *sometimes* be recognized by other states, depending on where the couple makes its home. Here, once more, it is helpful to consider the analogy with interracial marriage, which involved the most profound disagreement in American history over marriage recognition. In that charged context, a territorial solution prevailed: even Southern courts recognized interracial marriages of couples who made their homes elsewhere. Same-sex couples should not be treated worse than racist regimes treated interracial couples. If a state recognizes same-sex relationships, then couples who make their home in that state ought to have their relationship recognized everywhere in the country.

The first three chapters take up the constitutional issues. They examine in turn the claims that rely on equal protection, privacy, and sex equality. Chapter 4 turns to the moral arguments that have been offered for and against unequal treatment of gays. The next two chapters consider the conflict-of-laws question, how to structure a regime in which different regions arrive at different answers. Chapter 5 considers the choice-of-law problem that state courts will face. Chapter 6 examines the constitutionality of the Defense of Marriage Act, which withholds all federal recognition to same-sex marriages and authorizes states to ignore, not only the marriages themselves, but also judicial decisions that arise from such marriages. The epilogue considers the role of courts in social reform and the place of principled arguments, of the kind that this book has been making, in political debate.

CHAPTER ONE

EQUAL PROTECTION AND
INVIDIOUS INTENT

Laws that discriminate against gays will always be demonstrably rational, because such laws will always further the state's legitimate moral objection to homosexual sodomy. Thus teaches *Bowers v. Hardwick*.[1] Laws that discriminate against gays will always be constitutionally doubtful, however, because they will always arouse suspicion that they rest on a bare desire to harm a politically unpopular group. Thus teaches *Romer v. Evans*.[2] Both of these teachings are coherent, and neither of them is necessarily inconsistent with the other. They leave the courts, however, with a doctrinal dilemma that has no obvious solution.

In order to sustain this claim, I must defend the reading of *Romer* just stated. This puts me into a thicket of constitutional argument. The scholarly reaction to *Romer* was remarkable. The Supreme Court held that the Equal Protection Clause of the Fourteenth Amendment was violated by an amendment to the Colorado constitution that prohibited antidiscrimination protection of gays, because "the amendment seems inexplicable by anything but animus toward the class that it affects."[3] The Court's inference of unconstitutional animus was central to its holding, but almost no scholar who read the opinion was willing to believe that this was what really was going on.[4]

In this chapter, I will argue that *Romer* is defensible in the terms in which it was decided. The opinion is concededly puzzling. There are, as Lynn Baker has observed, "missing pages."[5] I will try to supply those pages, and to explain why they were absent from the opinion, without throwing away any of the pages that *are* there. I will offer a parsimonious defense of the decision, discarding as little as possible of the reasoning actually set forth by the Court and adding as little as possible that the Court did *not* say.

Romer is a case about impermissible purpose. It fits quite comfortably into a body of doctrine that has made purpose fundamental to the adjudication of equal protection claims. The missing pages can easily be filled in by the reader, who need only take note of the hatred and stereotyping of gays that has been ubiquitous in American culture for a long time. Once this obvious cultural fact is recognized as part of the context in which the Colorado amendment was enacted, then the

Court's attribution of invidious purpose to the law makes eminent sense.

The filling of this ellipsis has implications that go well beyond *Romer*. The Court's opinion implicitly invokes a defect in the political process that contaminates, at least to some extent, *all* laws that discriminate against gays. But that contamination implies that laws discriminating against gays should be presumptively unconstitutional. The principal doctrinal obstacle to this conclusion is *Bowers v. Hardwick*, which held that a state can have a legitimate moral interest in prohibiting homosexual conduct. *Hardwick* established that a state will always have an innocent explanation for a law that discriminates against gays. *Romer* implicitly recognized that the widespread animus against gays (which is *not* the same thing as moral objection to homosexual conduct) undermines, to an extent that is hard to determine, the credibility of such explanations. The constitutional status of laws that discriminate against gays, therefore, is uncertain after *Romer*.

*   *   *

Begin by looking at the bare bones of what the Court said. *Romer* involved an amendment to the Colorado constitution (referred to on the ballot as "Amendment 2"), which provided that neither the state nor any of its subdivisions could prohibit discrimination on the basis of "homosexual, lesbian or bisexual orientation, conduct, practices or relationships." [6] In his opinion for the court, Justice Kennedy observed that the Amendment "has the peculiar property of imposing a broad and undifferentiated disability on a single named group." [7] This was unusual, and called for " 'careful consideration to determine whether [this law was] obnoxious to the constitutional provision.' " [8] The state defended the law by citing "respect for other citizens' freedom of association, and in particular the liberties of landlords or employers who have personal or religions objections to homosexuality." [9] The amendment, however, was "[n]ot confined to the private sphere." [10] The state also cited "its interest in conserving resources to fight discrimination against other groups." [11] The amendment, however, seemed to "deprive[ ] gays and lesbians even of the protection of general laws and policies that prohibit arbitrary discrimination in governmental and private settings." [12] Such a universal license to discriminate against gays "would compound the constitutional difficulties the law creates." [13] "The breadth of the Amendment is so far removed from these particular justifications that we find it impossible to credit them." [14]

The Court thus felt compelled to "conclude that Amendment 2 classifies homosexuals not to further a proper legislative end but to make them unequal to everyone else." [15] The broad disability imposed on a targeted group "raise[d] the inevitable inference that the disadvantage imposed is born of animosity toward the class of persons affected. '[I]f the constitutional concept of "equal protection of the laws" means anything, it must at the very least mean that a bare . . . desire to harm a politically unpopular group cannot constitute a *legitimate* governmental interest.'"[16] *Romer*'s rule of decision may thus be summarized: if a law targets a narrowly defined group and then imposes upon it disabilities that are so broad and undifferentiated as to bear no discernible relationship to any legitimate governmental interest, then the court will infer that the law's purpose is simply to harm that group, and so will invalidate the law.

How defensible is this inference? Justice Scalia thought that, so far from manifesting a bare desire to harm gays, the amendment was "rather a modest attempt by seemingly tolerant Coloradans to preserve traditional sexual mores against the efforts of a politically powerful minority to revise those mores through use of the laws."[17] "The Court's portrayal of Coloradans as a society fallen victim to pointless, hate-filled 'gay-bashing' is so false as to be comical."[18]

> Of course it is our moral heritage that one should not hate any human being or class of human beings. But I had thought that one could consider certain conduct reprehensible—murder, for example, or polygamy, or cruelty to animals—and could exhibit even "animus" toward such conduct. Surely that is the only sort of "animus" at issue here: moral disapproval of homosexual conduct. . . .[19]

The inference of impermissible motive, he thought, was therefore uncalled for. The Court's opinion "disparaging as bigotry adherence to traditional attitudes," Scalia concluded, was "nothing short of insulting."[20]

Whether the Court correctly decided *Romer* (at least, according to the rationale on which the Court relied) would seem to depend on whether the Court's inference of animus was justified. As Scalia's response shows, however, any answer to that question is likely to rest on an unspoken response to other, and more fundamental, questions: why does motive matter, and what sort of motivation renders a law unconstitutional under the Equal Protection Clause of the Fourteenth Amendment? Only after we have determined just what "animus" is prohibited, and why it is prohibited, can we even begin to determine whether such animus underlay Colorado's Amendment 2.

Part I of this chapter, then, examines the way in which the Court has understood the Fourteenth Amendment. I shall show that the Fourteenth Amendment analysis that now prevails can be understood as a means of pursuing unconstitutional intent. I then consider the reasons for so understanding the Equal Protection Clause and how these reasons, in light of certain institutional constraints, justify the present doctrinal structure, which rarely focuses on intent directly.

Part II then examines the way in which the Court decided *Romer*. I will claim that the Court was wrong to say that no innocent explanation could be offered for the Amendment. The logic that led to the inference of animus was incomplete; there was a gap in the reasoning. Nonetheless, in the context of the widespread hatred and stereotyping that constitutes, in significant part, the stigmatization of gays in contemporary American society, it would have been inappropriate for the Court to apply only minimal scrutiny to a law that on its face singled out gays for special disadvantage.

Part III addresses the problem of reconciling *Romer* and *Hardwick*. I conclude that *Romer* is a hard case because the court was presented with an unsolvable tangle of permissible and impermissible motives. This difficulty, moreover, is not confined to *Romer,* but is likely to be present whenever a court must adjudicate an equal protection challenge to a law that facially puts gays at a disadvantage. Given this tangle, it is unsurprising that the Court did not even suggest in its opinion that, as a general matter, laws discriminating against gays would be subjected to heightened scrutiny. After *Romer,* however, it is clear that minimal scrutiny cannot be the answer, either.

HOW AND WHY THE COURT
FOCUSES ON INVIDIOUS INTENT
The Court's Equal Protection Analysis

The Equal Protection Clause of the Fourteenth Amendment states that "[n]o State shall . . . deny to any person within its jurisdiction the equal protection of the laws." The Supreme Court has interpreted this provision as prohibiting arbitrary discrimination, or treating similar things dissimilarly. Without more, this produces a very deferential standard of judicial review. "The general rule is that legislation is presumed to be valid and will be sustained if the classification drawn by the statute is rationally related to a legitimate state interest." [21] Because this stress on mere rationality threatens to transform the clause into a minor protection against legislative carelessness, the clause has been given teeth in cases where the challenged classification is based on race: "all legal restrictions which challenge the civil rights of a single racial group are immediately suspect." [22] When legislation employs such classifications, classifications, "these laws are subjected to strict scrutiny and will be sustained only if they are suitably tailored to serve a compelling state interest." [23] This higher level of scrutiny has been justified with the explanation that race is "so seldom relevant to the achievement of any legitimate interest that laws grounded in such considerations are deemed to reflect prejudice and antipathy—a view that those in the burdened class are not as worthy and deserving as others." [24] Almost no legislation has been able to satisfy that test, whereas almost any legislation can meet "minimal scrutiny," which asks whether the statute is rationally related to a legitimate state interest. In the 1970s, the Court devised a third, intermediate, level of scrutiny: classifications based on sex or illegitimacy are what has been infelicitously called "quasi-suspect"; they "will survive equal protection scrutiny to the extent they are substantially related to a legitimate state interest." [25] The Court has not, however, explained how it is determined whether a given type of classification is suspect or quasi-suspect. Moreover, it has been noted that the insistence on close fit between means and end, varying in strictness with the level of scrutiny, has only an indirect relation to the evils of racial oppression against which the clause was originally enacted. [26]

The prevailing understanding of equal protection builds on the famous footnote 4 in *United States v. Carolene Products Co.*, which declared that "prejudice against discrete and insular minorities may be a special condition, which tends seriously to curtail the operation of those political processes ordinarily to be relied upon to protect minorities, and which may call for a correspondingly more searching judicial inquiry." [27] The settled doctrine today is that "the invidious quality of a law claimed to be racially discriminatory must ultimately be traced to a racially discriminatory purpose." [28] This view draws its power from the fact that the idea of equality does not entail that any specific, substantive right should be guaranteed. John Hart Ely, the leading scholarly exponent of the theory that the Fourteenth Amendment is concerned primarily with prejudice infecting the legislative process, explains that "unconstitutionality in the distribution of benefits that are not themselves constitutionally required can intelligibly inhere only in the way the distribution was arrived at." [29]

Intent, then, obviously plays an important role in at least one part of the Court's equal protection doctrine—the part that deals with facially neutral classifications. [30] Ely has argued, moreover, that even the formalistic, levels-of-scrutiny approach that applies to suspect or quasi-suspect classifications is best understood as "a handmaiden of motivation analysis." [31] "Racial classifications that disadvantage minorities are 'suspect' because we suspect that they are the product of racially prejudiced thinking of a sort we understand the Fourteenth Amendment to have been centrally concerned with eradicating."[32] Even if a challenger cannot prove the discriminatory intent behind a statute, the demands of strict scrutiny will flush out that intent, since no goal will fit the statute perfectly except the unconstitutional one that the statute actually serves.[33]

Why should the judiciary think that it is entitled to police the motives of legislative decision-makers in this way? The best explanation is Ely's. Ely is troubled by Alexander Bickel's claim that "judicial review is a counter-majoritarian force in our system," and that "when the Supreme Court declares unconstitutional a legislative act or the action of an elected executive, it thwarts the will of the representatives of the actual people of the here and now. . . ."[34] Since Bickel, many constitutional theorists have seen their task as reconciling unpopular judicial decisions, such as *Brown v. Board of Education,* with Bickel's "counter-majoritarian difficulty."

Ely aspires to develop a constitutional theory in which "the selection and accommodation of substantive values is left almost entirely to the political process,"[35] and judicial review is concerned solely with "what might capaciously be designated process writ large—with ensuring broad participation in the processes and distributions of government."[36] Ely's answer to Bickel's counter-majoritarian difficulty is to assign to the judiciary only that task with which the legislature cannot be trusted: "to keep the machinery of government running as it should."[37] The basis of this concern about process is the theory of representative government, which requires that a representative actually represent all of his constituents. In order for legislation to be legitimate, even unpopular minorities must "be represented in the sense that their interests are not to be left out of account or valued negatively in the lawmaking process."[38] A law that is generated by a process tainted by prejudice, in which the legislators are biased against or hold stereotyped views of some of their constituents, is unconstitutional.

Philosophical Underpinnings

Ely's foundational commitment to "equal concern and respect" as a basis for lawmaking relies on the work of Ronald Dworkin, who has made this commitment the centerpiece of his political theory. Dworkin, however, has never undertaken to demonstrate why government is obligated to endorse this conception of equality.[39] Nonetheless, the idea has widespread appeal.

Walter Murphy has developed the most elegant demonstration that a constitution necessarily embodies certain substantive commitments that demand equal concern and respect for all citizens. Murphy observes that constitutional democracy is a hybrid of two political theories, constitutionalism and democracy. Constitutionalism holds that there are some fundamental rights that cannot be violated, even with the consent of the majority. Democratic theory holds that, in order for the people to have an obligation to obey the law, they must be in some sense its authors.[40]

Both constitutionalism and democracy imply limits to the scope of legitimate decisionmaking. "When such a polity consciously, seriously, and systematically violates its fundamental principles, it destroys its justification for existence, and public officials lose their authority to speak as agents of the people."[41] According to constitutionalism, "[a]ny change that would transform the polity into a political system that was totalitarian, or even so authoritarian as not to allow a wide space for human freedom, would be illegitimate. . ."[42] According to democratic theory, "a people could not legitimately use democratic processes to destroy the essence of democracy—the right of others, either of a current majority or minority or of a minority or majority of future generations, to meaningful participation in self-government."[43] Both theories presuppose some notion of human worth. That constitutionalism does so is self-evident, but democracy shares the same commitment. "A system that denies human worth cannot claim consent as the foundation of its legitimacy, for what is worthless can confer nothing."[44]

Any constitutional democracy, therefore, is committed to "acknowledging the right of each member to exist as a full human being."[45] This implies certain process rights that are relevant here. Specifically, every citizen has a right to "treatment as being equal in worth to every other person, whether private individual or public official."[46]

If Murphy is right, then, so long as there are cultural tendencies that devalue certain groups of people and so long as those tendencies are strong enough politically to contaminate the process of political decisionmaking, *any* coherent constitution logically must include at least some rights against discrimination. It does not *necessarily* follow, however, that these antidiscrimination rights must be judicially enforceable. As Jeremy Waldron has observed, moral realism does not entail the legitimacy of judicial review unless it can be shown that judges have greater expertise in moral matters than legislatures.[47] Nonetheless, as it happened, the decision to embody this kind of antidiscrimination right in the Fourteenth Amendment did entail a commitment to federal oversight of state decisions, and it is easy to see why it should. "The Equal Protection Clause reflects an unmistakable determination that state legislatures are not to be trusted to refrain from engaging in racial discrimination."[48] The basis of judicial review under the Fourteenth Amendment is not the special expertise of federal judges but rather the inability of legislatures to judge themselves impartially.

The Equal Protection Doctrine at Work

In practice, the equal protection doctrine of unconstitutional motive has given legislatures a great deal of freedom. As noted earlier, motive is often not at issue in Fourteenth Amendment litigation. "A racial classification, regardless of purported motivation, is presumptively invalid and can be upheld only upon an extraordinary justification."[49] In cases in which there is no suspect classification, the Court has constructed a doctrine that makes it exceedingly difficult for plaintiffs to prove discriminatory intent. Successful challenges to state action under the Equal Protection Clause hardly ever depend on a direct showing of invidious intent. Most often, the challenger points to objective facts from which bad intent is inferred. *Romer* is unusual only in that the Court indicates plainly that it relied upon an inference of bad intent.

Absent a suspect classification, Ely thought, "it will be next to impossible for a court responsibly to conclude that a decision was affected by an unconstitutional motivation whenever it is possible to articulate a plausible legitimate explanation for the action taken."[50] This is because, inasmuch as laws are never enacted with only one motive, "courts will be unable to determine—as between a rational and otherwise legitimate explanation for a choice and an unconstitutional explanation—which one in fact motivated the choice."[51]

Ely's view has been borne out in the Supreme Court's decisions. Daniel Ortiz has shown that the Court's approach to government decisions that have a disparate impact on minorities, at least with respect to housing and public employment, amounts in practice to minimal scrutiny. "Instead of asking whether the decisionmaker *would* have made the same decision without the discriminatory motivation, the Court asks something a bit closer to whether it *could* have done so."[52] This approach fails to satisfy the requirements of Ely's process theory because "the presence of permissible goals—even very substantial ones—does not reveal how important the impermissible goals were."[53]

Moreover, the Court has interpreted the concept of impermissible intent in a remarkably deferential way by holding that the Fourteenth

Amendment is not violated unless a state action was taken "'because of,' not merely 'in spite of,' its adverse effects upon an identifiable group." [54] It should not be surprising that courts applying this standard have almost never found state action to be unconstitutional.[55] David Strauss observes that by limiting unconstitutional intent to deliberate malice, the Court holds "that the government is free to undervalue the interests of a class of citizens, to treat them with indifference, to ignore the burdens it imposes on them, so long as it does so in order to achieve an objective other than injuring the group." [56] If this is the standard for a Fourteenth Amendment violation, then even the deliberate segregation invalidated in *Brown v. Board of Education* is probably constitutional, because "it is not obvious that the architects of Jim Crow invariably desired to hurt blacks." [57]

Strauss argues that the reason the court adopted the discriminatory intent standard was to contain the disruptive implications of the Equal Protection Clause. Alternative conceptions of discrimination, focusing on such results of decisionmaking as subordination, stigma, second-class citizenship, or encouragement of prejudice, were unacceptable to the Court, because "they seemed far more vague than the discriminatory intent standard, and they seemed far more threatening to established institutions." [58] The Court's cautious rationale for adopting the intent test may explain why it has applied the test itself in such a half-hearted way. Strauss argues convincingly that the intent test, "rigorously applied, . . . is no less threatening to established institutions" [59] than the alternatives. The problem with the intent test, on this account, is not that the underlying constitutional theories focus on motive rather than result, but that the Court has biased the test against the party challenging the law. A surgical technique is not discredited by a low success rate if it becomes clear that the surgeons were trying to kill their patients.[60]

There is, however, an alternative explanation for why the Court has not pursued the intent test with any zeal. Intent-based analysis is costly. As already noted, invidious intent must always be difficult to prove. Moreover, as Kenneth Karst argued soon after the Court adopted the intent test, such a doctrine inevitably will tend to validate official decisions because judges are reluctant to impugn the motives of other officials.[61] Finally, as Strauss observes, a serious application of the intent test necessarily leads to speculative or meaningless questions. A court must ask, "suppose the adverse effects of the challenged government decision fell on whites instead of blacks, or on men instead of women. Would the decision have been different?" [62] But this means that we must ask, for example, whether abortion would be outlawed if men could get pregnant. Such a question is unanswerable. Thus, any test that directly seeks to find unconstitutional intent is bound to fail. Like the sun, the thing can only be looked at indirectly.

There is, however, one other way of invalidating legislation that does not contain a suspect classification, but that is the product of an impermissible motive. This is to look to the objective purpose of the statute—the purpose that plainly appears from an examination of the face of the statute. Thus, at the same time that Justice Scalia has argued that "discerning the subjective motivation of those enacting the statute is, to be honest, almost always an impossible task," he has written that "it is possible to discern the objective 'purpose' of a statute (i.e., the public good at which its provisions appear to be directed)." [63]

This method of sticking to the facial purpose of the statute is not necessarily inconsistent with the process-based approach to the Equal Protection Clause. If directly searching for the legislature's subjective purpose is really a forlorn and doomed enterprise, then one needs proxies that have evidentiary value. One such proxy is the existence of a suspect classification. Another is the objective purpose of the statute.

The Court recently followed this objective approach in *Church of the Lukumi Babalu Aye v. Hialeah*,[64] in which it struck down four ordinances that a city had enacted with the avowed purpose of preventing a Santeria church from practicing animal sacrifice. The laws, the Court held, violated the Free Exercise Clause of the First Amendment, because their object was the suppression of a religious practice. Justice Kennedy, who wrote the majority opinion, was able to find lurid statements by Hialeah city officials indicating that they sought to "not to permit this Church to exist" and thought that Santeria was "an abomination to the Lord" and the worship of "demons." [65] But Justice Kennedy lost his majority in the section of the opinion that cited these facts; only Justice Stevens joined it. The majority portion of the opinion held that "suppression of the central element of the Santeria worship service was the object of the ordinances" [66] and cited the language and operation of the statutes, as well as the fact that almost all nonreligious killings of animals were expressly exempted.

The objective approach does not confine the court's attention to the four corners of the statute. The context in which the law was enacted is another objective fact that the court may properly take into account in discerning the law's purpose. This is always so when the suspect classification doctrine is used; it is only by reference to the tendencies in American culture to stigmatize and devalue certain groups that the

Court has been able to discern the "discrete and insular minorities" that need judicial protection. Even when a suspect classification does not appear on the face of the statute, context is relevant. Again, *Lukumi* is an illustration. The impermissible purpose was evident from the face of three of the statutes, which prohibited "sacrifice" of animals as part of a "ritual." The fourth statute, however, was facially neutral; Ordinance 87-72 merely prohibited "the killing of animals for food" outside of areas zoned for slaughterhouses. It only exempted the slaughter or processing for sale of "small numbers of hogs and/ or cattle per week in accordance with an exemption provided by state law."[67] The Court declared the ordinance "underinclusive on its face"[68] because the exempted activities implicated the city's professed concerns about public health and cruelty to animals as much as animal sacrifice did. This argument alone, however, could hardly have invalidated the law. The Court has often upheld arbitrarily underinclusive statutes.[69]

If any innocent-sounding explanation will save a statute that involves no suspect classification, then this law should have been upheld. The court conceded that, "unlike the other three ordinances," this one "does appear to apply to substantial nonreligious conduct and not to be overbroad."[70] Nonetheless, the Court held that the invidious purpose of the other three ordinances contaminated this one as well.[71]

The doctrine of impermissible intent that the Court has constructed, then, tends to ignore the subjective intentions of the lawmakers, but encourages inquiry into the objective purpose of the law. Moreover, knowledge of this purpose can be facilitated by knowledge of the context in which the law was enacted—once again, an objective question. The pursuit of illicit motivation has produced a procedure that, for sound institutional reasons, drives evidence of actual motive to the margins of judicial inquiry.

The case for this approach becomes strongest when we consider laws enacted by referendum, such as Amendment 2. Such laws are subject to the same equal protection scrutiny as any other laws. The problems of discerning the subjective intent of lawmakers obviously become insuperable when one confronts a lawmaking body composed of hundreds of thousands, or even millions, of voters.[72] The Court has struck down, on the basis of invidious purpose, three laws enacted by popular vote.[73] In each case there was enough evidence of racial motivation to warrant suspicion. And once suspicion is aroused, the presumptions that are put into play may appropriately—indeed, must— do all the rest of the work. The Sixth Circuit has gone so far as to hold that "in the referendum context, it is *impermissible* for the reviewing court to inquire into the possible actual motivations of the electorate in adopting the proposal." [74]

THE INTENT TEST IN *ROMER*

Let us at last return to the problem posed by *Romer.* Now that we understand why the Court is concerned about purpose, what shall we say about its inference that an impermissible purpose underlay Amendment 2?

The Innocent Explanation

The difficulty that Justice Scalia raises is that an innocent explanation for Amendment 2 seems to be available. Let us examine this innocent explanation in greater detail.

The application of antidiscrimination law to nongovernmental activities typically is predicated on the factual premise that the groups it seeks to protect are subject to *pervasive* discrimination. Opponents of antidiscrimination protection for gays claim that whatever discrimination gays suffer is too rare to have much impact on their lives or opportunities.[75] Some also think, without making any claim one way or the other about the pervasiveness of discrimination, that laws protecting gays from discrimination are so rarely invoked that they are not worth having.[76]

Moreover, even if nearly every employer and landlord is predisposed to discriminate against gays, it remains possible to avoid such discrimination. The price of doing so is the closet. Absent a massively intrusive investigatory apparatus,[77] it is impossible for anyone to discriminate solely on the basis of orientation, which is easily concealed.

Moreover, if the Court is really confining itself to minimal scrutiny, then it should not matter if gays *are* pervasively discriminated against, whether by the state or by private entities. Such pervasive discrimination might merely reflect a moral perspective that, the Court held in *Hardwick,* is a permissible basis for criminal prohibition (which is a far heavier imposition than private discrimination): the "belief . . . that homosexual sodomy is immoral and unacceptable."[78] A state might reasonably conclude that, if gays by their conduct are revealing themselves to be moral monsters, they ought not to complain when other citizens shun them as such.

Justice Kennedy declares that "[i]t is not within our constitutional tradition to enact laws of this sort,"[79] but the truth is that, not too long ago, pervasive discrimination against gays was regarded as a sort of moral imperative. In 1953, President Eisenhower issued an executive order barring gays from all federal jobs, and the FBI initiated a "widespread system of surveillance to keep homosexuals off the federal payroll."[80] Corporations under government contract applied the administration's security provisions to their own employees, and many states and municipalities followed the federal government's lead, while also enforcing similar standards in the licensing of many professions. One study in the mid-1950s estimated that over 12.6 million workers, more than 20 percent of the labor force, faced loyalty-security investigations as a condition of employment.[81]

The closest thing to a canonical rationale for this pervasive discrimination was set forth in 1950 by a Senate committee that investigated the employment of "homosexuals and other moral perverts" in government. Such people, the committee concluded, lacked "emotional stability," because "indulgence in acts of sex perversion weakens the moral fiber of an individual to a degree that he is not suitable for a position of responsibility." Even one "sex pervert in a Government agency," the committee warned,

> tends to have a corrosive influence upon his fellow employees. These perverts will frequently attempt to entice normal individuals to engage in perverted practices. This is particularly true in the case of young and impressionable people who might come under the influence of a pervert. . . . One homosexual can pollute a Government office.[82]

It is now clear that the committee was in the grip of a fantastic delusion. Hardly anyone believes this sort of stuff any more. Under minimal scrutiny, however, it ought not to matter. "[I]t has long been settled that a classification, though discriminatory, is not arbitrary nor violative of the Equal Protection Clause of the Fourteenth Amendment if any state of affairs reasonably can be conceived that would sustain it."[83] "This remarkable deference to state objectives," Tribe observes, "has operated in the sphere of economic regulation quite apart from whether the conceivable 'state of facts' (1) actually exists, (2) would convincingly justify the classification if it did exist, or (3) was ever urged in the classification's defense either by those who promulgated it or by those who argued in its support."[84] The Senate committee's claims, if believed, would obviously justify discrimination against gays by a broad range of private employers as well as by government.

Not only is it possible to doubt the need for antidiscrimination protection of gays, it is also possible reasonably to object to the expressive function of antidiscrimination ordinances such as Denver's. As Scalia observed, such ordinances are intended by at least some of their supporters to achieve "not merely a grudging social toleration, but full social acceptance, of homosexuality." [85] Some opponents of such laws also interpret them in just this way. [86]

The rationale for Amendment 2, then, might well be the following: Homosexual conduct is intrinsically evil and corrupting; so much so that it justifies discrimination in almost every context. In fact, however, such discrimination rarely occurs and, where it does occur, does little harm. Antidiscrimination law, then, does not protect gays in any tangible way. Its sole function is the expressive one of giving gays a legitimacy they do not deserve and giving moral scruples against homosexual conduct a stigma that *they* do not deserve. For these reasons, one might argue, the electorate of Colorado was entirely justified in seizing from gays the expressive machinery of the state and deploying it on their own behalf.

There is no question that many of Amendment 2's supporters had motives of this kind. Such motives do not per se deny anyone equal concern and respect. Dworkin argues that, in the context of Amendment 2, "there can be no difference" between moral disapproval and animus. This is because Dworkin thinks that *Romer* implicitly denies (what he explicitly denies) that it is legitimate "for a state to impose a disadvantage on a particular group just to express the majority's moral contempt for that group's practices, even when no other proper purpose, such as protecting anyone's economic or security interests, is served." [87] In so claiming, Dworkin relies on an argument that he has often made, that government fails to treat citizens with equal concern and respect whenever it restricts individual liberty on the ground that one citizen's conception of the good life is better than another's. [88] John Finnis adequately answered this claim long ago. Morals legislation

> *may* manifest, not contempt, but a sense of the equal worth and human dignity of those people, whose conduct is outlawed precisely on the ground that it expresses a serious misconception of, and actually degrades, human worth and dignity, and thus degrades their own personal worth and dignity, along with that of others who may be induced to share in or emulate their degradation. [89]

It is clear that the condemnation of homosexuality by the Catholic church, for example, takes precisely this form. Gays themselves are not condemned. Their equal dignity and worth is emphatically insisted upon. As Ely has pointed out, "a sincerely held moral objection to the act" of homosexual sex is not per se the same thing as "a simple desire to injure the parties involved." [90]

Does the Innocent Explanation Save Amendment 2?

If it's possible to imagine an innocent explanation, is the game over? Must we conclude that *Romer* is wrongly decided? The trouble with this kind of reasoning is that it proves far too much. There have always been innocent explanations for discriminatory laws, even those animated by the most sinister motives. The reason why the Court strikes down some laws, even those that can be given innocent explanations, is that there are objective indicia of invidious intent that dispose the Court toward suspicion.

The question, then, is whether Scalia's benign interpretation is persuasive, given the context in which Amendment 2 was adopted. Chief Justice Warren raised the same problem of innocent explanations when he wrote in *Brown v. Board of Education* that "separate educational facilities are inherently unequal." [91] The statement was correct insofar as it recognized the implausibility of the "separate but equal" claim in the context of Jim Crow, but incredible insofar as it was phrased in terms of what Charles Black called "the metaphysics of sociology: 'Must Segregation Amount to Discrimination?'" [92] Black's comment remains instructive:

> That is an interesting question; someday the methods of sociology may be adequate to answering it. But it is not our question. Our question is whether discrimination inheres in that segregation which is imposed by law in the twentieth century in certain specific states in the American Union. And that question has meaning and can find an answer only on the ground of history and of common knowledge about the facts of life in the times and places aforesaid. [93]

Just as Warren's opinion in *Brown* seemed to invite an irrelevant debate about the metaphysics of sociology, Kennedy's opinion in *Romer* seems to invite an irrelevant debate about the metaphysics of legislative draftsmanship: a debate about how narrow a class may permissibly be disadvantaged by a statute, how broad the disadvantaging may be, and how the narrowness and broadness should be calibrated in order to avoid unconstitutionality. This would be a silly direction for constitutional law to go in. In both cases, the issue is what the purpose of the law is in the context in which it was enacted. This question "has meaning and can find an answer only on the ground of history and of common knowledge about the facts of life in the times and places aforesaid." To say it again, context matters.

Up to this point, we have uncovered a gap in the Court's reasoning in *Romer*. The fact that a group, narrowly defined, is saddled with a broad range of disabilities does not, without more, warrant an inference of impermissible motive. If this gap cannot be filled, then *Romer* is wrongly decided. Conversely, if *Romer* is rightly decided, and if the opinion accurately represents at least a part of the sequence of reasoning that leads to that conclusion, then we must be able to point to facts that complete the logical circuit.

Invidious Motives

Given its context in American culture, is there any good reason to think that a law like Amendment 2, which on its face imposes unusual disadvantages on gays, is the product of impermissible motives? What do history and common knowledge tell us about the way in which gays are regarded in the contemporary United States?

HATRED First of all, raw hatred of gays has been and continues to be quite common. In the most extreme cases, it takes the form of random attacks on strangers. "Violence against gay men and lesbians," Kendall Thomas observes, "on the streets, in the workplace, in the home—is a structural feature of life in American society."[94] In a survey of anti-gay violence and harassment in eight major cities, "86.2 percent of the gay men and women surveyed stated that they had been attacked verbally; 44.2 percent reported that they had been threatened with violence; 27.3 percent had had objects thrown at them; 34.9 percent had been chased or followed; 13.9 percent had been spit at; 19.2 percent had been punched, hit, kicked, or beaten; 9.3 percent had been assaulted with a weapon; 18.5 percent had been the victims of property vandalism or arson; 30.9 percent reported sexual harassment, many by members of their own families or by the police."[95] A study commissioned by the National Institute of Justice, the research arm of the U.S. Department of Justice, found that gays "are probably the most frequent victims [of hate violence today]."[96] As a consequence, "gay men and lesbians always and everywhere have to live their lives on guard, knowing that they are vulnerable to attack at any time."[97]

Attacks on gays bespeak an astonishing rage, frequently involving torture and mutilation. Homophobic murders typically involve mutilation of the victim. The coordinator of one hospital's victim assistance program reported that "attacks against gay men were the most heinous and brutal I encountered."[98] A physician reported that injuries suffered by the victims of homophobic violence that he had treated were so "vicious" as to make clear that "the intent is to kill and maim."[99]

This extraordinary level of antipathy is the tip of a large iceberg. Those who attack gays are atypical, but they reveal much about the culture in which they have been socialized. Their behavior can hardly be characterized as aberrant or isolated when it is so common throughout the United States.

According to Gordon Allport's classic study of prejudice, patterns of behavior rejecting out-groups form a continuum, from verbal denunciation (what Allport calls "antilocution"), to avoidance, to discrimination, to physical attack, to organized extermination. The milder forms of prejudice are the most common: "most people are content to express their hostility verbally to their own friends and never go further. Some, however, reach the stage of active discrimination. A few take part in vandalism, riots, lynchings." [100] When violence does occur, it "is always an outgrowth of milder states of mind. Although most barking (antilocution) does not lead to biting, yet there is never a bite without previous barking." [101] The perpetrators of hate violence are predominantly young males, who are distinguished from their elders primarily in that they "have a thinner layer of socialized habit between impulses and their release." [102] Others, however, are likely to manifest similar attitudes in other, more socially acceptable ways. "[A]ny negative attitude tends somehow, somewhere, to express itself in action. Few people keep their antipathies entirely to themselves. The more intense the attitude, the more likely it is to result in vigorously hostile action." [103]

While few Americans actually engage in violence against gays, many more dislike them intensely. Gays are among the least liked groups in the United States, according to Kenneth Sherrill's analysis of the Feeling Thermometers of the American National Election Study. Respondents were asked to rate their feelings toward a variety of groups on a scale of 0 to 100. In four surveys spanning a ten-year period, the lowest score, zero, was consistently assigned to gays and lesbians by more respondents than any other group; next in order were illegal immigrants, people on welfare, and Christian fundamentalists. (In 1994, the most recent year, 28.2 percent assigned gays a zero ranking, as compared with 24.2 percent for the next most unpopular group, illegal immigrants, and 9.1 percent for the third most unpopular group, people on welfare. The figure for blacks was 2.0 percent.) Sherrill concludes that "such hostility does not face any other group in the electorate." [104] The hostility is not only intense, but widespread. Gays and lesbians also have consistently received one of the lowest mean FT scores, although in recent years they have escaped the lowest average rating by being 2 to 4 points above illegal immigrants. "Among American citizens included in these studies only lesbians and gay men were the objects of cold feelings from a majority of Americans." [105]

The idea that gays are inferior human beings is not the only reason they are discriminated against, but it is plainly one of the reasons. What is stigmatized is not only homosexual activity, but homosexual desire. The stigma cannot simply be explained in terms of the perceived immorality of the desired conduct. The trouble is not homosexual conduct, but gay identity.

This can be shown by focusing on the mildest form of prejudice in Allport's continuum: verbal denunciation. Richard Mohr notes that the English language does not treat gays merely as persons who engage in certain sexual activities. Dictionary definitions of "homosexual" refer to desire rather than conduct. Anti-gay slurs also target status rather than behavior:

> With the apparent exception of "cocksucker," no widespread anti-gay slur gives any indication that its censure is directed at sex acts rather than despised social status. Group-directed slurs (dyke, queer, fag) place gays in a significant social category along with blacks (nigger, shine, shitskin), other racial groups (chink), women (cunt, gash), various ethnic groups (wop, dago, gook, jap, JAP, mick, kike). . . . They do not place gays in the same category as liars, hypocrites, murderers, and thieves—those who commit immoral and criminal actions and yet for whom culture in no case has coined group-based invectives. This schema of slurs strongly suggests that gays are held to be immoral because they are hated, rather than hated because they are immoral.[106]

Even gays who do not act on their inclinations, or even openly repudiate them, still bear the stigma of their status, if it is known. In 1976, presidential candidate Jimmy Carter told an interviewer, "I've looked on a lot of women with lust. I've committed adultery in my heart many times. This is something God recognizes I will do—and I have done it—and God forgives me for it." [107] The statement caused a minor flap at the time, but Carter went on to win the election. Imagine the reaction if he had said that he had looked on a lot of men with lust.

STEREOTYPING Stereotyping of gays is problematic, even if it is not merely a manifestation of hatred. Consider the Senate Committee's fantasies described earlier,[108] or, more pertinently here, the mendacious stereotypes about gays that were deployed by Amendment 2's supporters. Colorado for Family Values was the organization that drafted and principally led the campaign for Amendment 2. Its principal pamphlet, delivered to 800,000 Colorado doorsteps before the election, claimed, inter alia, that "sexual molestation of children is a large part of many homosexuals' lifestyle," that such molestation "is actually an accepted part of the homosexual community!", that gays are "rich, 'horny,' political power brokers," and that gay rights ordinances protect sexual intercourse in public places, would require employers to construct separate bathrooms for gays, would impose legal penalties upon churches and individuals that preach that homosexuality is wrong, and "could force churches to unite homosexuals in marriage." [109] Colorado for Family Values evidently judged that at least some of their audience was predisposed to credit silly claims of this sort.

Ely explains why stereotyping of this kind violates the Fourteenth Amendment. "The cases where we ought to be suspicious are . . . those involving a generalization whose incidence of counterexample is significantly higher than the legislative authority seems to have thought it was." [110] This is because such a generalization denies those people who are counterexamples, and to whose existence the decision-maker is oblivious, "*their* right to equal concern and respect, by valuing their welfare at zero." [111] The danger of such devaluation is particularly great where the group in question is one to which the decision-makers do not belong. People are especially likely to subscribe to self-flattering generalizations, and to negative myths about outsiders. "Just as we would want reconsidered any important decision that was made under the influence of an erroneous assumption about the relevant facts, so should we here." [112]

It seems likely that the Court recognized the existence of both of these motives. Moreover, in assessing whether *Romer* was correctly decided, we ought also to take note of one other constitutionally impermissible purpose that is pervasive in American society and is closely connected to the stigmatization of homosexuality, but which appears to have escaped the Court's notice.

SEXISM This is the desire to impose traditional sex roles on others. Any action that singles out gays facially classifies on the basis of sex. The point ought to be obvious, but I explain it in detail in chapter 3, below.

Doubtless it never occurred to the Court that discrimination against gays is a kind of sex discrimination. If it had, then *Romer* would have been an easy case, squarely controlled by *Hunter v. Erickson,*[113] which invalidated a law specifically protecting race discrimination. Amendment 2 involved an explicit gender classification: under the amendment, men, but not women, who sleep with men may freely be discriminated against. Viewing Amendment 2 as sex discrimination would have been a simpler and more automatic path to heightened scrutiny, but it is not the path that the Court took.

Invidious Motive and Amendment 2

Laws, such as Amendment 2, that target gays for disadvantage thus are the product of a political process contaminated by constitutionally impermissible motives.[114] It is only when this cultural background is kept in view that it becomes clear why Amendment 2's singling out of gays for broad disadvantage is constitutionally fatal.

The core constitutional objection to Amendment 2 is that, absent such motives, it probably would not have passed. This judgment of probability can of course be disputed. Invidious prejudices certainly contribute to the passage of laws of this kind, but they are mixed with motives that are permissible ones. Scalia's claim that "the only sort of 'animus' at issue here" was "moral disapproval of homosexual conduct"[115] was surely a correct description of many, perhaps most, of those who voted for Amendment 2. On the other hand, these voters had some allies who had pretty unsavory motives. Sorting them out, and determining whether the impermissible motives were the determinative ones, seems an impossible task.

The existence of such mixed motives is not a new difficulty, however. It is the innocent explanation problem again. Almost any law can be given *some* innocent explanation. What's more, any such innocent explanation usually will correctly characterize the motives of some of its supporters. For example, probably the most severe attribution of invidious legislative purpose in any Supreme Court opinion was its declaration, in *Loving v. Virginia*,[116] that laws prohibiting interracial marriage were "measures designed to maintain White Supremacy."[117] The Court stated this in the teeth of a perfectly innocent alternate explanation that Virginia had offered. In its brief, Virginia had argued that if the Court were to undertake an inquiry into the rationality of the challenged legislation, "it would quickly find itself mired in a veritable Serbonian bog of conflicting scientific opinion upon the effects of interracial marriage, and the desirability of preventing such alliances, from the physical, biological, genetic, anthropological, cultural, psychological and sociological point of view."[118] It argued that the decision not to allow such marriages rested on the acceptance of scientific arguments put forth by respectable authorities. If an innocent explanation was all that was needed, here it was. Moreover, it is nearly certain that at least some of Virginia's leaders had managed to persuade themselves that these scientific claims were true. The appellants responded that "there is not a single anthropologist teaching at a major university in the United States who subscribes to the theory that Negro-white matings cause biologically deleterious results,"[119] but the Court was certainly not competent to adjudicate this dispute. Moreover, under motive-based analysis, even if the law rested on bogus science, this would not necessarily have impugned the legislators' motives. Innocent mistakes are not invidious.

Instead, the Court emphasized that "Virginia's miscegenation statutes rest solely upon distinctions drawn according to race."[120] Such distinctions are "'odious to a free people whose institutions are founded upon the doctrine of equality.'"[121] The Court supported its attribution of invidious purpose by noting that "Virginia prohibits only interracial marriages involving white persons,"[122] but it also indicated that Virginia would not be able to cure the difficulty by enacting a more broadly worded statute.[123]

In both *Loving* and *Romer,* the kind of classification that was used itself triggered a presumption of unconstitutionality, which the state was unable to overcome. In both cases, the triggering of that presumption was appropriate, because the classification in question was one that was widely understood to separate those citizens who were fully human from the *Untermenschen.* The use of such a classification sufficed to raise a serious doubt about the legitimacy of the law's motivations. Once such a doubt has been raised, legislation can no longer be presumed to be constitutional. "When there is proof that a discriminatory purpose has been a motivating factor in the decision . . . judicial deference is no longer justified."[124]

The doctrine of suspect classification rests on a judgment that, whenever a classification of a certain sort is used, a court is justified in presuming that "a motivating factor in the decision" was the illicit motive ordinarily associated with that classification in the minds of at least some of the citizenry. A classification should be suspect, then, if it is the case that many citizens think that the classification in question does distinguish those persons who are entitled to a full measure of concern and respect from those who are inherently degraded and inferior. Sexual orientation is a classification of that sort.

Richard Duncan has argued that *Romer* is wrongly decided, because the draconian or unconstitutional applications that worried the Court were unlikely ever to occur, and in any event were not the law's primary effect.[125] At oral argument, the justices had wondered whether the amendment would authorize libraries to refuse to lend books to gays, hospitals to deny gays access to kidney dialysis, or the police, the health department, and the insurance commissioner to engage in similar discriminatory denials of services.[126] The amendment's literal language might have authorized such discrimination, but these scenarios were unlikely and might have been cured by a narrow interpretation of the amendment. Duncan tellingly cites Justice Kennedy's observation, in another context, that courts should not invalidate laws "on a facial challenge based upon a worst-case analysis that may never occur."[127]

Duncan's question—"But why should we think these scenarios will ever occur or were intended by the voters of Colorado when they approved the initiative?"[128]—deserves an answer. The evidence of actual discriminatory animus is sparse. The offending, overbroad language of the amendment did not even appear on the ballot, which contained only a summary of the law. Survey data does not turn up convincing evidence of impermissible animus in the Colorado electorate.[129] Michael Dorf observes that if the reason objective impermissible purpose voids a statute "is because the objective features of the statute provide clear evidence of the subjective goals of the legislature," then "one would expect that on occasion a statute with an objective impermissible purpose could be defended on the ground that although the statute appears to serve only an impermissible purpose, in fact it was enacted for different, permissible purposes."[130] This is just what Duncan is saying. Duncan concedes that Amendment 2 may look as though it was animated by a bare desire to harm gays, but he thinks that the totality of the evidence of the lawmakers' subjective purposes should lead us to a different conclusion.

The judicial limitations already noted forbid this move, however.[131] We decided in the first place to look to objective rather than subjective purpose because (a) it is very hard confidently to attribute any particular motive to a collective group; (b) courts are rightly reluctant to challenge other officials' motives; (c) this reluctance means that a motive-based test will bias the judiciary in favor of validating statutes, even those that are in fact contaminated by impermissible motives. All of these considerations militate against permitting a motive-based defense to a finding of impermissible objective purpose. It will be as difficult confidently to attribute a good subjective motive to the decision-makers as it was to attribute a bad one to them. The courts' reluctance to impugn the lawmakers' motives will again bias adjudication, to the detriment of Fourteenth Amendment protections. If it was hard, in assessing the prima facie case against a statute, to say that a lawmaker had a bad motive, it will be equally hard at the rebuttal stage to *deny* that the lawmaker had a good one. The only way to avoid the difficulty is to forbid any of the parties to the litigation from putting in issue the subjective motives of the lawmaker.

Thus we come to the following paradox. Following the Court's interpretation of the Equal Protection Clause, the *sine qua non* of a violation of that clause, is unconstitutional subjective motive. A well-crafted set of implementing rules, however, will push subjective motive so far outside the scope of inquiry (at least in cases where the person challenging the law does not directly put motive in issue) that evidence of motive in fact will become entirely irrelevant to the adjudication of the law's constitutionality, perhaps to the point of being inadmissible in court.

I recognize the contingent and contestable nature of my judgment. Reasonable people disagree about whether hatred and stereotyping of gays is sufficiently pervasive in our society to warrant judicial suspicion of laws that discriminate on the basis of sexual orientation. *Romer* is therefore a hard case. An objective test of suspectness must rely on objective social meanings, and these are always going to be contested. But this does not, without more, impugn the result. If the Court is not going to abdicate its Fourteenth Amendment role, then it has to make its own best judgment.

Doubt in *Romer* itself was properly resolved by the language of the amendment, which had "the peculiar property of imposing a broad and undifferentiated disability on a single named group."[132] Kennedy was right to focus on this unusual property, which appears to have turned the scales against the law (though the opinion would have made a good deal less sense if some other group had been named). Akhil Amar observes that the amendment that was actually enacted was only a partial repealer of local antidiscrimination ordinances; heterosexuals continued to be protected from discrimination on the basis of sexual orientation.[133] A law that did not thus single out a "named group"— for example, a slightly redrafted Amendment 2, merely substituting "sexual orientation" for "homosexual, lesbian or bisexual orientation"[134]—would present a harder case. But unless there were reliable background knowledge of hatred and stereotyping of gays, even the inference of animus in *Romer* would have been unwarranted.

Although *Romer* indicates a critical awareness of the prejudice against gays, a later decision suggests that at least some members of the Court have an imperfect grasp of these issues. *Boy Scouts of America v. Dale*[135] invalidated a New Jersey law prohibiting the Scouts from discriminating against gays. The Scouts' brief before the U.S. Supreme

Court claimed that private, noncommercial expressive associations have a right to choose their own members and an unqualified right to choose their leaders.[136] The Court held instead that the Scouts had a right to be free from laws that would impair their freedom of expression, and that "Dale's presence in the Boy Scouts would, at the very least, force the organization to send a message, both to the youth members and the world, that the Boy Scouts accepts homosexual conduct as a legitimate form of behavior."[137]

Steven D. Smith observes that perceptions of what behavior constitutes endorsement is parasitic on one's background norms of appropriate, neutral behavior. Thus, for example, it is widely thought that the Establishment Clause prohibits the state from supporting religion, but no one thinks that this is what is happening when the church is burning and the fire department puts it out. That's not endorsement; it's just what fire departments do. On the other hand, the state would certainly be sending a symbolic message if the firemen stood by and watched the church burn.[138]

The question of whether the Scouts have "endorsed" homosexuality, then, depends on one's background assumptions about what sort of action is normally appropriate. The Court's analysis assumes that, if the Scouts had not expelled Dale in response to the mere knowledge that he was gay, the organization would send a message of endorsement of homosexual conduct. The day the Supreme Court ruled against him, James Dale declared in an interview: "I'm not a message. I'm not a symbol. I'm not a sign. I'm just a person who happens to be gay."[139] The Court evidently thinks that a gay person *is*, by virtue of his mere existence, a message and that anyone who wishes to avoid endorsing the message must avoid contact with the person. The unspoken background assumption is that the neutral, nonexpressive thing to do is to discriminate against gays. This view is unsurprising coming from Justice Rehnquist, who dissented in *Romer*, but it is remarkable that Justice Kennedy, the author of *Romer*, and Justice O'Connor, who joined his opinion, were ready to sign onto this.[140]

WHAT ABOUT *HARDWICK*?

If this reading of *Romer* is correct, then the case has far-reaching implications. Charles Black wrote of *Brown* that "the venial fault of the opinion consists in its not spelling out that segregation . . . is perceptibly a means of ghettoizing the imputedly inferior race."[141] The *Romer* opinion has a similar fault. In neither case, however, does this fault necessarily impugn the result. The cultural information that is omitted from the opinion is easily supplied by the reader. If, however, the key element in this equation is the recognition of the invidiously stigmatized status of gays, that recognition cannot be confined to the facts of *Romer*. It is precisely this kind of background knowledge that the Court relies on when concluding that a given type of classification warrants heightened scrutiny as a general matter. For this reason, even though *Romer* does not so much as intimate that sexual orientation is a suspect classification, it is nonetheless a step in that direction. *Romer* found that there exists a non-empty set of laws targeting gays that are unconstitutional because they reflect an impermissible animus against the group.[142] Once that finding has been made, it becomes reasonable to ask, of *any* law that facially discriminates against gays, whether it is a member of the set.

Given the widespread prejudice against gays, minimal scrutiny of laws that target them is at least sometimes inappropriate, and *Romer* shows that the Court is disposed at least implicitly to recognize this. But if that is so, then has the way been paved for heightened scrutiny of such laws as a general matter? Will sexual orientation become at least a quasi-suspect classification? *Romer* can easily be read as a precursor of that development. But there is an alternative explanation of why the Court did not drop the other shoe.

Return to the problem with which we began. Can *Romer* be reconciled with *Bowers v. Hardwick*,[143] in which the Court held that a law criminalizing homosexual sodomy does not violate the Due Process Clause? Kennedy did not mention the earlier case in his opinion, and when asked the question in an interview, he would not answer it.[144] In this final section of this chapter, I will suggest that *Hardwick* is an obstacle, though not necessarily an insuperable one, to heightened scrutiny for sexual orientation classifications. It is this obstacle—not merely the precedent, but the defensible principle for which it stands— that is the reason for the Court's hesitation.

Citing with approval several lower court opinions, Justice Scalia reasoned that, after *Hardwick*, it would be anomalous to deem gays a protected class under the Equal Protection Clause.[145] Without more, this argument is a non sequitur. The *Hardwick* Court expressly declared that it was not deciding the equal protection question.[146] It is embarrassing to need to point out that due process and equal protection are two distinct constitutional provisions.[147] The argument implicitly assumes that if there is any provision of the Constitution that a law does not violate, the law cannot violate any other constitutional command either. That proposition is insane. The fact that, in the context of gay rights, it has been solemnly assumed by panel after panel of federal judges deserves more comment than it has gotten.

There is, however, an argument that can be made for linking the Due Process and Equal Protection Clauses in the way that Scalia attempts to. The Court has sometimes suggested that in order to be a fundamentally unfair basis of classification, which is the gravamen of an equal protection claim, a trait must be irrelevant to any (or almost any) legitimate state purpose. This means that, in order to adjudicate an equal protection claim, a court must canvass the range of possible legitimate state purposes and decide whether the purposes proffered on behalf of the challenged law are legitimate. But that same extratextual inquiry undergirds a due process claim, in which the issue is whether the state has a sufficient basis for infringing on the liberty of the person challenging the law.

This means that when courts decide whether homosexuality should be deemed a suspect classification, it is relevant that the legitimacy of the state's purposes in suppressing homosexual conduct was already put into question in *Hardwick*. In *Hardwick,* the Court decided that the promotion of morality was a sufficient basis for criminalizing sodomy.[148] There is, then, according to *Hardwick,* a legitimate state interest in discouraging homosexual conduct. If that is true for due process purposes, it must also be true for equal protection purposes.

The existence of a legitimate purpose is not, however, dispositive for equal protection analysis. The Due Process Clause protects citizens from being injured in important ways and is indifferent to the state's motives. In equal protection analysis, on the other hand, motive is central.

The analysis in *Hardwick* turned on the importance, or lack thereof, of the asserted liberty. The Court rejected Hardwick's claim because the right to engage in homosexual sodomy is neither "implicit in the concept of ordered liberty" nor "deeply rooted in this Nation's history and tradition."[149] Hardwick's interest in engaging in sodomy was deemed (at least constitutionally) trivial, so that the state did not need much justification in order to infringe on that interest. When the Court suspects invidious motive, on the other hand, it does not matter if the discrimination is about something trivial. A city could not permissibly distribute one lollipop to each white child who resides within its limits. If the Court suspects that illicit motive is involved, then the state has a serious burden of proving the relevance of laws that discriminate against the group.

Still, a realistic analysis properly concludes that, after *Hardwick,* the granting of protected status to gays under the Equal Protection Clause would be surprising. *Romer* upsets a sound realist prediction. But it is not clear that this gives anyone a right to complain. Realist predictions are not the law.

There is no doctrinal inconsistency between the two Court's decisions in *Hardwick* and *Romer,* but this is not to say that the result in *Hardwick* is secure. Numerous statutes in American history have specifically prohibited interracial fornication. Since fornication is not a fundamental right, any privacy-based challenge to such laws would have failed. If there had been precedents rejecting such privacy claims, the Court would not have needed to overrule them in order to hold the very same statutes unconstitutional under the Equal Protection Clause.[150] Similarly, a sodomy law that facially discriminates against gays, such as remains on the books in seven states,[151] is valid under *Hardwick* but might still be invalidated on equal protection grounds.[152]

The real stumbling block in this analysis is an ambiguity in the Court's equal protection doctrine. Suspect classifications are sometimes described as those that are "seldom relevant to the achievement of any legitimate interest,"[153] but that makes little sense; why make it hard for government to rely on such classifications on the rare occasions when they *are* relevant? The real problem is that suspect classifications signal invidious intent. But if government can often, even if insincerely, point to a colorable reason for relying on that classification, then it is not clear whether a presumption of unconstitutionality is justified.

Hardwick establishes that sexual orientation is a "distinguishing characteristic[ ] relevant to interests the state has the authority to implement."[154] Once it is stipulated that homosexual acts are harmful in some way that the state can permissibly cognize, then discrimination against gays is indisputably rational. There will always be room for dispute as to what the government's real reason is for enacting any particular law. Perhaps that is why the Court avoided formulating any presumption about laws that discriminate against gays.

The reasoning of *City of Cleburne v. Cleburne Living Center,*[155] in which the Court enjoined the application of a law discriminating against the mentally retarded because it reflected "irrational prejudice,"[156] but refused to declare the retarded a quasi-suspect class, may have influenced the Court's decision in *Romer* to remain silent on the question of suspectness:

Doubtless, there have been and there will continue to be instances of discrimination against [gays] that are in fact invidious, and that are properly subject to judicial correction under constitutional norms. But the appropriate method of reaching such instances is not to create a new quasi-suspect classification and subject all governmental action based on that classification to more searching evaluation. Rather, we should look to the likelihood that governmental action premised on a particular classification is valid as a general matter, not merely to the specifics of the case before us. Because [sexual orientation] is a characteristic that the government may legitimately take into account in a wide range of decisions . . . we will not presume that any given legislative action, even one that disadvantages [gays], is rooted in considerations that the Constitution will not tolerate.[157]

Romer, therefore, can be viewed as a case in which, as in *Cleburne,* the Court intervened against a particularly abusive law, while prudently avoiding a sweeping declaration of suspectness. But this cannot conclude the inquiry. The Court in *Cleburne* thought that the retarded had been the beneficiaries of beneficial legislation that "belies a continuing antipathy or prejudice and a corresponding need for more intrusive oversight by the judiciary."[158] Such beneficial legislation, the court worried, might well be chilled by heightened scrutiny.[159] The same arguments, it appears, weighed against judicial protection of other groups who "can claim some degree of prejudice from at least part of the public at large,"[160] such as "the aging, the disabled, the mentally ill, and the infirm."[161] None of those groups, however, has been subject to the degree of antipathy that gays have experienced and continue to experience. In each of those cases, there was less warrant for a presumption of impermissible motive.

Our answer to the suspectness question will depend on whether we think it likely that, in most cases, laws that discriminate against gays primarily reflect impermissible prejudice or a permissible moral judgment. An honest answer will not cheat by collapsing one of these into the other; both are invariably present. Reasonable people can and do disagree about which of them, in the general run of cases, has a greater effect on gays' legal status. Those who think that condemnation of homosexuality rests on a sound moral judgment will find such a judgment reflected even in the most vicious antigay violence. Those who think that the condemnation of homosexuality mainly reflects irrational prejudice will find such prejudice reflected even in overtly religious objections. Whether it is appropriate for laws that discriminate against gays to be presumed unconstitutional, depends on which of these sides is right. No wonder the Court hesitates.

I think it likely that, absent motives of raw hatred of gays, sexism, and stereotyping, the legal status of gays would be very different from what it is now. Because other reasonable people have different views, I am not serenely confident of this judgment. I *am* certain, however, that deferential judicial review, resting on the easy assumption that all such laws are innocently motivated, *can't* be the right answer.

CHAPTER TWO

THE RIGHT TO
PRIVACY?

By this point, many readers are sure to feel that we have started in the wrong place. They will say that the equality concerns raised by *Romer*, which focuses on the motives of the lawmakers, are tangential to the real issues raised by the gay rights question. Those issues are not so much questions of equality as of privacy. The appropriate starting point for any discussion of the legal rights of gay people, many think, is the idea that certain private matters are none of the law's business.[1] Certainly this has been, for a long time, the most commonly made argument for the legal equality of gay people. This argument must contend with the contrary precedent of *Bowers v. Hardwick*, which held that the constitutional right of privacy does not protect consensual homosexual sex committed within a person's home. This is not an insuperable obstacle, however, because the overwhelming majority of commentators think that *Hardwick* is wrongly decided.[2]

To evaluate the privacy argument, we must begin with its constitutional basis. There is no enumerated right to privacy in the Constitution. Nonetheless, the Court has held for a long time that there is such a right and that it includes the right to marry[3] and to divorce,[4] the right of married and unmarried persons to use contraceptives,[5] the right of extended families to live together,[6] and, most controversially, the right to abortion.[7]

The privacy question has tended to dominate gay rights discussions because the criminalization of homosexual activity has been the most important legal disadvantage that gays have faced and the keystone of a pattern of other disadvantages. The sodomy statutes brand all gays as criminals and so legitimize discrimination against them.[8] These statutes' centrality has been reinforced by the *Hardwick* decision, which focused solely on the privacy issue and which has been most students' introduction to issues of gay rights in the law.

Privacy, however, is a weak basis for gay rights claims. It has no textual basis. It cannot be deduced from earlier privacy decisions. It inappropriately requires judges to decide what is important in life. It excessively disables the state from legislating on the basis of morality. Moreover, privacy is a poor characterization of what is at stake in the gay rights debate, which turns primarily on public status rather than private conduct. The argument has great rhetorical power, of course and has produced notable successes in litigation. It would be foolish for advocates not to deploy it. But its weaknesses suggest that even advocates should not place too many of their eggs in this basket. And courts can always rely on better arguments.

THE BASIS OF PRIVACY RIGHTS

The germinal privacy case is *Griswold v. Connecticut,*[9] which invalidated a Connecticut statute that prohibited the use of contraceptives. Justice Douglas's opinion for the Court holds that the statute violated the constitutional right to privacy, which is not enumerated in the text but which, Douglas argued, could nonetheless be derived from the text.

The logic of Douglas's derivation was as follows. (1) "[S]pecific guarantees in the Bill of Rights have penumbras, formed by emanations from those guarantees that help give them life and substance."[10] (2) "Various guarantees create zones of privacy. The right of association contained in the penumbra of the First Amendment is one. . . . The Third Amendment in its prohibition against the quartering of soldiers . . . is another. . . . The Fourth Amendment [which] explicitly affirms the 'right of the people to be secure in their persons, houses, papers, and effects, against unreasonable searches and seizures.' . . . [and the] Fifth Amendment in its Self-Incrimination Clause" are still others.[11] (3) "The Ninth Amendment provides: 'The enumeration in the Constitution, of certain rights, shall not be construed to deny or disparage others retained by the people.'"[12] (4) "The present case . . . concerns a relationship lying within the zone of privacy created by several fundamental constitutional guarantees. And it concerns a law which, in forbidding the use of contraceptives rather than regulating their manufacture or sale, seeks to achieve its goals by means having a maximum destructive impact upon that relationship."[13] (5) The statute is invalid because it sweeps "unnecessarily broadly" in its regulation of privacy within the marriage relationship.[14]

The basic problem with this argument is that steps (4) and (5) do not follow from the preceding steps. As Justice Hugo Black's dissent insisted, the provisions cited by Douglas do not protect any general right to privacy, but only "privacy at certain times and places with respect to certain activities."[15] Nothing in the specific provisions enumerated by the Court in step (2) implies that the statute challenged in *Griswold* is unconstitutional.

I am not challenging the idea, derided by many critics of the decision, that specific constitutional guarantees can have penumbras. That idea is sound and important. Douglas correctly argued that some unenumerated rights had been protected by the Court because "[w]ithout those peripheral rights the specific rights would be less secure." [16] The strongest case he cited for this proposition was *NAACP v. Alabama*,[17] which blocked an attempt by the local courts of Alabama to force the NAACP to disclose the names of its members. The NAACP had shown that "on past occasions revelation of the identity of its rank-and-file members ha[d] exposed these members to economic reprisal, loss of employment, threat of physical coercion, and other manifestations of public hostility." [18] These circumstances persuaded the Court that an unenumerated right—here, the right to keep one's membership secret—was necessary to the exercise of enumerated rights of free speech and association. Indeed, it was clear that the real reason Alabama wanted the list was that, by disclosing the names, it could stifle unwelcome political dissent.

No such argument was available in *Griswold*. Douglas acknowledges at the end of his opinion that marriage "promotes a way of life, not causes; a harmony in living, not political faiths." [19] Douglas is left with the claim that the marriage relationship is specially protected in its privacy because it is "an association for as noble a purpose as any involved in our prior decisions." [20] The issue raised by the penumbras argument is not, however, whether the privacy right is for a noble purpose, but whether it is necessary to the exercise of an enumerated right and therefore qualifies as an implied right.

The weakness of the majority's opinion led the dissenters to conclude that the Court's decision was a reprise of the "substantive due process" cases of the early twentieth century, in which the Court had often invalidated social and economic legislation on the ground that it unduly infringed on constitutionally protected liberty. The leading case of that period is *Lochner v. New York*,[21] which struck down a New York statute providing a maximum sixty hour work week for bakers. The Court held that the Fourteenth Amendment protected liberty from unjustified state interference and that the maximum hours law unduly violated the freedom of contract between employer and employee. *Lochner* has become notorious as an unjustified usurpation of judicial power, and it was repudiated by the Court in the 1930s.

Douglas began his opinion in *Griswold* by rejecting the suggestion that *Lochner* be resuscitated in order to invalidate the Connecticut statute. "We do not sit as a super-legislature to determine the wisdom, need, and propriety of laws that touch economic problems, business

affairs, or social conditions."[22] Black, on the other hand, thought that
the basis of the Court's decision was "the same natural law due process
philosophy found in *Lochner*."[23]

The weaknesses of Douglas's opinion led other members of the
Court to attempt other paths to the same result. Justice Goldberg
thought that the Ninth Amendment was the basis of a right to liberty,
which the statute violated.[24] Justice White thought the law unconstitutional because it did not promote any of the purposes that the state
claimed for it.[25] Justice Harlan, in what was to become the most influential of the opinions, thought that the law violated the Due Process
Clause of the Fourteenth Amendment, which he understood to reflect
"basic values that underlie our society."[26]

Harlan's approach, which is frankly based in substantive due process, is the one that has commanded the crucial swing votes on today's
court. The most controversial extension of the right to privacy has
been the Court's decision that protected the right to abortion. The crucial votes to reaffirm the right to abortion in *Planned Parenthood v.
Casey* were Justices O'Connor, Kennedy, and Souter, who wrote a joint
opinion that repeatedly quoted Harlan's formulation. The following is
perhaps the core of Harlan's argument:

> [T]he full scope of the liberty guaranteed by the Due Process Clause . . .
> is a rational continuum which, broadly speaking, includes a freedom
> from all substantial arbitrary impositions and purposeless restraints, . . .
> and which also recognizes, what a reasonable and sensitive judgment
> must, that certain interests require particularly careful scrutiny of the
> state needs asserted to justify their abridgment.[27]

This approach to privacy is untroubled by the privacy right's lack of
textual basis and simply takes it as a given part of doctrine. It assigns
considerable power to the Supreme Court. It is the Court that gets to
decide which laws are "substantial arbitrary impositions and purpose-
less restraints," and it is the court that decides which interests cannot
be abridged without "particularly careful scrutiny" of the state's needs.
Can the Court's course be defended? And even if it can, what follows
for *Hardwick*?

BORK'S CRITIQUE

Robert Bork is the most prominent and persistent critic of the right to
privacy. His attack has been twofold. First, he claims that the right
does not exist; it has no basis in the Constitution. Second, even if it

exists, it is indeterminate; there is no way to know what liberties are or are not protected by this right.

The first point is a simple one, already made by the dissenters in *Griswold*. There is no right to privacy enumerated in the Constitution. "Where constitutional materials do not specify a value to be preferred, there is no principled way to prefer any claimed human value to any other. The judge must stick close to the text and the history, and their fair implications, and not construct new rights."[28] If the Constitution does not speak, and if lawmaking authority is placed with the elected representatives of the people, then those representatives should be permitted to exercise their power to make law without interference from the judiciary.

This argument, relying on the weaknesses of the opinions in *Griswold*, is an intellectually powerful one, because those opinions, and scholarly efforts to improve them, are indeed weak. "None of the theories [of unenumerated rights] offered to date is wholly satisfying,"[29] concedes Laurence Tribe, who was Hardwick's attorney before the Supreme Court.

Nonetheless, Bork is fairly isolated in his repudiation of the privacy doctrine, as became clear when he was nominated by President Reagan to the Supreme Court in 1987. The Senate rejected Bork by the largest margin of any nominee in American history, largely because of his critique of *Griswold*, which was capitalized upon by his opponents in public statements and advertisements.[30] Afterward, many commentators agreed that the Bork hearings had enshrined the unenumerated right to privacy as an unquestionable article of Constitutional faith.[31] Subsequent Supreme Court nominees have evidently taken this lesson to heart. Each of them has been questioned about his or her view of the right to privacy, and each, while generally declining to comment on legal questions that might come before the Court, has thought it prudent to declare allegiance to this doctrine.[32] The security of the privacy doctrine in the American mind is evidenced by one poll, which found that 73 percent of respondents thought that the Constitution guarantees a right to privacy and that 51 percent thought that it was written in the Constitution.[33]

Moreover, Bork's clause-bound textualism appears to be repudiated by the Constitution itself in the Ninth Amendment, which states: "The enumeration in the Constitution, of certain rights, shall not be construed to deny or disparage others retained by the people." Bruce Ackerman has observed that Bork's constitutional theory comes close to amending this provision by deleting the word "not."[34]

Bork's argument against the existence of unenumerated rights misconstrues both American law and its cultural background. In his book, *The Tempting of America,* he generalizes the claims of his 1971 article in a survey of American constitutional law since the founding. He concludes that "the heresy of political judging is systemic."[35] There has, he concludes, been no time in American history when judges have resisted the temptation to find unenumerated rights in the Constitution. This conclusion however undermines his claim that that this heresy is inconsistent with "the basic American plan: representative democracy."[36] Whatever is wrong with political judging, it cannot be that it is un-American if such judging has been systemic since the country was founded.

The basic problem is Bork's obliviousness to the felt necessities that elicit the judicial heresies that he condemns. In the cases that he most vociferously condemns, he is strangely evasive about the concrete effects of the laws that the Court struck down. Thus he claims that "[t]here was, of course, no prospect that [the statute challenged in *Griswold*] ever would be enforced. If any Connecticut official had been mad enough to attempt enforcement, the law would at once have been removed from the books and the official from his office."[37] The law had, however, operated very efficiently to prevent Planned Parenthood from operating a birth control clinic in the state. This meant that methods of contraception controlled by women, such as diaphragms, were unavailable to poor women who did not have their own doctors; middle-class women had no trouble getting *their* doctors to break the law by quietly providing them with diaphragms. With respect to birth control clinics, the law was enforced regularly and predictably for decades, with the police reliably showing up whenever the attempt was made to operate such a clinic. The first such raid was in 1938; the last led to the *Griswold* litigation.[38]

Similarly with another case Bork condemns, *Bolling v. Sharpe,* which invalidated school segregation in the District of Columbia. The Fourteenth Amendment rationale of *Brown v. Board of Education* could not apply to this case, because that amendment does not apply to the federal government, so instead the Court relied on substantive due process, as it was later to do in *Griswold.* Bork predictably condemns the Court's reasoning. Yet he also writes: "Congress would not and could not have permitted that ugly anomaly to persist, and would have had to repeal the District's segregation statutes."[39] He does not explain what would have compelled this result in a Congress whose most powerful posts were disproportionately held by Southern segregationists. Evidently he judges that his audience is sufficiently result-oriented that he must distort his reasoning to suit its sensibilities.

Bork nonetheless has a point. The problem with deducing the law from felt necessities is that different people feel different necessities.[40] *Griswold* was generally well-received at the time it was handed down,[41] but this was largely symptomatic of the fact that the statute was already doomed politically. The Catholic Church had relaxed its opposition to repeal.[42] Public opinion had turned quite sharply against the statute, compared to what it had been only a few years earlier.[43] The Connecticut legislature's reluctance to act was, in the end, less a response to political pressure from a determined minority than a prudent desire to let the Supreme Court do the legislature's work for it.[44]

The bottom line appears to be that the privacy doctrine has no sound theoretical basis, but that this defect is not a fatal one. The Court is inventing the law, but this does not undermine its legitimacy; sometimes, indeed, the Court's inventions enhance its popularity. There is plenty of room for argument about whether it has been wise to allow the Court this power, which has led to disasters such as *Dred Scott v. Sandford*[45] and *Lochner,* but the power certainly seems to be there. It has been relied on by several state supreme courts (some, unlike the U.S. Supreme Court, relying on explicit privacy protections in the constitutions they were interpreting) to invalidate their sodomy laws, and it helped produce a similar result in South Africa.[46] Since it has sometimes been used well, it can perhaps be defended on pragmatic grounds.[47]

But then, everything depends on the wisdom of the judges. It ends up mattering enormously, for example, that in *Hardwick* Justice Powell, who was the crucial swing vote, lacked even the dimmest comprehension of gay people's lives.[48] Perhaps Plato was right that we ought to be governed by the best and the wisest, but it's hard to come up with a reliable method for finding personnel who meet that description.

THE SCOPE OF THE PRIVACY RIGHT

There is a second prong to Bork's attack on the privacy doctrine, and this prong does problematize the application of the privacy doctrine to any controversial case such as Hardwick's. His objection is not only to the derivation of the principle; he also claims that there is no coherent way to apply it. Even if one assumes for the sake of argument that there are unenumerated rights in the Constitution, how does one decide what they are?

In a well-known article published in 1971, Bork objects that the Court's choice of the level at which to define the protected liberty was necessarily arbitrary. *Griswold* certainly did not adopt the very broad principle that "government may not interfere with any acts done in private," but it is hard to explain why the principle should be defined narrowly, as "government may not prohibit the use of contraceptives by married couples."

> Why does the principle extend only to married couples? Why, out of all forms of sexual behavior, only to the use of contraceptives? Why, out of all forms of behavior, only to sex?
>
> To put the matter another way, if a neutral judge must demonstrate why principle *X* applies to cases *A* and *B* but not to case *C* . . . , he must, by the same token, also explain why the principle is defined as *X* rather than *X minus*, which would cover *A* but not cases *B* and *C*, or as *X plus*, which would cover all cases, *A, B*, and *C*.[49]

Thus, Bork argues, there is no principled way to distinguish the economic liberty at issue in *Lochner* from the sexual liberty at issue in *Griswold*. In each case, those whose conduct is restricted by the law would prefer to be unburdened by the restriction, while the majority has a different preference. The United States is a democracy; the majority wins unless the Constitution contains some command to the contrary. Both of these decisions are therefore illegitimate.

Bork's criticism problematizes the application of the privacy right to any controverted case, such as the right to homosexual sex. When Bork was a Court of Appeals judge, he observed that the privacy cases "contain little guidance for lower courts."[50] *Griswold*, for example, "did not indicate what other activities might be protected by the new right of privacy and did not provide any guidance for reasoning about future claims laid under that right."[51] The same critique applies to explicit privacy protections in state constitutions. What can they mean?

Some constitutional interpreters have argued that the solution is to define rights as broadly as possible.[52] Bork has, however, correctly observed that one cannot, as a practical matter, abstract all the way to a general right to freedom, since some legal constraints on freedom must, as a practical matter, exist.[53]

An obvious candidate for a limiting principle is John Stuart Mill's dictum that "the only purpose for which power can be rightfully exercised over any member of a civilized community, against his will, is to prevent harm to others. His own good, either physical or moral, is not a sufficient warrant."[54] Mill's principle has been cited by some state courts when they interpreted their own constitutions to vindicate claims like Hardwick's.[55] Mill's essay is a great work of political theory, and it has always held a strong attraction for those friendly to the rights of gays, but his line would secure liberty for gays at far too high a price. Social Security would have to be abolished; prescriptions could no longer be required for powerful drugs; cocaine would have to be legalized, and the formidable persuasive resources of modern advertising permitted to be mobilized on that substance's behalf. (Imagine what Joe Camel could do with those enormous nostrils.)[56]

Mill's principle also constitutionalizes a highly controversial theory of the meaning of life, one that holds that the most fundamental task of a human being is that of defining oneself. This view, Gerard Bradley has pointed out, is "quite culturally specific."

> That the uniqueness of each person should lead to a conception of life in which the goal is the formation and expression of one's own personality is an idea foreign to ancient or medieval thought. Any society, past or present, determined by Eastern religion and spirituality would find the cult idolatrous, worshipping an illusion. But the notion of a self-defining individual, creating an identity through successive choices which are themselves no subject of moral evolution save for harmful effects on others, also could not be sustained—even if thinkable at all—until recently in Western societies. The apex of the moral life until recently was attunement to an order of being not of one's making, and the medium was freely willed acts.[57]

It is doubtful whether it is appropriate for the Court to read such a [sub!]culturally specific philosophy into the Constitution.[58]

And, once again, look at how little Mill's principle accomplishes. Even if private sex acts between consenting adults are not properly within the reach of the criminal law, this falls far short of equality for gays. It is entirely consistent with pervasive discrimination. One can coherently think that certain sexual conduct is immoral and that the state should denounce its citizens who engage in it, even though such conduct, when private and between consenting adults, is outside the state's legitimate jurisdiction.[59] (And even this defense of privacy is a fragile one, since it is doubtful whether there can be a fundamental right to do wrong.)[60]

Some members of the Court have tried to rely on tradition as a way of restricting the scope of the privacy right, holding that in order to qualify for protection, a liberty must be "deeply rooted in this Nation's history and tradition."[61] This strategy has elicited the persuasive rejoinder that tradition is too indeterminate for the task.[62] The reliance on history appears now to be part of the Court's official line on the boundaries of privacy, but it is hard to believe that the Court's decisions do not have other determinants.

Defenders of Blackmun's position in *Hardwick* have tried to identify the more abstract interests at stake in that case. Kendall Thomas has noted three broad conceptions of the constitutional right to privacy in the case law and commentary: zonal, relational, and decisional.[63]

The zonal paradigm focuses on the constitutional significance of the home, recognized in the text of the Third and Fourth Amendments and in a number of the Court's decisions. "The behavior for which Hardwick faces prosecution," Blackmun noted in his dissent in *Hardwick,* "occurred in his own home."[64] This implicated the Fourth Amendment's protection of "the right of the people to be secure in their . . . houses." Blackmun concluded that "the right of an individual to conduct intimate relationships in the intimacy of his or her own home seems to me to be the heart of the Constitution's protection of privacy."[65]

The scope of the zonal claim is unclear, however. Justice Blackmun plainly did not mean to say that any conduct engaged in in the privacy of one's home is protected. "The Court," Bork observes, "we may confidently predict, is not going to throw constitutional protection around heroin use or sexual acts with a consenting minor."[66] Blackmun did not explain how to distinguish protected from unprotected conduct. Moreover, even if Blackmun had prevailed on this issue, the result would be a very modest victory for gays. Much of what is at stake in the gay rights issue is public equality and recognition, not simply a right to conduct secret liaisons undisturbed by the law.[67] Thomas notes that "'the closet' is less a refuge than a prisonhouse."[68]

The relational paradigm "focuses on persons rather than places."[69] It holds that certain associations are specially protected from state interference, because of "the fundamental interest all individuals have in controlling the nature of their intimate associations with others."[70] Here, too, the boundaries of this principle are unclear. If *all* associations were protected, then the prohibition of criminal conspiracy and solicitation would be unconstitutional. Evidently there is some distinction between protected and unprotected associations, but the doctrine does not make it clear where the boundary lies. Hardwick was not arrested because he was associating with another person; he was arrested because he and the other person were collaborating in conduct that was made criminal by the laws of Georgia.

The decisional paradigm, which is the most important of the three, holds that individuals are entitled to "freedom to choose how to conduct their lives."[71] Certain rights are protected, Blackmun observes, "because they form so central a part of an individual's life."[72] It is possible to derive, from "the freedom an individual has to *choose* the form and nature of these intensely personal bonds,"[73] a right not to be discriminated against on the basis of that protected choice.

The fact that a choice is important does not, however, mean that it is protected. Otherwise there would be a constitutional right to suicide, not just for terminally ill patients, but in all circumstances. The general right to autonomy in important decisions does not necessarily entail a right to any particular option.

The common response to this argument is that gay relationships *are* acceptable and valuable. When the law tries to interfere or assign second-class status to gay people's sexual relationships, it is harming them for engaging in conduct that is innocuous or even praiseworthy. Such laws are perverse and wrong. Thus, David Richards writes that "[t]o deny the acceptability of such acts is itself a human evil, a denial of the distinctive human capacities for loving and sensual experience without ulterior procreative motives—in a plausible sense, itself unnatural."[74] Richards articulates the ultimate wellspring of the privacy argument, denouncing laws that attempt to regulate homosexual sex as pernicious obstacles to human happiness.

As a moral argument, then, the autonomy argument is sound. The trouble with this kind of argument, when it is presented as a *constitutional* argument, is the core difficulty with the privacy doctrine: it requires judges to decide, with no apparent guidance from any legal authority, what parts of an individual's life are so central as to warrant protection. In another context, the Court acknowledged that the question of what a person's "ultimate concerns" are is basically a religious question.[75] The courts have no superior competence in answering such questions, which are really not questions of law at all. The Court should not be making pronouncements on such matters.

In defense of Blackmun, Morris Kaplan has written that the right to privacy is not peripheral to the Constitution, but rather is "the belated formulation of a conception of the relation between individuals and their government that is central to the political philosophy of the Constitution."[76] The basic idea is that individuals have rights that are not subject to the whims of government, and that, as the Ninth Amendment declares, these rights are not exhausted by the enumeration in the Constitution. The process of determining the right balance between individual rights and legitimate public objectives "is inherently contestatory and subject to political and intellectual challenge, but it is just the sort of task entrusted to judges within a constitutional democracy." [77]

The question remains, however, how judges can know how to perform that job. The question is not resolved simply by asking whether human rights exceed the constitutional enumeration. I have many interests that government ought to secure for me. I have important interests in life, health, protection from violence, including foreign invasion, and being part of a prosperous economy. Even a right to sexual freedom doesn't do me much good unless I can find a partner. Judges can't give me these things. One needs some account of judicial competence to supplement one's moral realism. As I noted in chapter 1, moral realism does not entail the legitimacy of judicial review unless it can be shown that judges have greater expertise in moral matters than legislatures. Justice Iredell's classic denunciation of natural justice as a source of constitutional law did not deny moral realism; he merely noted the absence of any "fixed standard" for determining what natural justice required, so that "the ablest and purest men have differed upon the subject." [78]

Moreover, as Jed Rubenfeld has observed, the defense of privacy rights that relies on "personhood," the freedom of self-definition, cuts more than one way. "[P]ersonhood," Rubenfeld observes,

> seeks to protect the freedom of individuals to define themselves in contradistinction to the values of the society in which they happen to live. The premise of such freedom is an individualist understanding of human self-definition: a conception of self-definition as something that persons are, and should be, able to do apart from society. [79]

As communitarian and republican theorists have insisted, [80] however, self-definition is a communal activity for at least some people, and intolerance of unorthodox identities may be an indispensable component of this activity.

> In just those cases personhood considers most important, the individual identity sought to be protected can be seen as most clearly conflicting with the collective identity society seeks to maintain. On what ground can personhood uphold one person's right to define himself at the price of ignoring or even destroying an entire community's right to define itself? [81]

If values of self-definition are equally at stake on both sides, then the judiciary ought to leave the weighing to the presumptively legitimate decision-maker, the legislature. "Indeed, in such a balance, personhood would presumably weigh more heavily in favor of those appealing to tradition in their self-definition, for the simple reason that there are likely to be more of them." [82] In short, if autonomy and self-direction are valuable, as the traditional privacy argument insists, then moralistic legislation may be indispensable to the autonomy and self-direction of those who define themselves in terms of their communities.

Rubenfeld has also observed that there are dangers in the suggestion that sexuality is a matter of fundamental self-definition. That suggestion reproduces certain invidious assumptions that gay rights advocates should be wary of endorsing. The notion of homosexual identity begins with the notion of an essential division separating those who engage in homosexual as opposed to heterosexual sex. Moreover, that identity is assumed to be deviant. There is no notion of "heterosexual identity." Persons don't define themselves when they engage in heterosexual sex, because "heterosexuality is merely normality, and the heterosexual must make some further, more particular decisions—pursuing certain kinds of partners or forms of sexual pleasure—before he will be said to have defined his identity according to sexual criteria." [83]

Finally, it's not clear that the decisional account of privacy succeeds in distinguishing *Lochner*. It would be dubious to assume that sex is an important part of self-definition, while the work that one does in the world as an economic actor is less important.[84] "Mark Twain would surely have felt constrained in the most fundamental sense, if his youthful aspiration to be a river-boat pilot had been frustrated by a State-ordained system of nepotism." [85]

Bruce Ackerman responds to the *Lochner* question and the concern about judicial competence by citing Justice Jackson's pronouncement that "we act in these matters not by authority of our competence but by force of our commissions." [86] For Ackerman, the question presented to the Court after the discarding of *Lochner* was one of the meaning of the New Deal:

> How sweeping was the New Deal transformation? Should it be interpreted as completely obliterating the Founding affirmations of private ordering previously expressed in the rhetoric of freedom of contract? Or should the courts continue to re-present the Founding concern for personal liberty by marking off for special protection areas of life that seem far removed from the New Dealers' demand to regulate "free" markets for the general welfare? [87]

It is in response to this problem that *Griswold* should be understood as offering an important interpretive proposal: "Granted, when the

Founders thought about personal freedom, they used the language of property and contract; but given the New Deal deflation of the constitutional status of this language, isn't the most meaningful way *we* can interpret these Founding affirmations through the language of privacy?" [88]

This nicely explains the persistence of substantive due process after the New Deal's repudiation of *Lochner*, but still leaves unanswered the key question: *which* areas of life are to be immunized from government regulation? Ackerman offers no answer to this question, and so his defense of privacy rights remains as incomplete as those of his predecessors.

Finally, there is the matter of state interests. Certain state interests seem to be sufficient to overcome the presumption of privacy, understood according to any one of these paradigms. For example, the zonal, relational, and decisional paradigms are all implicated by the prohibition of incest, which remains on the books in all fifty states. [89] In his majority opinion in *Hardwick*, Justice White stressed the analogy with the incest taboo, which he evidently regarded as an ancient prohibition, the reasons for which are not clear, but which appears somehow so necessary to the functioning of civilized society that it should not be disturbed. Seeing no plausible distinction between the two prohibitions and assuming that it would be plainly unacceptable to invalidate the incest prohibition, the Court concluded that the sodomy prohibition must similarly be sustained. [90] Blackmun responded that "the nature of family relationships renders true consent to incestuous activity sufficiently problematical that a blanket prohibition of such activity is warranted." [91] But this misses at least part of the rationale for the prohibition. One concern that underlies the prohibition of adult incest is that the dynamics between parents and children will be poisoned if parents are encouraged to regard their children as sexual objects, even with the proviso that consummation must be postponed to the more or less distant future.

If it is conceded that such considerations may be given any weight at all, it is hard to resist the inference that society has a legitimate interest in regulating the expression of sexuality. [92] If the social consequences of sexual mores can appropriately be taken into account by lawmakers, it is exceedingly difficult to draw any abstract limit on government's power to regulate sexual behavior. [93] Defenders of the homosexuality taboo argue that the taboo is necessary to preserve the monogamous family. The argument is, I think, unpersuasive, but it is the same *kind* of argument that is necessary to the defense of the incest taboo.

The same kind of difficulty is raised by the claim, similarly grounded in substantive due process, that gays should be able to avail themselves of the constitutional right to marry. The Supreme Court has held that there is such a right, but it must have implicit limits. It cannot mean that I have a right to marry my goldfish, or my sofa. And the Court has never explained what these implicit limits are.[94] Opponents of same-sex marriage say that the right to marry declared by the Court is implicitly limited to heterosexual marriage.[95] The Delphic statements of the Court offer no way to know whether those opponents are wrong.

In short, because it is hard to determine the boundaries of the right to privacy, it is hard to determine whether homosexual sex is protected by that right. And so long as that is the case, gays' constitutional privacy claims must be doubtful.

JUDGING HARDWICK

What then is one to think of the *Hardwick* case?

Many commentators have suggested that Hardwick's claim cannot be distinguished from the earlier privacy cases.[96] Cass Sunstein, in a nicely nuanced treatment, notes the difficulty of the levels of generality problem, but suggests that it can be resolved by reference to precedent. "At the level of generality that best explains such decisions as *Roe* and *Griswold,* the governing tradition would require far stronger justifications than did the *Hardwick* Court for criminal bans on sexual activity between consenting adults."[97]

A close reading of the privacy cases indicates, however, that they are less concerned with promoting sexual liberty than they are with promoting social cohesion and deference to traditional institutions. The decisions preceding *Hardwick* are not purely libertarian in their tendency. The Court has rejected at least as often as it has sustained privacy claims involving private conduct between consenting adults. *Griswold* itself relied heavily on the traditionally high status of marriage, and the concurring opinions likewise embraced that tradition while rejecting sexual libertarianism.[98] *Eisenstadt v. Baird*[99] extended the right of contraception to unmarried couples while reaffirming that the state had a legitimate interest in preventing fornication.[100] *Roe v. Wade* specifically rejected the proposition "that one has an unlimited right to do with one's body as one pleases."[101] A particularly striking illustration is a pair of cases, only three years apart, in which the Court protected traditional families from zoning laws, while withholding similar protection from households made up of unrelated persons.[102] In short, the line of cases preceding *Hardwick* suggested that sexual morals legislation was constitutionally legitimate and suggested this too many times for *Hardwick* to be plausibly characterized as an anomaly in an otherwise libertarian jurisprudence. Even the contraception and abortion cases can be understood as concerned with social stability, which is threatened by single-parent families, irresponsible youthful parents, and neglected children. Thomas Grey's survey of the cases concludes:

> [T]he Court has consistently protected traditional familial institutions, bonds and authority against the centrifugal forces of an anomic modern society. Where less traditional values have been directly protected, conspicuously in the cases involving contraception and abortion, the decisions reflect not any Millian glorification of diverse individuality, but the stability-centered concerns of moderate conservative family and population policy.[103]

Laurence Tribe and Michael Dorf concede that Grey's observation is "realistic," but argue that the approach he describes "is not something that deserves to be called constitutional interpretation."[104] It is inappropriate, they argue, for the court to define basic liberties "by applying the views of the Mayo Clinic or of Planned Parenthood, whether or not one regards those views as socially enlightened."[105] But the subjective balancing of interests that they condemn seems to be an indispensable prerequisite to the adoption of the principle that *they* propose, which is that "consensual intimacies in the home are presumptively protected as a privilege of United States citizens."[106]

The principle of the privacy cases may simply be that in the area of sexual conduct, regulations will be subject to heightened scrutiny if they infringe on interests that the *judges* deem to be important. Once the judges decided that they had a low opinion of "homosexual sodomy," that was the end of the matter. *Hardwick* can, in short, be understood not as a constitutional anomaly, but rather as a reflection of an authoritarian tendency that was present in the privacy cases from the beginning. One can condemn that tendency—I do—but one cannot say that the result in *Hardwick* is not consistent with the preceding privacy case law.

None of this can defend the Court's opinion in *Hardwick*, which is a disastrously bad piece of judicial craftsmanship. Part of the problem may be that the task the Court set itself is insoluble; there seems to be no principled way to draw the boundaries of the privacy doctrine, so that one can have no more confidence in the conclusion that Hardwick's conduct was *not* protected by the privacy right than that his conduct *was* protected. Justice White worried that "[t]he Court is most vulnerable and comes nearest to illegitimacy when it deals with judge-made constitutional law having little or no cognizable roots in the language or design of the Constitution." [107] The problem with this way of putting matters, Rubenfeld observes, is that "the Court in *Hardwick* necessarily drew a line: the right to privacy stops here. That act of line-drawing was a quintessentially normative judgment." [108] That sort of judgment is, of course, the very kind of "imposition of the Justices' own choice of values" [109] that Justice White seeks to avoid.

Moreover, the values on which the Court relies are decidedly unappetizing. The central defect of the opinion is what Blackmun called its "almost obsessive focus on homosexual activity." [110] The statute upheld in *Hardwick* defined sodomy as "any sexual act involving the sex organs of one person and the mouth or anus of another." [111] The category of homosexuality did not appear in the statute. The record in the case did not even disclose the gender of Hardwick's partner.[112] The Court's declaration that "[t]he issue presented is whether the Federal Constitution confers a fundamental right upon homosexuals to engage in sodomy" [113] was thus about as strange as if it had said that the issue presented was whether persons with the initials M. H. had such a right. Whatever the rational basis of the statute might be, it could not have been, as the Court claimed, the "belief of a majority of the electorate in Georgia that homosexual sodomy is immoral and unacceptable." [114] Moreover, when the Court tried to apply its test of whether the asserted liberty was "deeply rooted in this Nation's history and tradition," [115] it looked to the traditional common-law prohibition of sodomy, not noticing that that definition did not differentiate between homosexual and heterosexual sodomy, nor that the conduct with which Hardwick was charged, fellatio, was not part of the common-law definition of sodomy.[116] The Court anachronistically assumed that the category of "homosexual" was part of the ancient prohibition. Thus, the Court forcibly imposed the category of "homosexual" on the statute it was construing, the rationale for that statute, and the scope of the constitutional privacy right.

This would be poor craftsmanship under any circumstances, but it was particularly disastrous where, as the Court well knew,[117] there was an unsettled question about the status of anti-gay discrimination under the Equal Protection Clause—a question that the Court declared that it was not reaching. The Court's blithe use of a category whose suspect character had not yet been adjudicated is so disastrously inappropriate as to cast a pall on Byron White's entire judicial career. It is roughly analogous to a (thankfully imaginary) case in which a pre-*Brown v. Board of Education* court, upholding a conviction of an African-American defendant for some crime of which race was no element, might have added in dicta that it expressed no opinion as to whether the result would be different if the defendant were white.

As I have already noted, the privacy doctrine reflects powerful felt necessities. Many of those necessities can, however, be grounded on a firmer textual basis than privacy. The rights of contraception and abortion, for example, both involve the right of women to be free from the traditional burden of motherhood and thus implicate sex equality and the right to be free of involuntary servitude.[118] But no involuntary servitude is imposed by the prohibition of homosexual sex. The sex equality implications of that prohibition are considered in the following chapter.

The same problem of having judges decide what is important in life plagues the result-based equal protection approach that retains a powerful hold on the academy, although it has become marginal in the Supreme Court. This approach focuses on the effect discrimination has on its victims, rather than on the motives of discrimination's perpetrators.[119] (*Romer v. Evans*, examined in chapter 1, is a specimen of the motive-based approach.) If one holds that what the Constitution prohibits is stigma or material disadvantage, then (since these things are ineradicable aspects of social life) one must offer a theory of when they are justified and when unjustified.[120] And this theory will entangle one in the same difficulties presented by the privacy argument: one must, again, decide what discriminations are so injurious as to require special justification, which again calls upon courts to decide what is important in life. Once more, it is unclear whether this is an appropriate matter for judicial resolution. Thus, the arguments considered in this chapter are weaker than those considered in the preceding and following chapters. The privacy claim, often taken to be central to the question of gays' constitutional status, is actually peripheral to that question. A defense of constitutional protection for gays must look elsewhere.

CHAPTER THREE

THE SEX DISCRIMINATION ARGUMENT, AND OBJECTIONS

While I was writing the first draft of this chapter, the oral argument took place before the Vermont Supreme Court in *Baker v. State*, a case in which three same-sex couples claimed that they had a constitutional right to marry. The Associated Press reports the following exchange between one of the justices and a lawyer.

> Justice Denise Johnson questioned how refusing to grant marriage licenses to the three couples was anything but discrimination.
>
> "Why are people being excluded from a marriage license here?" she asked. "A man can't marry a man because he's a man. A woman can't marry a woman because she's a woman. Why isn't that gender discrimination?"
>
> Assistant Attorney General Timothy Tomasi said it was not because both men and women were given the right to marry in Vermont. "There's no benefit given to males that isn't given to females," he said.[1]

The news story doesn't give many details about the argument, but this fragment alone tells us something important. The sex discrimination argument is being made in the courts. It is being heard and understood by judges. And, through news of the litigation, the public is finding out about it.[2]

The argument that discrimination against gays is sex discrimination is starkly simple; Justice Johnson stated it in three sentences.[3] It is also powerful; Tomasi's response to the argument is weak, and there's no better counterargument that he overlooked.

The basic argument can be stated in two syllogisms.

First syllogism:

(1) Laws that make people's legal rights depend on their sex are sex-based classifications.

(2) Laws that discriminate against gay people are laws that make people's legal rights depend on their sex.

> *Illustrations:* If Lucy may marry Fred, but Ricky may not marry Fred, then (assuming that Fred would be a desirable spouse for either) Ricky is suffering legal disadvantage because of his sex. If a business fires Ricky, or if the state prosecutes him, because of his sexual activities with Fred,

while these actions would not be taken against Lucy if she did exactly the same things with Fred, then Ricky is suffering legal disadvantage because of his sex.

Therefore,

(3) Laws that discriminate against gay people are sex-based classifications.

Second syllogism:

(1) Sex-based classifications are subject to heightened scrutiny.

(2) (from the first syllogism) Laws that discriminate against gay people are sex-based classifications.

Therefore,

(3) Laws that discriminate against gay people are subject to heightened scrutiny.

The argument is straightforward. I have just stated it. Elaboration, to the extent that it is needed, must take the form of responses to objections. Since Sylvia Law and I revived the then-dormant sex discrimination argument ten years ago,[4] a considerable literature has grown that argues about its merits. Some who were initially skeptical of the argument have become converts,[5] but the argument has also elicited numerous criticisms, from both the left and the right.[6] In this chapter, I shall describe and respond to these criticisms. They boil down to six objections:

1. *There is no discrimination, because both sexes are treated alike.*

2. *There is sex discrimination, but the discrimination is not impermissible, because both sexes are discriminated against in the same way.*

3. *The discrimination is justified by real differences between men and women.*

4. *Sexual-orientation discrimination is distinct from sex discrimination; they aren't the same thing.*

5. *The discrimination is not the kind of discrimination that sex discrimination law prohibits, because it has nothing to do with the subordination of women.*

6. *The discrimination is connected to the subordination of women, but it's not connected in the right way: the causal link between women's subordination and heterosexism is not sufficiently clear and strong for the argument to work.*

In this chapter, I shall address these objections in turn.[7] Some of these objections rest on conceptual confusion. Others depend on a mistaken view of sex discrimination law. The last of the objections rests on a valid concern about marginalizing the distinct moral claims of gay people. However, I will argue, this concern is not sufficiently powerful to defeat the argument's considerable strengths.

1. There is no discrimination, because both sexes are treated alike.

The sex discrimination argument has been accepted by a few courts, but it as been rejected by many more. Of those that have accepted it, some did so conclusorily and without argument.[8] The standard response to this argument, cited by virtually every court that has rejected it (and repeated by Assistant Attorney General Tomasi, quoted above), is that both sexes are treated alike by sanctions against homosexuality, because no one of either sex may engage in sexual conduct with another person of the same sex.[9] Ricky can't marry Fred, it's true, but Lucy likewise can't marry Ethel.

This response happens to be the same one that was made on behalf of the laws against interracial sex or marriage: both races are equally forbidden to engage in the prohibited sexual conduct, so there is no race discrimination.[10] That argument was rejected in *McLaughlin v. Florida*,[11] in which the Court unanimously invalidated a criminal statute prohibiting an unmarried interracial couple from habitually living in and occupying the same room at night. "It is readily apparent," wrote Justice White for the Court, that the statute "treats the interracial couple made up of a white person and a Negro differently than it does any other couple."[12] Racial classifications, he concluded, can only be sustained by a compelling state interest. Since the State had failed to establish that the statute served "some overriding statutory purpose requiring the proscription of the specified conduct when engaged in by a white person and a Negro, but not otherwise,"[13] the statute necessarily fell as "an invidious discrimination forbidden by the Equal Protection Clause."[14]

McLaughlin stated the obvious. If prohibited conduct is defined by reference to the actor's own race or sex, the prohibition is not neutral with reference to that characteristic.[15] Indeed, in the states that specifically prohibit homosexual sex, the defendant's own sex would appear to be one of the essential elements of the crime that the prosecution must prove.[16]

2. There is sex discrimination, but the discrimination is not impermissible, because both sexes are discriminated against in the same way.

Another response that has been made is that parallel discriminations, while impermissible in the race context, are just fine in the sex context. Thus, David Orgon Coolidge has argued that sex discrimination doctrine should apply only to "classifications that disadvantage individuals on the basis of preferring one sex over another."[17] But this doesn't explain the Court's hostility to, say, single-sex schools.[18] Could a state require all girls and women to attend one set of schools, and boys and men to attend another, and then defend the law by arguing that there's no sex discrimination because members of both sexes are equally required to attend same-sex public schools?

The fact of classification itself raises constitutional difficulties. The Court has held that "the party seeking to uphold a statute that classifies individuals on the basis of their gender must carry the burden of showing an 'exceedingly persuasive justification' for the classification."[19] "The burden of justification is demanding and it rests entirely on the State."[20]

3. The discrimination is justified by real differences between men and women.

Lynn Wardle points out that the Court has upheld sex-based classifications when they are based on "physiological" or "demonstrable" differences between men and women.[21] The laws upheld in those decisions, however, reflected accurate empirical rather than normative generalizations. More importantly, *the generalizations they reflected were exceptionless.* If it were otherwise—if a sex-based classification could be justified by what is usually the case, or what is true about most members of either sex—then the constitutional doctrine would be eviscerated, because even the most invidiously sexist laws have been justifiable in terms of some argument of this sort.

The strongest support for Wardle's claim may be found in two decisions written in 1981 by Justice (as he then was) Rehnquist, who had previously sought without success to adopt a rule of minimal scrutiny for sex-based classifications. In these two cases, Rehnquist attempted to construe "intermediate scrutiny" in the most deferential possible way. But these decisions have had no generative power, and the Court has gone in a very different direction.

In *Rostker v. Goldberg,*[22] the Court upheld a law requiring men, but not women, to register for the draft. Justice Rehnquist reasoned that the law reasonably reflected real differences between the sexes, given the statute excluding women from combat (the validity of which was not before the Court). Combat readiness was an important governmental interest, and registering women would not advance that interest. "Men and women, because of the combat restrictions on women, are simply not similarly situated for purposes of a draft or registration for a draft."[23] Justice Marshall correctly observed that this reasoning turned established sex discrimination doctrine on its head. The relevant inquiry, he wrote, "is not whether a *gender-neutral* classification would substantially advance important governmental interests. Rather, the question is whether the gender-based classification is itself substantially related to the achievement of the asserted governmental interest." [24] This inversion of the doctrine was not repeated in any subsequent case, and Laurence Tribe is probably right that the case should be understood as an example of the Court's extraordinary deference to Congress with respect to military affairs. [25]

In *Michael M. v. Superior Court*, [26] the Court upheld a statutory rape law that punished the male, but not the female, participant in intercourse when the female was under 18 and not the male's wife. "Because virtually all of the significant harmful and inescapably identifiable consequences of teenage pregnancy fall on the young female," Justice Rehnquist's plurality opinion explained, "a legislature acts well within its authority when it elects to punish only the participant who, by nature, suffers few of the consequences of his conduct." [27] Thus, Rehnquist claimed, the statute did not rest merely on " 'the baggage of sexual stereotypes.' " [28] Rehnquist nowhere suggests that such stereotyping is permissible; instead he relies on the fact that "this Court has consistently upheld statutes where the gender classification is not invidious, but rather realistically reflects the fact that the sexes are not similarly situated in certain circumstances." [29]

Rehnquist's reasoning relies on the fact that no young males, not even a single one, can become pregnant. This is an exceptionless generalization about the sexes. It is a long leap from the holding of *Michael M.* to the conclusion that the state can impose sex-based classification on the basis of generalizations that are only statistically accurate, such as the generalizations that many heterosexual couples produce children and same-sex couples tend to be childless. [30] Such generalizations have been relied on by courts seeking justifications for denying gays the right to marry. [31] But such generalizations have also been relied on to justify *all* forms of sex discrimination. [32] It is now firmly established that generalizations of this sort, even if largely accurate, can never justify sex-based classifications. The Court has held that the justification for a sex-based classification "must not rely on overbroad generalizations about the different talents, capacities, or preferences of males and females." [33] "[G]eneralizations about 'the way women are,' estimates of what is appropriate for most women, no longer justify denying opportunity to women whose talent and capacity place them outside the average description." [34]

Some have objected that an interpretation of sex discrimination doctrine that applied heightened scrutiny to "mirror image restrictions" would entail, absurdly, that single-sex toilets are unconstitutional.[35] The Court has (to my knowledge) only considered the issue of single-sex toilets once, and that indirectly, when in *United States v. Virginia* it declared that admitting women to a previously all-male residential college, as the Constitution required, "would undoubtedly require alterations necessary to afford members of each sex privacy from the other sex in living arrangements."[36] The Court thus assumed without explanation that these were innocuous, while holding that sex-based classifications were presumptively invalid as a general matter.[37]

Even if one accepted as an unshakable premise that single-sex toilets must be permissible, however, this hardly entails that such facilities do not classify on the basis of sex. The sign MEN on the door plainly indicates that only males may enter. Moreover, if it is insisted that mirror-image treatment keeps something from being a classification, then this insulates from scrutiny not only miscegenation prohibitions, but also the separate-race toilets that were one of the most insulting manifestations of segregation in the Jim Crow South.

A defense of single-sex toilets under heightened scrutiny would doubtless rely on the widespread desire for "privacy from the other sex in living arrangements." The basis for this desire is obscure, psychologically complex, and culturally contingent. (Sex-segregated toilets are not universal even in the United States.) Part of it is the felt need to preserve a sense of secrecy about the genitalia of the other sex, and women's fear of male violence also has something to do with it. Whatever the roots of this desire, single-sex toilets satisfy it at little tangible or intangible cost. The tangible burden of sex-segregated restrooms is fairly de minimis.[38] Intangible costs matter as well: single-race toilets were generally understood to connote that blacks were filthy, animal-like, and too polluted to be permitted to perform intimate functions in the same space as whites. Single-sex toilets, however, do not connote the inferiority of women.[39] All these considerations, taken together, should satisfy intermediate scrutiny.

No one who has raised this objection has explained just how the toilet exception to the sex discrimination prohibition could be generalized to include antigay discrimination. Two possibilities present themselves.

One might read the exception to mean that law should accommodate widespread, deeply felt anxieties about sexual boundaries. Sex-segregated toilets reflect those anxieties, and so does the prohibition of homosexual sex. But this principle proves far too much. *All* sex discrimination has sometimes reflected such anxieties. This exception would swallow the rule.

A second possibility is to say that the interest protected by sex-segregated toilets is freedom from the unwanted sexual gaze. That same interest is protected by some antigay rules, such as the exclusion of gays from the military, which (purportedly) shields soldiers from being seen naked by persons who might regard them as sexual objects. This argument, too, proves too much. It, like the other, has been used to justify all kinds of sex discrimination. It is impossible for any policy to shield persons from the sexual gaze, and it can be destructive to try. Humanity cannot neatly be divided into "homosexuals" and "heterosexuals." In situations in which women are unavailable for prolonged periods (such as the military in wartime), men sooner or later will start staring at each other in the shower. A policy that zealously strove to eradicate the sexual gaze would require an Orwellian regime of extraordinarily minute surveillance.[40] Acceptance of sex-segregated toilets hardly entails this.

The principal difference between the segregated-toilet exception to the prohibition of sex discrimination and any form of antigay discrimination is that the toilet exception does not impose any serious burden or insult on anyone. Discrimination against gays is always stigmatizing, and it usually involves serious tangible disadvantages as well, such as the military exclusion. If sex-segregated restrooms had such consequences, they, too, would be unconstitutional.

The only exceptionless "real difference" that could be cited between homosexual and heterosexual couples is one that depends on the new natural law theory, which I shall examine at length in chapter 4. This somewhat mysterious doctrine holds that marriage is inherently heterosexual, because only a heterosexual couple can achieve the "two-in-one-flesh" communion that comes from being an organic unit of the procreative kind. This argument, if accepted, could provide the basis for two answers to the sex discrimination argument. First, it may be argued that laws allowing only different-sex couples to marry classify on the basis of *marriage*, not on the basis of sex.[41] The most supportive precedent for this claim is *Geduldig v. Aiello*,[42] in which the Supreme Court held that discrimination against pregnant women is not sex-based. Pregnancy, the Court noted, is "an objectively identifiable physical condition with unique characteristics."[43] A state disability insurance program that did not cover pregnancy, the Court reasoned, "divides potential recipients into two groups—pregnant women and non-pregnant persons. While the first group is exclusively female, the second includes members of both sexes."[44] "There is no risk from which men are protected and women are not. Likewise, there is no risk from which women are protected and men are not."[45] Similarly, it might be argued, marriage is an objectively identifiable *moral* condition with unique characteristics; a law extending marriage to persons of both sexes divides citizens into two groups, married persons and unmarried persons, both of which include members of both sexes; there is no benefit that men receive and women do not, and vice versa.[46]

The trouble with this argument is that the persuasive authority of *Geduldig* is weak. The decision has not been overruled, but similar reasoning in the Title VII context has been rejected by Congress, and *Geduldig*'s reasoning has been almost universally condemned by scholars.[47]

For these reasons, a second legal strategy may be more attractive: even if it is conceded that the marriage laws classify on the basis of sex, it can be claimed that this discrimination is necessary to the compelling interest in promoting the realization of one of the highest goods that human beings can achieve, the good of marriage. A law that mapped this good in a misleading way (for example, by giving legal recognition to same-sex "marriages") would miseducate the public about the goods that are really worth pursuing.[48] Moreover, the laws reflect real differences between the sexes: only one man and one woman can become one flesh, and there are no exceptions to this generalization.

The philosophical difficulties raised by these claims are examined in chapter 4. The trouble with this argument as a *legal* argument is that it relies on a highly contestable set of ontological claims that probably make no sense outside the context of a certain flavor of conservative Christianity.[49] The Supreme Court has held that, to be constitutional, a law must "have a secular legislative purpose."[50] The promotion of one-flesh unity does not appear to be capable of being plausibly characterized as such a purpose. Recall that, when a sex-based classification must be defended, "[t]he burden of justification is demanding and it rests entirely on the State."[51] It is hard to imagine how a state could meet its burden by invoking this peculiar philosophical theory of marriage, because it is hard to imagine a court endorsing these metaphysical claims.

4. Sexual-orientation discrimination is distinct from sex discrimination; they aren't the same thing.

A number of courts have held without further argument that, since sexual orientation isn't the same thing as sex, sexual orientation discrimination just *can't* be a kind of sex discrimination.[52] The objection, which has also been presented to me many times in conversation, seems to be the following: it's not sex discrimination, because it's *really* sexual-orientation discrimination. To see what's wrong with this reasoning, consider the following case.

I have been ordered by my doctor not to eat any sour foods, because they will upset my stomach. This morning I find in my refrigerator a nice big lemon, which it would be pleasant to chew on this unusually hot day. But I remember my doctor's orders. I mustn't eat anything sour. Lemons are sour. But, aha, here's a way out of the difficulty: lemons are also *yellow*! And my doctor didn't say a word to me about not eating yellow things. So it's fine to eat the lemon, isn't it? Since the lemon is *really* yellow, it can't be sour. But of course a thing can be yellow and sour at the same time. In law, it often happens that a breach of warranty is also a products liability tort. Murder is always tortious. So there is no reason why a single act of discrimination cannot be based on sex and on sexual orientation at the same time.

Caroline Lindberg has stated a related objection. The sex discrimination claim, she argues, covers only a subset of the claims of discrimination against gays:

> Although the sex discrimination approach has obvious utility and appeal when used to secure the recognition of gay and lesbian families, it fails to offer much to the individual who experiences discrimination that is not directly related to his or her partner. This approach necessarily makes the gay man or lesbian a relative creature, defined only by reference to his or her relationship. In the absence of anti-discrimination legislation that focuses on the individual's sexual orientation, the single gay man or lesbian remains vulnerable to discrimination just for being homosexual. For example, a lesbian living in Hawaii might well be entitled to legally marry her partner, but in the absence of protection for sexual orientation, she could be summarily fired when she sends her boss an invitation to her wedding and he discovers that she is a lesbian.[53]

This objection misapprehends the nature of sexual-orientation discrimination. Such discrimination always has reference to a person's relationships, actual or imagined. I am sexually attracted to women and have engaged in sexual relations with women, but you cannot tell from this information alone whether I am gay; you also need to know what sex I belong to. In the hypothetical, the lesbian has been fired by her boss because of her attraction to women, but the boss does not fire all employees who are attracted to women. There is no case imaginable in which discrimination on the basis of sexual orientation will not also be discrimination on the basis of sex.

It is also hard to imagine a case of sex discrimination that cannot be *characterized* as a case of sexual-orientation discrimination, if the defendant is clever enough to think of it. Francisco Valdes's extensive study of the caselaw finds that, in cases involving straightforward sex discrimination, defendants have often succeeded by imputing homo-sexuality to the plaintiff on the basis of the plaintiff's purported gender-atypical behavior. Gender stereotyping is supposedly forbidden by sex discrimination law, but the decision to permit sexual-orientation discrimination has created a huge loophole that has been deployed even against heterosexual plaintiffs.[54]

John Gardner is thus mistaken to argue that "those committed to the moral wrongfulness of sex discrimination should not be delighted to find sexuality discrimination campaigners out on their moral margins trying to turn the marginal cases into central cases, distracting in the process from the real central cases of direct sex discrimination."[55] Discrimination against gays *is* a core case of sex discrimination. Mary Anne Case has argued persuasively that the principle that underlies the constitutional norm against sex discrimination is that "sex should be irrelevant to an individual's treatment by the law and, more broadly, to his or her life chances."[56] This principle comes directly into play when a person is told that he may not marry the person he loves, though he would be permitted to do so if his own sex were different.

5. The discrimination is not the kind of discrimination that sex discrimination law prohibits, because it has nothing to do with the subordination of women.

This objection depends on a false legal premise. A party challenging a sex-based classification is not required to show anything about the relation between the statute and the subordination of women. The Supreme Court has never asked anyone who challenged a sex-based statute to make such a showing; given the difficulties of demonstrating such complex propositions of social causation, no plaintiff could possibly satisfy such a demand.[57] A requirement of this sort would be tantamount to minimal scrutiny.[58]

Thus, for example, in *Craig v. Boren*,[59] the case that first announced that sex-based classifications would be subject to heightened scrutiny, the Court invalidated a law that prohibited the sale of 3.2 percent beer to males under the age of 21 and females under the age of 18. The Court did not hold that the classification at issue tended to subordinate women. Nor did it hold that male eighteen- to twenty-year-old beer drinkers had been subjected to a history of discrimination. It held merely that the state had not met its heavy burden of justification for the classification.

The analogy with the miscegenation[60] cases has confused some commentators, because they think that the Court's holding in *Loving v. Virginia*,[61] which invalidated laws against interracial marriage, depended on its finding that such laws endorsed the doctrine of "White Supremacy." [62] But, as already noted, *Loving* was not the first case in which the Court invalidated a miscegenation law. It was preceded by *McLaughlin*, in which the Court did not say a word about white supremacy; addressing the question of the law's relation to racism was not necessary to the decision. In fact, *Loving* is the *only* Supreme Court decision that has ever directly relied on the idea of white supremacy as a basis for invalidating a law.[63] Once more, a party challenging a racially discriminatory statute does not need to show anything about the statute's relation to racism. She does not need to show that the statute is caused by racism, and she need not show that the statute has the effect of reinforcing racism. Equal protection doctrine does not require a challenger to a statute to address such intractable sociological questions. The challenger has to show that there is a classification of a kind that is subject to heightened scrutiny; once that is shown, the state has to show sufficient justification for the law.

Still, there is a valid worry about the formal argument. Even if discrimination against gays is, as a formal matter, a kind of sex discrimination, is this argument merely a sort of clever lawyer's trick, or does protecting gays from discrimination really further the underlying purposes of sex discrimination law? If the argument is a mere trick, then even if the rejection of the sex discrimination argument would require the courts to carve out a new, ad hoc exception to the general rule against sex-based classifications, perhaps the exception should be made.

The answer depends on what one thinks sex discrimination law is for. If the purpose of the law is to prevent the imposition of gender classifications on people's life choices, then the argument is over; this is just what the formal argument shows that anti-gay discrimination does. If, however, one thinks that it exists in order to end the subordination of women, then one would have to demonstrate some link between anti-gay discrimination and the subordination of women. Any such showing will necessarily wade into deep social-psychological waters. Nonetheless, the showing can be made.

The argument I have offered in the past is the following. Here, as in other areas of antidiscrimination law, the facial classification reveals something important about purpose. The link between heterosexism and sexism is common knowledge if anything is. Most Americans learn no later than high school that one of the nastier sanctions that one will suffer if one deviates from the behavior traditionally deemed appropriate to one's sex is the imputation of homosexuality. It is an obvious cultural fact that the stigmatization of homosexuality is closely linked to gays' supposed deviation from the roles traditionally deemed appropriate to persons of their sex. Moreover, both stigmas have gender-specific forms that imply that men ought to have power over women. Gay men are stigmatized as effeminate, which means, insufficiently aggressive and dominant. Lesbians are stigmatized as *too* aggressive and dominant; they appear to be guilty of some kind of insubordination. The two stigmas, sex-inappropriateness and homosexuality, are virtually interchangeable, and each is readily used as a metaphor for the other. As was true in *Brown v. Board of Education*, the findings of scholarship reinforce what common sense already tells us. Numerous studies by social psychologists have found that support for traditional sex roles is strongly correlated with (and, in some studies, is the best single predictor of) disapproval of homosexuality. Historians chronicling the rise of the modern despised category of "the homosexual" have found similar connections with sexism.[64]

The connection is also a particularly malign one. The homosexuality stigma is part and parcel of some of sexism's worst manifestations. Christine Korsgaard observes that

> whenever individuals deviate very far from gender norms, gender ideals become especially arbitrary and cruel. Human beings are fertile inventors of ways to hurt ourselves and each other, and gender ideals are one of our keenest instruments for the infliction of completely factitious pain. People are made to feel self-conscious, inadequate, or absolutely bad about having attributes that in themselves are innocuous or even admirable.[65]

If one were to search for illustrations of Korsgaard's concluding sentence, one could hardly find more telling examples than those involving the stigmatization of homosexuality. Men who are patient, aware of others' feelings, good with children, appreciative of beauty, or women who are active and competent, athletic, good with tools, are always in danger of being labeled "queer." The fear of this type of stigma plays a potent role in inducing members of both sexes to adhere to the roles traditionally assigned to their own sex—roles that are, of course, structured hierarchically. This is yet another reason for rejecting Gardner's claim, noted earlier, that sexuality discrimination is on the "moral margins" of the case against sex discrimination. It is not, any more than discrimination against interracial couples was on the moral margins of the case against race discrimination.

6. *The discrimination is connected to the subordination of women, but it's not connected in the right way: the causal link between*

women's subordination and heterosexism is not sufficiently clear and strong for the argument to work.

The argument that heterosexism is linked to sexism has been subject to a lot of misunderstanding. Most importantly, it has been misconstrued as an extraordinarily strong causal claim, when in fact its causal claims are exceedingly weak. My claim emphatically is not that gender role deviance is "the total explanation for homophobia." [66] My claim is a good deal more modest. In an earlier article, I wrote that the homosexuality taboo

> is crucially dependent on sexism, without which it might well not exist. And when the state enforces that taboo, it is giving its imprimatur to sexism. As with the miscegenation taboo, the effect that the taboo against homosexuality has in modern American society is, in large part, the maintenance of illegitimate hierarchy; the taboo accomplishes this by reinforcing the identity of the superior caste in the hierarchy, and this effect is at least in large part the reason why the taboo persists. [67]

The claim I made here about social causation was a weak one, supplemented with an argument that a weak claim about causation ought, in this context, to suffice. I now think that there is a better way to attack the problem. [68]

Consider how one would address the analogous objection to the claim that the miscegenation prohibition functions to maintain white supremacy. How could one have responded to a claim that that prohibition had nothing to do with the subordination of blacks?

If one understood the issue to be one of social causation, one could rely on several different kinds of evidence to show such causation. Since the association of the prohibition with racial prejudice is a matter of psychological fact, one might try to draw upon psychological evidence, either by examining the prejudice through the lenses of depth psychology or by examining group studies to determine whether the prohibition is correlated with prejudice. One might examine the history of the prohibition to determine whether it has evolved together with the prejudice, such that historians have found it difficult to discuss one without discussing the other as well. This kind of evidence might lead one to conclude that the prohibition's causal relation to the prejudice is one of *function*—that the prohibition is caused by, and helps to maintain, the prejudice. [69]

There is, however, a shorter and surer road to the same conclusion. Instead of speculating about modes of causation, one may look directly at the discourse that surrounds the prohibition, in order to see whether that discourse persistently invokes and relies upon the prejudice. Unlike the other approaches described in the preceding paragraph, this one remains resolutely on the surface of the challenged prohibition, eschewing deep questions of social theory.

With the miscegenation prohibition, the link between the prohibition and the prejudice was so much taken for granted that the Supreme Court was able to infer it easily from some statements of lower courts, of a kind that had often been given a more benign interpretation.[70] With homosexuality, the link is disputed, and evidence is needed. The link seems obvious to me, but how am I to show that my views are not idiosyncratic? Fortunately, the link has been documented in abundance by Francisco Valdes, who has shown in luxuriant detail the ways in which sex, gender, and sexual orientation have been constantly conflated for the last century in literature, the discourse of scholarly psychologists, politics, public opinion, popular culture, and judicial decision making. His evidence is too voluminous to summarize, so I simply incorporate it by reference here. Valdes concludes that "sex, gender, and sexual orientation *never* have been constructed independently of each other in our society."[71] I suppose that anyone who wanted to refute him could begin by citing instances of discourse in which sexual orientation is constructed *without* reference to gender norms. It would not be an easy task. I cannot imagine where to begin.

The claim that heterosexism and sexism are linked in the way that I have just described is entirely consistent with the claim made by some critics of the sex discrimination argument, that sexual-orientation discrimination is distinct in its social operation from sex discrimination.[72] I do not know how to evaluate that claim, which pertains to complex social and psychological processes that are largely mysterious. What Charles Stember wrote about the basis of the miscegenation taboo is equally true of the homosexuality taboo; any explanation must rely upon "speculation and deduction."[73] I do not know whether sexism or heterosexism (understood as a distinct social force) plays a more central role in maintaining these laws. I don't think anyone knows.[74] I prefer to rely on weak causal claims because I think that, with respect to these questions, weak causal claims are the only ones we can endorse with any confidence. It seems to me pointless to argue about which strong causal explanation is the correct one. Surely we can work against these forms of oppression, and even perceive a functional connection between them, without first understanding every detail of how they came into existence or perpetuate themselves!

I am similarly bemused by Cheshire Calhoun's claim that "[e]ven if empirically and historically heterosexual dominance and patriarchy are completely intertwined, it does not follow from this fact that the collapse of patriarchy will bring about the collapse of heterosexual dominance."[75] She is right. That certainly doesn't follow.[76] It is also true that the two forms of oppression are different in kind: women, like racial minorities, are disproportionately concentrated in disadvantaged places in society, while gay people have no legitimized place at all in civil society. Perhaps those who seek to end heterosexual dominance shouldn't worry at all about patriarchy; perhaps the strategy of fighting heterosexism by fighting sexism is ill-conceived. The strategy may or may not pay off, and one can't tell what the payoff will be until the strategy is tried. The same objection can be made against any particular attempt to fight a pervasive cultural form of oppression: who could be sure, in advance, that school desegregation would help, even a little bit, in ameliorating racial oppression? Even if St. George doesn't know anything about the arrangement of the dragon's innards, though, he's still well advised to stick his sword into it, as often and in as many places as he can. One doesn't need a detailed anatomy of the beast in order to tell the difference between stabbing it and waving one's sword in some other direction.[77]

There are, to be sure, differences between male supremacy and heterosexual supremacy. One can certainly say a lot about each system of dominance before mentioning the other. A social scientist, or even an interested observer of social phenomena, will probably want to study those differences. But that doesn't mean that male supremacy and heterosexual supremacy have nothing to do with one another.

Many writers have worried that the sex discrimination argument marginalizes gays' moral claims. Jack Balkin writes that the sex discrimination argument implies "that discrimination against homosexuals is merely a 'side effect' of discrimination against women, and therefore somehow less important." John Gardner writes that "those committed to the moral wrongfulness of sexuality discrimination should not be at all happy to find this wrongfulness appended to the moral margins of somebody else's grievance, namely the grievance of those who are victims of sex discrimination."[78] William Eskridge writes that the sex discrimination argument has "a transvestite quality," because "[i]t dresses a gay rights issue up in gender rights garb."[79] Danielle Kie Hart argues that the sex discrimination argument "makes the lives of homosexuals invisible; it sends a clear message to society that it is not acceptable to discuss homosexuality in a public forum; and it reflects and may perpetuate negative attitudes about lesbians and gay men."[80]

All these concerns are valid. One can make the same point about the interracial couple that was prosecuted under the miscegenation laws:

the racist system primarily harmed blacks, but the white husband's interests were hardly unimportant.

The problem here is the problem with any legal claim. Law always picks and chooses among facts in the world, deeming some relevant and ignoring others. It thus flattens the richness of human life. Law isn't literature. When we evaluate a human life, we don't just ask whether the person followed the rules. Othello and Iago both killed their wives; the law would make no distinction between them, even though any reader of Shakespeare's play knows that the two men lived in different moral universes. Facts are messy; legal categories make them clean, usually by stripping off all the living flesh. We've already seen the danger that the causal claim behind the sex discrimination argument will be taken to be stronger than it actually is. There is a similar danger, which should always be resisted, that stories deemed irrelevant for legal purposes will be deemed irrelevant simpliciter.

The sex discrimination argument relies on settled law that was established for the benefit of women, not of gays. It can be relied on because it is settled, but it is settled only because it was devised without thinking about—to some extent, by deliberately ignoring—the claims of gays. Accepting and relying on the sex discrimination argument thus means accepting and relying on a view of the world in which gays are at best marginal.

On the other hand, the marginalization of gays is precisely why the argument has the comparative advantages that it does. Each of the other principal arguments for gay equality, the privacy and suspect classification arguments, depend on an extension of existing law to cover gays. The sex discrimination argument does not depend on any extension of existing laws. On the contrary, it is its opponents who must ask for legal innovation, by carving out a new exception to a rule that is settled.

The argument's strengths are not accidental. The relation between the stigmatization of gender nonconformity and that of homosexuality is too close for the argument to be dismissed as a mere technical trick. But it does abstract from the particularity of gays' lives.

And from the particularity of some conservatives' objections to homosexuality. The objection from the left that I have just considered, in its insistence on particularity, resembles the objection from the right that has been articulated by Lynn Wardle.

> The heterosexual dimension of the relationship is at the very core of
> what makes marriage a unique union and is the reason why marriage is
> so valuable to individuals and to society. The concept of marriage is

founded on the fact that the union of two persons of different genders creates a relationship of unique potential strength and inimitable potential value to society. The essence of marriage is the integration of a universe of gender differences (profound and subtle, biological and cultural, psychological and genetic) associated with sexual identity. . . . Legalizing same-sex marriage, on the other hand, would send a message that a woman is not absolutely necessary and equally indispensable to the socially valued institution of marriage, weakening rather than strengthening equality for the vast majority of women.[81]

Wardle's complaint is oddly similar to those of Balkin, Gardner, and Eskridge, all of whom are his political adversaries. He, too, complains that the sex discrimination argument ignores social meanings that are salient in *his* culture. And the aspects of his culture to which the claims don't correspond should be acknowledged, even if they're legally irrelevant.

Conservative critics of the sex discrimination argument have never addressed the evidence that heterosexism and sexism are culturally linked, just as they have never deigned to notice in print that gay people are the objects of insane hatred in the United States. It would be unfair to attribute sexism or hatred to these writers; the conservative Christianity that they all endorse condemns both the oppression of women and violence against gays. On the other hand, I do not suppose that they would attempt to deny that these vicious tendencies are at least reinforced by laws that discriminate against gays. There are men whose conceptions of heterosexual masculinity is very much bound up with rage toward women; the statistics on wife battering teach us that there are quite a few men of that sort. Violence against gays is a fact of life throughout the United States.

The conservatives' argument must be that even if these unwelcome phenomena are made more likely by laws that discriminate against gays, and even if such laws get some of their support from people who have these immoral prejudices, those laws nonetheless reflect benign purposes. This defense of laws that reinforce invidious prejudices would resemble the doctrine of double effect in Catholic casuistry: it is morally permissible to bring about a bad result, such as someone's death, so long as that result is not what you intend either as end or as means, but is only an unwelcome side-effect of your act. Even if one accepts this doctrine, however, the doctrine requires "that the good effect or aspect, which is intended, should be proportionate (say, saving someone's life), i.e. sufficiently good and important relative to the bad effect or aspect."[82] That is, the purpose being served by laws that discriminate against gays would have to be shown to be, not merely rational, but so important that it justifies the reinforcement of sexism. Perhaps another way of saying this is that such laws would have to withstand heightened scrutiny. I have already explained why I think that they cannot survive such scrutiny.

*   *   *

The sex discrimination argument has, of course, usually been rejected by the courts, but this does not distinguish it from any other argument that has been made on behalf of gays. The rule of law is always an aspiration, never perfectly realized. Courts have for a long time been predisposed to reject claims made by gay people regardless of their merits.[83]

The sex discrimination argument has an important analytic strength, particularly when one compares it to the other arguments that are available. The equal protection argument for judicial protection of gays as such is supported by the long history of anti-gay discrimination, but the indeterminacy of equal protection doctrine makes this strategy an uncertain one. The privacy argument is even less certain, since it is most unclear how one determines whether any particular conduct is protected by it.

The sex discrimination argument is not free from indeterminacy, to be sure. With any presumptively unconstitutional law, the question inevitably arises whether the state can offer an adequate justification for what it has done, and then a court will have to balance the interests involved in a way that will unavoidably leave some room for judicial discretion. With the sex discrimination argument, I noted earlier, it is uncertain what distinguishes sex discrimination in marriage from similarly separate-but-equal discrimination in restrooms. By contrast, with the sex discrimination argument, the prima facie case has been made, and the burden is on the state to get out from under it. The indeterminacy works, to that extent, to the advantage of the person challenging the law. With liberty or sexual-orientation-as-a-suspect-classification, on the other hand, the indeterminacy plagues the plaintiff at the level of his prima facie case. The law's inertia is in favor of validation. In short, it matters a lot at what stage of the argument the indeterminacy comes in.[84]

The sex discrimination argument's comparative moral strengths are less stark than its doctrinal advantages, but they are worth noting. The privacy and suspect class arguments do point to important and valid moral claims, even if it is hard to translate those claims into legal doctrine. Sodomy laws do intrude into matters that are none of the state's business. Gays have been the object of vicious prejudice. But the sex discrimination argument shows that the oppression of gays has destructive effects that reach far beyond the impact on gays themselves. The subordination of the feminine oppresses everyone. A moral assessment of anti-gay prejudice that leaves this factor out is as incomplete as a moral assessment of the miscegenation taboo that forgets to mention racism.

One is still entitled to wonder why the argument has been so often rejected. I would suggest three reasons. One is that the argument is simply not understood. Another is that it has struck observers as a mere trick, one that misses the real issue of discrimination that is in question. (I have already cited instances of both these phenomena.) The third, and perhaps the most powerful, is that, from a political standpoint, the argument proves too much. If accepted, the sex discrimination argument would entail that *all* laws discriminating against gays, notably marriage laws, must be swept away at a single stroke. Judges are understandably hesitant to begin down that road.

Such prudential judgments have a long and honorable history. "A universal feeling," Lincoln observed, "whether well or ill-founded, can not be safely disregarded."[85] Lincoln was speaking of the feeling against the political and social equality of blacks—a feeling that was certainly more universal in 1854 than the feeling against same-sex marriage is today.[86] Yet, while his account of universal feeling was probably accurate at the time, the belief that this feeling had no foundation in justice had a corrosive effect upon it, to the extent that today nearly no one will admit to such a sentiment. Moral and legal arguments can change even universal feelings. That is why I keep talking about the sex discrimination argument. It captures an aspect of the wrong of discrimination against gays that other, more familiar arguments miss. It is important that the argument be repeated and understood. Many people who are otherwise oblivious to the plight of gays do understand what is wrong with sexism.

This is not to say that the other arguments are wrong. Anti-gay laws reflect a multitude of sins. Their unconstitutionality is overdetermined. One can only enumerate their defects one by one. As one enumerates each, one necessarily neglects the others. The proper response to this situation is not to try to decide which of the various charges is the most serious, but simply to state them all. I have never said, and I have never heard anyone say, that the sex discrimination argument is the only one that should be made. It is one arrow in the quiver. There is plenty of room for, and use for, the others.

CHAPTER FOUR

WHY DISCRIMINATE?

If the arguments that I have developed so far are persuasive, then when the state seeks to discriminate against gays, it has a heavy burden of justification. Even if these constitutional claims are rejected, however, the question remains whether such discrimination is appropriate. What defenses can be offered for discrimination against gays?

This chapter will survey the most intellectually respectable arguments that have been made. In chapter 1, I argued that much of the reason for the second-class status of gay people in America is irrational hatred. The legal disadvantages of gays have also been defended, however, on the basis of thoughtful arguments that have persuaded many people. Those arguments deserve to be taken seriously.

Americans have become more tolerant of gay people than ever before, but this tolerance has definite limits. A clear majority now think that gays should be protected from employment discrimination and that gay partners should have some of the legal rights of a married couple, such as inheritance, Social Security benefits and health insurance. Marriage, on the other hand, is where they draw the line. Here, most are sure that homosexual acts are in some way per se inferior to heterosexual acts.[1]

The importance of the idea that marriage is inherently heterosexual was recently shown dramatically in a series of cases in which state courts attempted to mandate legal recognition of same-sex couples. In Hawaii and Alaska, judicial decisions that seemed likely to require recognition of same-sex marriages prompted amendments to those states' constitutions that passed by overwhelming margins. In Vermont, however, a decision that offered gays exactly the same benefits, but not the honorific "marriage," not only did not produce any such amendment but was met with prompt cooperation by the state legislature.[2]

Evidently, many Americans share the intuition that marriage is inherently heterosexual, and that intuition plays a powerful role in determining the changing legal status of gays. How is this intuition to be evaluated? Is it a mere prejudice, or perhaps the manifestation of a religious dogma that is incapable of rational justification? Or is it a window into moral reality—a moral reality that is perhaps less well understood now than it was in the past, but that continues to exercise strong moral authority over us?

The question just posed is related to a deeper one, having to do with the law's treatment of homosexuality generally. The question whether the law should or may discourage and morally condemn homosexual conduct has become a pressing political issue all over the world. Homosexual conduct has been discouraged and, in some places, even prohibited for centuries, but in recent years there has been a growing movement to repeal laws based on negative moral judgments of homosexuality.

The central claim of gay liberation is that there is no moral distinction between homosexual and heterosexual conduct per se. The question of same-sex marriage and the question of legal equality for gays are therefore closely related. If there is a distinctive good achievable by heterosexual marriage that cannot possibly be achieved by same-sex couples, then perhaps the traditional disfavoring of homosexuality by the law can be justified. If, on the other hand, the goods achievable by heterosexual couples are in no way superior to the goods achievable by gay couples, then indeed legal discriminations against the latter are arbitrary and indefensible.

I will conclude that there is no good reason to regard the sex of one's partner as a morally significant factor in evaluating sexual conduct. This claim puts me in the awkward position of having to prove a negative. A great many arguments that have been made why sexual orientation is relevant to legitimate governmental purposes; these must be taken up, one by one, and rebutted. This work is Herculean; the killing of the hydra, which grew two heads for every one that was cut off, is the most pertinent of Hercules' tasks.

Some of the commonest claims, to the effect that gays are child molesters, miserable psychopaths, or persons who cannot sustain lasting relationships, are easily discredited.[3] Others deserve closer examination. The most popular, the idea that homosexual acts are wrong because unnatural, rests on a logical fallacy. Others, such as the idea that homosexuality is a mental illness, rest on false empirical claims. The most interesting argument, because it is the only argument that is logically coherent and not empirically falsifiable, is that offered by the new natural law theorists. I shall devote the first part of the chapter to showing that the new natural law theory really is the final redoubt of the traditional moral view, and then show that this theory is itself unsustainable.

THE "PERVERTED FACULTY" ARGUMENT

The traditional view in Anglo-American law, that homosexual conduct is per se immoral, has its roots in classical thought and in Jewish and Christian philosophical and religious ideas. It holds that homosexual conduct is morally wrong because it is contrary to nature. The argument is most intelligible as a theological one—a claim that the purposiveness of organs in nature indicates an artificer who created them. From the purposiveness of these organs, new conclusions are inferred about these natural phenomena: specifically, that the natural order of things reflects the will of God. It is God's will that human beings ought to act in accordance with the patterns laid down in nature. From this it follows that any departure from the natural order of things is a defiance of the will of God, and is therefore evil. Since sex organs are intended by God for reproduction, any nonreproductive use of the sex organs is evil.

A teleological account of this kind appears to be the most plausible explanation for St. Thomas Aquinas's strange conclusion that homosexual intercourse is one of the worst of the vices of lust, worse in a certain respect (though not in others) even than rape: "God himself arranged the natural orders. And so a sin against nature in which the natural order itself is violated is a sin against God who is the creator of that order. . . . [T]he individual is more bound to the nature of species than he is to other individual members of that species and therefore the sin which attacks nature itself is more grievous."[4]

The fundamental difficulty with this way of reasoning is that urged by Hume, who argued that any attempt to infer the existence of God from natural phenomena "is useless; because our knowledge of this cause being derived entirely from the course of nature, we can never, according to the rules of just reasoning, return back from the cause with any new inference, or making additions to the common and experienced course of nature, establish any new principles of conduct and behaviour."[5] Even if the existence of God is stipulated, the same logical fallacy plagues any attempt to infer divine intentions from natural phenomena. One can attribute no intention to the artificer of nature (if there was or is one) that is not apparent from the observation of nature itself. This destroys the teleological objection to homosexuality. Observation of nature alone does not reveal that there is anything wrong with deviating from what ordinarily and typically happens in nature. Anything that is physically possible may well have been intended by the designer of the universe, who made it possible. Nature makes possible both procreation and other uses of the sexual faculties, and even if nature was created for a purpose, there is no way to infer from nature itself which of these was intended or whether that intent ought to be binding on us.[6] As Germain Grisez acknowledges, any moral argument that relies entirely on natural patterns without more is untenable, because it "moves by a logically illicit step—from human nature as a given reality, to what ought and ought not to be chosen."[7]

The impulse reflected by this view is understandable, but it ultimately rests on bad theology as well as bad philosophy. The desire to see God's design in the world produces a characteristic vice, the temptation to suppress evidence that spoils the pattern we thought we saw (such as the testimony of others who do not see it, or who see a different pattern). This is reflected most strikingly in the trial of Galileo: his opponents insisted that, since their understanding of the divine plan was incompatible with Copernican astronomy, the old Ptolemaic system must be the correct one. Galileo's findings have now been assimilated by the religious, but even at this late date Darwin is still giving indigestion to some. In the same way, homosexuality seems to many to signify a disenchanted universe, in which, for all we can tell, there is no plan or purpose at all. This disenchantment is particularly troubling in matters sexual, which many people feel a special need to integrate into a religious narrative.

It is, of course, a fallacy to think that a disenchanted view of nature is irreconcilable with belief in God. It is at least equally consistent with the Judeo-Christian tradition to consider it impious for one to presume knowledge of God's intentions in creating the universe: "Where wast thou when I laid the foundations of the earth? Tell me if thou hast understanding."[8] The theories of Galileo and Darwin, and the rejection of natural teleology are all compatible with religion. There is no reason in principle why one cannot believe in God without also believing that He is a kind of cosmic Kilroy, Who feels impelled to leave His initials carved on every tree. On the other hand, these theories do place greater demands on religious faith than their predecessors. They demand that faith stand on its own bottom, rather than leaning on comforting hints drawn from observed phenomena. And this is, perhaps, why they are resisted so fiercely. Faith is hard.

THE DISEASE CONCEPTION

More modern writers abandon the theological trappings of Aquinas's argument in favor of more scientific claims. This development may perhaps be dismissed, as Eskridge does, as the "modernization of justification"—a manifestation of the tendency, first named by Reva Siegel, for opposition to minority rights to be rejustified by modernized rhetoric.[9] Nonetheless, these arguments, too, must be addressed on their merits.

Once arguments that rely on the naturalistic fallacy are discarded, there remain arguments that attempt to show that homosexual conduct will in some way be detrimental to human well-being. The most influential version of this argument is that made by certain psychiatrists (now a distinct minority in their profession) who argue that sexual attraction to members of one's own sex is a kind of mental disease.[10] This position only solidified after some early equivocation about what is to count as a disease. The earliest proponents of the disease view in the late nineteenth and early twentieth centuries defined disease in terms of deviation from customary standards of acceptable behavior. They "un-self-consciously invoked morality—God, country, family— in describing their treatment of homosexuals."[11] Similarly, the American Psychiatric Association's first listing of mental disorders stated that homosexuals were "ill primarily in terms of society and of conformity with the prevailing cultural milieu."[12] This naive valorization of social custom is hopelessly question-begging. Why should the individual have to conform to the custom, rather than the custom be relaxed to suit the individual?

The modern psychiatric proponents of the disease view have therefore relied on the claim (disagreeing with Freud) that all human beings were constitutionally predisposed to heterosexuality and that only overwhelming environmental forces, specifically massive fears induced during childhood, could divert sexual object choice toward a same-sex object. These writers all thought that this diversion is caused by severe early developmental disturbances. All therefore concluded that homosexuality must invariably be associated with severe personality disorders.[13] The only gays any of these doctors knew, of course, were their patients, who had come to them precisely because they were leading troubled lives. "Since it was assumed that all homosexuals suffered from a pathological condition there was no question about the methodological soundness of relying upon patients for a more general understanding of the disorder."[14]

The reason why the disease theory has now been abandoned by most psychiatrists and psychologists is that this prediction has been demonstrated to be false, most importantly by Evelyn Hooker's studies, which found that psychologists judging projective test results of matched pairs of male gays and heterosexuals could not distinguish the homosexuals from the heterosexuals, and categorized two-thirds of the members of both categories as of average adjustment or better.[15]

The disease theory also misconstrued the nature of homosexual desire, which it held could not be the basis of enduring, loving relationships. It has since been documented that many homosexual relationships are, except for the sex of the participants and the legal status of the union, indistinguishable from heterosexual marriages.[16]

THE RELEVANCE OF PROMISCUITY

The collapse of the disease conception has left a considerable gap in public policy, which for a long time was parasitic on that conception. The most recent claims about the inferiority of homosexual to heterosexual sex that focus on gays themselves (as opposed to others' reactions to gays) tend to emphasize the promiscuity of gay men. (As often happens in public discourse, women are ignored.) A typical formulation is stated by Norman Podhoretz:

> [M]en tend by nature to be promiscuous, and they only become monogamous when women force them to "settle down" in exchange for the comforts and pleasures of a stable home and the delights and the troubles, the challenges and the anxieties, that together constitute the rich fascination of fathering and raising children. It is because [male] homosexuals have no women to restrain them that they are generally so promiscuous (whereas lesbians, being women, do tend toward monogamy); and because they are so promiscuous they are doomed to an endless series of anonymous and loveless encounters—not to mention the risk of disease and early death.[17]

There are several things wrong here. First of all, the promiscuity of gay men is often exaggerated by writers who make this kind of claim. They often cite Bell and Weinberg's 1978 study of San Francisco gays, which notoriously found that 43 percent of the white males surveyed had had 500 or more partners in their lifetimes, and 28 percent had had 1000 or more partners.[18] But a nonrandom sample taken from San Francisco at the height of the sexual revolution is not a reliable index of the country as a whole.[19]

The University of Chicago study of sexual practices, which was the most extensive ever undertaken in the United States, found that "the group of people with same-gender partners (or who define themselves as homosexual or bisexual) have higher average numbers of partners than the rest of the sexually active people in the sample," but that the differences in the mean number of sexual partners between those with exclusively heterosexual partners and those with at least some same-gender activity "do not appear very large."[20] Sexually active men who had ever had any same-sex partners since age 18 had a mean number of sex partners (of either sex) since age 18 of 44.3, though the small sample size indicates that the mean can only be specified with 95 percent confidence as lying somewhere between 22.2 and 66.5 partners. Sexually active men who had never had any same-sex partners had a mean number of partners since age 18 of 15.7, with the 95 percent confidence interval ranging between 12.9 and 18.4 partners. Sexually active women who had ever had any same-sex partners since age 18 had a mean number of partners since age 18 of 19.7, with the 95 percent confidence interval ranging between 13.0 and 26.3 partners. Sexually active women who had never had any same-sex partners had a mean number of partners since age 18 of 4.9, with the 95 percent confidence interval ranging between 4.4 and 5.5 partners.[21]

Gay male relationships do appear to have more permissive attitudes about sexual fidelity than do heterosexuals. Blumstein and Schwartz' comparative study, the most extensive comparative survey to date, found that for men in couples, monogamy is thought to be important by 75 percent of husbands, 62 percent of heterosexual cohabitors, but only 35 percent of gay men. For women, 84 percent of wives, 70 percent of heterosexual cohabitors, and 71 percent of lesbians believe that monogamy is important. Among couples together for more than 10 years, 22 percent of wives, 30 percent of husbands, 43 percent of lesbians, and 94 percent of gay men reported at least one instance of nonmonogamy.[22] A survey of other research concluded that "nonmonogamy is not necessarily a sign of problems or dissatisfaction in the primary relationship. What seems most important is that partners in a relationship reach some degree of agreement about this issue."[23]

Surveys have found that between 40 percent and 60 percent of gay men, and between 45 percent and 80 percent of lesbians, were currently in a steady relationship.[24] Gay and heterosexual couples who are matched on age and other relevant background characteristics don't differ in standardized measures of love and relationship satisfaction.[25]

It is hard to tell how long these partnerships tend to last, since marriage records don't exist. Most studies have been of younger adults, whose relationships have, of necessity, lasted only for a few years. Blumstein and Schwartz's study followed a large sample of couples over an 18-month period. At the beginning of the study, lesbians, gay men, and heterosexuals were about equal in predicting that their current relationship would continue. After 18 months, the breakup rate was 22 percent for lesbian couples, 16 percent for gay male couples, 17 percent for cohabiting heterosexual couples, and 4 percent for married couples. Breakups were far more rare among couples who had already been together for more than ten years: 6 percent for lesbians, 4 percent for gay men, 4 percent for married couples. (None of the cohabiting heterosexuals had been together for more than ten years.) In sum, even in the present regime in which they are not permitted to marry, same-sex couples don't seem to be much more unstable than heterosexual couples.

Lawrence Kurdek's five-year longitudinal study of 236 married, 66 gay male, and 51 lesbian couples found that same-sex couples were not significantly different from heterosexual couples in their satisfaction with their relationships or their ability to solve problems, and that lesbian couples reported higher levels of intimacy than other couples. The only consistent differences between same-sex and opposite-sex couples were that the same-sex couples perceived fewer barriers to leaving their relationships and that the same-sex relationships were slightly more likely to dissolve. Kurdek concluded that the higher dissolution rates were most easily explained by the lack of formalized social and cultural support for same-sex relationships.[26] If same-sex marriages were recognized, the differences in dissolution rates might diminish or even disappear.

This data suggests that same-sex couples aren't all that different, in terms of their capacity to function or to remain stable, from heterosexual couples. Even those who are more impressed than I am by the statistical differences that do exist need to explain why those differences should justify discrimination against the millions of gays who *are* in stable relationships.

THE NEW NATURAL LAW THEORY

Our inquiry so far has shown that psychological and sociological arguments against gay equality do not withstand empirical scrutiny. It is a mistake to attempt to translate into instrumental terms what is essentially a moral argument. Moral argument can no longer, if it ever could, rely on the sciences to do its work. The traditional position, if it is to be made persuasively, must show that homosexual conduct is morally harmful and wrong even if it does not produce subjective unhappiness, is part of an enduring relationship, and for some people is the only possible basis for an enduring sexual relationship.

The most thoughtful attempt to meet this challenge emerges from the natural law tradition. Within this tradition, there are various schools of thought about moral theory and its implications for homosexuality and sexual ethics generally. The most interesting is that recently developed by the "new natural law theorists," Germain Grisez,[27]

John Finnis, Robert P. George, Gerard V. Bradley, and Patrick Lee. As Stephen Macedo has observed, the argument developed by these writers "is by far the most elaborate intellectual case for distinguishing between homosexual and heterosexual activity."[28] The remainder of this chapter will be devoted to describing and rebutting that argument, which is the last redoubt of the traditional view.[29]

One of the new natural law theory's (hereinafter NNL's) central claims is that marriage is *necessarily* a relation between persons of different sexes. Some of the premises of NNL will seem strange to many readers. Consistent with the Catholic ethical tradition from which it emerges,[30] NNL condemns not only homosexual conduct, but other sexual behaviors that are widely engaged in and considered innocuous, such as contracepted sexual intercourse. On the other hand, there are intuitions that most Americans share, specifically with regard to homosexuality, that the NNL theorists have defended more thoughtfully and coherently than anyone else. Most pertinently, NNL claims that, whatever goods a same-sex couple is capable of achieving together,[31] marriage is simply impossible for them, because of the kind of thing that marriage is. Most Americans believe this. Even those who are friendliest to gays' claims draw the line here.[32] They certainly do not believe that sex is valuable only for purposes of procreation. They approve of heterosexual marriages of the elderly and infertile, for example. But they think that even these cases realize something uniquely valuable that is not realized by the same-sex couple. So NNL's views, while they are often obscure, are not idiosyncratic. On the contrary, they are the most fully worked out statement of a position that is widely held and politically powerful. (Whether it coheres with other widely held views is a different question.) Thus, it is a matter of great urgency whether NNL is right.

In the following section, I will summarize the NNL argument. I will then state the objections.

The New Natural Law Argument

A foundational concept of NNL is that certain identifiable goods are intrinsically and not just instrumentally worthy of being pursued. These "basic goods" are intelligible ends, capable of motivating us to act as a matter of free choice by appealing to our practical understanding. Such goods are worth pursuing even at the price of discomfort or pain. In the earlier work of Grisez and Finnis, the "rea[s]ons for acting which need no further reason"[33] include life and health; knowledge and aesthetic experience; excellence in work and play; friendship; self integration (what I shall later refer to as "integrity");

peace of conscience; and peace with God.[34] (An important later addition will be considered below.) Each of these is an end in itself. None of them is reducible to any of the others, or to some common factor (such as utility) which they essentially share. Each, as an end, can provide a sufficient explanation for a human action; if we are told that a given action is done for the sake of one of these goods, we need no further explanation.[35]

The basic goods as they figure in options for morally significant choosing are incommensurable. "No basic good considered precisely as such can be meaningfully said to be better than another."[36] It follows from this that it can never be morally justified to act in a way directly contrary to one of the basic goods:

> For: The proposed destroying, damaging, or blocking of some basic aspect of some person's reality provides, of itself, a reason not to choose that option—the reason constituted (in the way that all basic, noninstrumental, more-than-sensory reasons for action are constituted) by that aspect of that person's fulfillment. And that reason could be set aside, and the option reasonably adopted, only if one could, prior to choice, identify some rationally preferable reason for choosing that option: that is, some greater good involved in or promised by that option than is involved in and promised by the options which do not include that choice to destroy, damage, or block a basic human good. But . . . such a commensurating of goods is rationally impossible.[37]

It is therefore wrong and unreasonable ever to destroy, damage, or impede a basic good, even when this would produce desirable results. "Evil may not be done for the sake of good."[38] This conclusion immediately entails, for example, the wrongness of acts of contraception, "acts whose exclusive intention is to impede the coming-to-be of a human life."[39] For life is a basic good, and contraceptive acts have as their aim the impeding of this good. Such acts could be rational only if it could be shown that the good sought to be damaged was outweighed by other goods. But, for reasons just given, this could never be shown.

Homosexual acts are always wrong, NNL teaches, because they directly violate two basic goods: marriage and integrity. NNL's description of these two basic goods is complex. I begin with integrity, which is the less complex of the two.

The integrity of the self, "harmony among all the parts of a person which can be engaged in freely chosen action,"[40] is a basic good—a good that is intrinsically worthy of pursuit. It is self-evidently good to be a single, coherent self rather than a mess of conflicting desires and impulses. This good of integrity is violated when one acts for the sake of bodily pleasure or emotional satisfaction, for example when one uses psychoactive drugs in order to produce a desired sensation, or when one masturbates. In all such actions, in which one uses one's bodily powers as an extrinsic means to producing an effect in one's consciousness, "one separates in one's choice oneself as bodily from oneself as an intentional agent. The content of such a choice includes the dis-integration attendant upon a reduction of one's bodily self to the level of an extrinsic instrument."[41]

The realm of sexuality is one in which the danger of such disintegrity is particularly strong, since most of the forms of possible sexual conduct aim precisely at bodily pleasure or emotional satisfaction. But there is one kind of sexual act that does not violate the good of integrity, because participants in that kind of sex act as unified persons who are realizing an intelligible good that is not reducible to pleasure.

The one and only morally permissible sex act is the marital act—the intercourse of married couples, which (for reasons shortly to be discussed) must be heterosexual. In his recent work, Grisez has added an item to the list of "basic goods" enumerated above, and now claims that "marriage itself is a basic human good."[42] The reduction of marriage to other basic goods, such as friendship and the transmission of life, is unsatisfactory, for three reasons:

> First, in marrying, people seem to intend only one many-faceted good rather than several distinct goods. Second, since the good of anything is the fullness of its being, and since basic goods of diverse sorts are irreducible to one another, either there is one basic human good proper to marriage or marriage is not one reality; but recent Church teaching, which resolves the tensions in the tradition, presents an integrated view of marriage; therefore, marriage is one reality having a basic good proper to it. Third, while marital friendship and fidelity might be reducible to the reflexive good of friendship, the core of the good of marital communion is the good which Augustine calls the "sacramentum." . . . Now, this good, the couple's one-flesh unity itself, is not reducible to the existential good of friendship, for, while the couple's consent gives rise to the marital bond, it transcends the moral order: unlike a friendship, a marriage is indissoluble.[43]

The character of marriage as a basic good arises out of the fact that in a unique way, it constitutes "a full communion of persons: a communion of will by mutual covenantal commitment, and of organism by the generative act they share in."[44] The communion of will is constituted by a commitment to exclusive and indissoluble partnership.[45] The organic communion consists in the fact that, when husband and wife engage in marital intercourse, they literally become a single organism. Reproduction differs from other biological functions in that with respect to it,

> each animal is incomplete, for a male or a female individual is only a potential part of the mated pair, which is the complete organism that is capable of reproducing sexually. This is true also of men and women: as mates who engage in sexual intercourse suited to initiate new life, they complete each other and become an organic unit. In doing so, it is literally true that "they become one flesh" (Genesis 2:24).[46]

For the married couple, sexual union is not extrinsic to their friendship with one another. It is not a mere means to their experience of bodily pleasure. It does not violate their integrity in the way that other sexual acts would. On the contrary, it preserves their integrity within a larger community.

> In sexual intercourse they unite (become one) precisely in that respect in which their community is distinct and naturally fulfilled. So this bodily unity is not extrinsic to their emotional and spiritual unity. The bodily, emotional and spiritual are the different levels of a unitary, multileveled personal communion. Therefore, in such a community sexual intercourse actualizes the multi-leveled personal communion.[47]

Marital acts preserve the participants' integrity precisely because they actualize and enable spouses to experience the basic good of their marital communion.

Nonmarital sex acts—irrespective of whether performed by same-sex or opposite-sex participants—cannot achieve this bodily unity. At best, they can achieve the illusory *experience* of unity. "For a truly common good, there must be more than experience; the experiences must be subordinated to a truly common act that is genuinely fulfilling (and as such provides a more than merely instrumental reason for action)."[48] When gay couples (or heterosexual couples, for that matter) achieve sexual satisfaction by means other than marital intercourse, the act "is really an instance of mutual masturbation, and is as self-alienating as any other instance of masturbation."[49]

Homosexual acts are wrong, not only because they violate the good of integrity, but also because they "violate the good of marriage."[50] A choice of nonmarital sex, Grisez writes, "damages the body's capacity for the marital act as an act of self-giving which constitutes a communion of bodily persons."[51] This damage, Finnis explains, "is not, of course, a matter of physiological damage. Rather, it is a damage to the person as an integrated, acting being; it consists principally in that disposition of the will which is initiated by the choice to engage in an act of one or other of the kinds in question."[52] If one regards nonmarital sex as morally permissible, then one violates the good of marriage in the same way that the good of life is violated by cowardly weaklings who would never try to kill anyone themselves, but who approve of terrorists who kill innocents.

The plainest illustration of the point is that of a married man who has never committed adultery, but who would be willing to do so if, say, his wife were not around when he felt a strong desire for sex. That man's exclusive intercourse with his wife cannot be an expression of his commitment to monogamy, because his conditional willingness to commit adultery precludes that commitment. But the same is true of any person who thinks that sex acts outside of marriage are ever permissible. Such a person must judge that the conduct in question has some value, and when that person engages in intercourse with his own spouse, he is pursuing that value, thus is motivated by something other than the good of marriage itself. Here, too, "one's performances in moving towards one's own and/or one's spouse's orgasmic satisfaction cannot express the exclusiveness of marital commitment and marital communion, because one is here and now (albeit conditionally) willing to do that sort of action for motives other than the expression of marital commitment."[53]

"Thus one's conscience's complete exclusion of nonmarital sex acts from the range of acceptable and valuable human options is existentially, if not logically, a precondition for the truly marital character of one's intercourse as and with a spouse."[54] When one damages that precondition, one is damaging marriage, since "to damage an intrinsic and necessary condition for attaining a good is to damage that good itself."[55] But, once again, it is always wrong to act in a way that intentionally damages a basic good. It follows that homosexual conduct (as a form of intrinsically nonmarital sexual activity) is always wrong.

Objections

The argument has called forth many objections.[56] Here, I want to focus on the three that are, in my view, the most fundamental. One is that the requirement never to act against a basic good bears too little relation to human well-being to be a requirement of morality. The second is that integrity is not violated by human actions that aim specifically at bodily pleasure. And the third is that the account of the good of marriage that NNL offers is inadequately defended.

1. Begin with the theory's fundamental requirement, that one never act contrary to a basic good. The difficulty this raises is clearest in the

case of contraception. Life is indeed a good thing, but when contraception is used, no damage is done to the life of any existing entity. The aim of contraception, "to prevent a possible baby's coming-to-be," [57] does not harm any *actual, existing* baby in any way. In NNL's moral scheme, respect for an exceedingly abstract good—a good that is "in the air," unattached to anyone in particular—requires that one tolerate severe impairment of the well-being of actual human beings, which may include permanent sexual abstinence by married persons or unwanted and perhaps even life-threatening pregnancy.[58] Charles Larmore has argued that this sort of deontology can be accepted only if it is undergirded with theological guarantees, so that one is reassured that the damage that one tolerates will be ultimately corrected by divine providence.[59]

2. The instrumentalization argument claims that it is always wrong to manipulate the body (one's own or another's) for the sole purpose of producing pleasure. This claim has led many to object that one often acts for the sake of pleasure and that this cannot be morally problematic as such. Often, the pursuit of pleasure responds to a bodily need, rather than inducing one: the arousal typically precedes the act. I feel an itch before I scratch it. In scratching an itch, I am not abusing my body or regarding it as "a lower form of life with its own dynamism," [60] but tending respectfully to its needs, which are my needs. And when A sexually pleasures B, by whatever means, A is tending respectfully to the needs of B's body, which are B's needs. Lee and George respond that "such acts as twiddling one's thumbs, tapping one's foot, or chewing sugarless gum, are rightly enjoyed simply as physical activities, exercises of one's physical capacities; but that, of course, is not the central reality in a sexual act." [61] Rather, in nonmarital sex, "the physical activities (stroking, rubbing) are chosen merely as extrinsic means of producing an effect (gratification) in consciousness, the only thing chosen for its own sake." [62] This, however, misunderstands what people want from sex. It may be that some of the sex acts that NNL condemns aim solely at a sensory pleasure that would be equally welcome if it were achieved in some other way, say by an "experience machine" that triggered pleasant sensations in one's consciousness,[63] but this seems to be the exception rather than the rule. Sexual desire as such (whether or not it is "marital" in the sense in which NNL uses the term) appears to be directed, not at a mere sensory gratification, but rather specifically at the bodily particularity of another person.[64]

Moreover, the prohibition on seeking pleasure for its own sake would appear to problematize sex even for the married couple that NNL idealizes. Even a married couple, NNL teaches, can fail to achieve unity if their pleasures are divorced from their marital acts. "If Susan, for example, masturbates John to orgasm or applies oral stimulation to him to bring him to orgasm, no real unity has been effected." [65] What, though, if he does it to her? The possibility of female orgasm appears to be an embarrassment to the theory. Most women cannot come to orgasm during vaginal sex. [66] Is it ever licit, according to the theory, for these women to orgasm? Is it appropriate before intercourse (perhaps because it prepares the vagina for penetration, with the pleasures of orgasm being an unintended side-effect), but not afterward? [67] Finnis deplores the widely held "assumption that regular sexual satisfaction is a natural right and a kind of obligation for a married couple," [68] but it is not clear whether he goes so far as to draw *these* conclusions. NNL has not refuted the alternative view (which accords with common sense much better than their view) that bodily pleasure is itself a good thing, and that when people cooperate to produce it, they are producing a common good.

3. Finally, there is not adequate warrant for accepting the NNL definition of the good of marriage. That definition includes the infertile heterosexual couple, but it excludes the same-sex couple. The basis of the distinction is the capacity of the heterosexual couple to engage in acts of the reproductive kind. Even when a heterosexual couple cannot reproduce, Finnis writes, "[t]he union of the reproductive organs of husband and wife really unites them biologically (and their biological reality is part of, not merely an instrument of, their *personal* reality). . . ." [69] The gay couple differs from the heterosexual couple, Finnis explains, precisely in that "their reproductive organs cannot make them a biological (and therefore personal) unit." [70]

Everything here turns on what constitutes an act of the reproductive kind.

> People who are not temporarily or permanently infertile could procreate by performing exactly the same type of act which the infertile married couple perform and by which they consummate or actualize their marital communion. The difference between sterile and fertile married couples is not a difference in what they do. Rather it is a difference in a distinct condition which affects what may result from what they do. [71]

What sense does it make to postulate one type of sexual activity as normal in this way, so that heterosexual intercourse is held to be an act of a reproductive *kind* even if reproduction is not intended and is known to be impossible? Why is it not equally plausible to say that all acts of seminal ejaculation are reproductive in kind, or to say that no acts of seminal ejaculation are reproductive in kind, and that reproduction is only an accidental consequence that may ensue under certain conditions? There is nothing in nature that dictates that the lines have to be drawn in any of these ways. Moreover, even if heterosexual sex is normal, it does not follow that it is normative. Why is an act of the reproductive kind valuable in the way that NNL asserts?

It appears that the argument can be salvaged, if at all, only by silently presupposing a kind of Aristotelian hylomorphism, in which the infertile heterosexual married couple participates imperfectly in the *idea* of one-flesh unity, but the gay couple does not participate at all. The infertile heterosexual couple does become one organism, albeit an organism of a handicapped sort, that cannot do what a perfectly functioning organism of that kind can do. The heterosexual couple is only accidentally infertile, while the gay couple is essentially so. But as with the "perverted faculty" argument, unless one posits a divine artificer whose intentions are knowable, it is not clear how the essence/accident distinction can do any moral work. In what sense *are* they one flesh? Procreative unity isn't realized *in them*. Their unity, if it exists outside of the ideational community in which they participate (and in which the gay couple obviously can also participate), consists in their membership in a class, a natural kind that ideally *can* procreate.

Why should we think that such a natural kind is a real thing, rather than an ex post mental construct? An unloaded gun remains a *gun,* a device designed for shooting, because it was constructed by an intelligent designer for a purpose. In contrast, it's far from clear in what sense, that has any moral weight, the genital organ of a sterile man can properly and precisely be called a *reproductive* organ. It is not fit for reproduction. Moreover, if the Darwinian model is correct, it cannot be said to be *designed* for reproduction, except in a metaphorical sense that can only mislead in this context. The structure is what it is because it just happened, in the past, to increase the gene's likelihood of reproducing itself. The gene wasn't *trying* to reproduce itself. A gene has neither mind nor intention.

"Biological union between humans," Finnis writes, "is the inseminatory union of male genital organ with female genital organ; in most circumstances it does not result in generation, but it is the behavior that unites biologically because it is the behavior which, as behavior, is suitable for generation." [72] Whether such behavior "is suitable for generation" would seem to depend, however, on whether the organs that are used are suitable for generation. A sterile person's genitals are no more suitable for generation than an unloaded gun is suitable for shooting. If someone points a gun at me and pulls the trigger, he exhibits the behavior which, as behavior, is suitable for shooting, but it still matters a lot whether the gun is loaded and whether he knows it. Intent matters: the act is a homicidal kind of act even if the actor mistakenly thinks the gun is loaded, when in fact it is not. Material reality matters, too: if, knowing the gun is unloaded, he points it and pulls the trigger, intending homicide, then indeed fantasy has taken leave of reality. But the only aspect of material reality that matters is whether the gun, as it now is, is in fact capable of killing. Contingencies of deception and fright aside, all objects that are *not* loaded guns are morally equivalent in this context: it is not more wrong, and certainly not closer to homicide, to point a gun known to be unloaded at someone and pull the trigger than it is to point one's finger and say, "bang!" And if the two acts have the same moral character in this context, why is the same not equally true of, on the one hand, vaginal intercourse between a heterosexual couple who know they cannot reproduce, and on the other, anal or oral sex between any couple? Just as, in the case of the gun, neither act is more homicidal than the other, so in the sexual cases, neither act is more reproductive than the other.

One may, finally, insist on the essentialism implied by the ordinary meaning of words. The heart of a dead man, which will never beat again, is still a heart. His stomach is still a digestive organ. Similarly, the penis of a man who is sterile is still a reproductive organ. But the only aspect of reproductiveness that is relevant to the natural lawyers' argument, namely the reproductive *power* of the organ, does not inhere in *this* organ. It is not a reproductive organ in the sense of power or potential, even if it is a reproductive organ in the taxonomic sense.[73] And, once more, it remains mysterious why its being a reproductive organ, in either sense, should have the moral significance that the new natural lawyers want to assign to it.

Finnis has responded to this objection by arguing that a marital act "is a distinct rational kind—and therefore in the morally relevant sense a natural kind—because (i) in engaging in it one is intending a *marital* act, (ii) its being of the reproductive kind is a necessary though not sufficient condition of it being marital, and (iii) marriage is a rational and natural kind of institution."[74] The institution "is rational and natural primarily because it is the institution which physically, biologically, emotionally, and in every other practical way is peculiarly apt to promote suitably the reproduction of the couple by the generation, nurture, and education of ultimately mature offspring."[75]

Here, the ground has suddenly shifted, from intercourse as a biological phenomenon to marriage as an institution. Finnis would, of course, deny that any shift has occurred, since he thinks that the biological and social are aspects of a single reality. Marriage "as a morally coherent institution or form of life . . . is fundamentally shaped by its dynamism towards, appropriateness for, and fulfillment in, the generation, nurture, and education of children who each can only have two parents and who are fittingly the primary responsibility (and object of devotion) of *those two parents.*"[76] Nonetheless, the emphasis on the social weakens the significance of the purported *biological* unity of the infertile heterosexual couple, since its status as a natural kind now seems to depend on the naturalness of marriage as an institution. Social practice is a good deal more variable than biology.[77] It is true that children typically are raised by their biological parents, but that social practice does not constitute a natural kind, much less a natural kind that includes instances that don't produce or raise children and excludes instances that do.[78]

Among the more difficult aspects of marriage as NNL describes it is the mental disposition that one must have in order to engage in it. NNL teaches that a gay couple can violate the good of marriage even if neither of them is capable of heterosexual marriage[79] and no existing marriage is harmed by their conduct. The difficulty here is related to the first difficulty discussed above. NNL's demand that persons respect goods that are "in the air," unattached to any actual human being, appears to be an integral part of the argument. One cannot accept the claim that homosexual conduct violates the good of marriage while rejecting the claim that contraception violates the good of life.[80]

What reason could there be for accepting NNL's account of the good of marriage? Here, we come at last to the difficulty of resolving any dispute about the nature of the basic goods. George observes that "intrinsic values, as *ultimate* reasons for action, cannot be deduced or inferred. We do not, for example, infer the intrinsic goodness of health from the fact, if it is a fact, that people everywhere seem to desire it. . . . We see the point of acting for the sake of health, in ourselves or in others, just for its own sake, without the benefit of any such inference."[81] The intrinsic nature of these goods can only be defended dialectically:

> While they may be defended by dialectical arguments designed either to rebut arguments against them, or to show up the defects or inadequacies of ethical theories that attempt to do without them, they cannot themselves be deduced or inferred or derived from more fundamental premises. One cannot argue one's way to them (the way one can, on the basis of more fundamental premises, argue one's way to a conclusion). The claim that they are self-evident does not imply that they are undeniable or, still less, that no one denies them. What it does imply is that the practical intellect may grasp them, and practical judgment can affirm

them without the need for a derivation. (Which is not to say that they can be grasped without an understanding of the realities to which they refer.) [82]

In order to show that the basic good of marriage has the dimensions they claim, then, the new natural law theorists would have to offer a dialectical defense of their view.

One piece of evidence that NNL offers is the law of marriage, which for centuries has held that marriage can only be consummated by reproductive-type acts. [83] This requirement does not necessarily indicate recognition of the moral reality that they assert, however. It could also simply manifest the law's recognition that, once intercourse has occurred, (1) the woman may be pregnant (and, given the primitive state of science when these rules of law were formulated, there was no way for a court to know if she was pregnant), so that annulment of the marriage would produce an unsupported child, and (2) the loss of the woman's virginity diminishes the willingness of other men to marry her (again, when these rules of law were formulated).

The other piece of evidence that NNL can rely on is the intuitive sense of limitations on licit sexuality that many people share. "Most people recognize that incest, bestiality and pedophilia, as well as promiscuity, prostitution, and group sex, are morally wrong. Nevertheless, it is not clear how such activities could be immoral if the explanation of the meaning and nature of sexual acts proposed by those opposing our view were correct." [84]

This invites two responses. The easy response is to notice how common contraception, masturbation, abortion, and oral sex are in America, even among married heterosexual couples and even among Catholics. [85] If Finnis is correct that one cannot achieve the marital good unless one understands that these practices are always wrong for anyone, then "marriage" as he understands it is an exceedingly rare phenomenon in the United States.

But this is too easy. As I noted earlier, there is a lot of overlap between NNL and most Americans' intuitions, particularly with respect to same-sex marriage. Finnis has written that my account of sex and friendship has "*nothing* to show why a currently two-person same-sex liaison should have the exclusiveness-and-intended-permanence-in-commitment that is inherent in the idea of marriage (including the marriage of a sterile couple)." [86] The only way to respond to Finnis's challenge is to offer a theory of marriage which accounts for those intuitions, such as unease about adultery, as well as his theory does. I will now sketch out such a theory.

Marriage is a traditional practice that realizes ends that are intrinsically good. It is uncertain whether those goods can be realized equally well in some other way. Marriage has no meaning or reality outside this traditional practice (and the ways in which that practice may be modified in the future). In other words, marriage is an historical cultural formation, not a timeless essence. Finnis is right when he observes that the idea of same-sex marriage "corresponds to no intrinsic reason or set of reasons at all," [87] at least if a one-to-one correspondence between practices and goods is what he is referring to. The question is not whether the practice corresponds to a metaphysical reality, but whether the goods that have traditionally been realized (when all went well) in that practice can also be realized in other social units that don't exactly correspond to the traditional definition. (The word "traditional" is, of course, tendentious here, since there are cultural traditions that have recognized same-sex marriages.)

Alasdair MacIntyre defines a "practice" as "any coherent and complex form of socially established cooperative human activity through which goods internal to that form of activity are realized in the course of trying to achieve those standards of excellence which are appropriate to, and partially definitive of, that form of activity, with the result that human powers to achieve excellence, and human conceptions of the ends and goods involved, are systematically extended." [88] Among examples of practices MacIntyre includes "the making and sustaining of family life." [89] Practices, as MacIntyre understands them, don't have essences. They have histories. The standards of excellence that guide them are not immune from criticism.

Proponents of gay rights are frequently challenged to explain why their position does not also require equality, not only for polygamists, but also for pedophiles, sadists, practitioners of incest, and necrophiliacs. Some, of course, would be happy to include those categories as well, but the logic of gay equality does not demand this. The distinction need not be drawn from high theory; it is enough to notice that none of these sexual practices have become the basis of a worldwide liberation movement whose moral claims persuade increasing numbers of citizens, legislatures, and courts. (If some want to argue that these other practices are as good as the ones that are now valued and honored, they must make their case, as gays have done.)

A proposal to modify marriage is ontologically similar to a proposal to modify the game of chess. Chess, too, "corresponds to no intrinsic reason or set of reasons at all," if, again, this means a one-to-one correspondence between practices and goods. Consider a proposal to change the rules so that the rook can now move one space diagonally, in addition to the other moves it is already permitted to make. Well, you'll say, if we adopted that rule we wouldn't be playing chess any more; we'd be playing some other game. (I don't follow baseball, but I'm told that a similar debate was undertaken some years ago, quite passionately, about the designated-hitter rule: "That's not baseball!") But perhaps this other game would be a better one than the one we play now. I don't think that this question can be resolved by trying to figure out what the essence of Chess is. Chess hasn't got an essence. Doubtless the present game of chess was developed through just such fiddling; perhaps someone once thought that the drunken reel of the knight was hostile to the essence of Chess. The question is what sort of chess rules are likely, under the circumstances, to best realize the good of play. (Actually, "chess" already denotes several different games. The dynamic is very different if you play with a chess clock.)

"A practice," MacIntyre observes, "involves standards of excellence and obedience to rules as well as the achievement of goods. To enter into a practice is to accept the authority of those standards and the inadequacy of my own performance as judged by them." [90] If marriage is understood as a practice in this sense, then one need not rely on any metaphysical claims about marriage as a basic good in order to explain why, at least sometimes, "faithfulness—reservation of one's sex acts exclusively for one's spouse—is an intelligible, intelligent, and reasonable requirement." [91]

As it happens, I am a married heterosexual. I understand my own marriage as instantiating a practice that I've inherited from earlier generations, and that has certain characteristic, intrinsic goods associated with it, having to do with friendship and the raising of children. There are certain rules associated with the practice of marriage that I adhere to, just because a practice without those rules taxes my imagination too much: perhaps some people can make polygamous marriages work, but I know that I couldn't do it, so I'm monogamous. My reasons for rejecting polygamy do not appear to be different in kind from my reasons for rejecting the diagonal-rook-move rule. I'm not prepared to condemn as morally corrupt those who structure their marriages or other relationships according to different rules; I simply wonder, as a practical matter, whether those different rules can sustain the game as an ongoing enterprise. I suspect that monogamy is a virtue in marriage, in MacIntyre's sense of virtue: "A virtue is an acquired human quality the possession and exercise of which tends to enable us to achieve those goods which are internal to practices and the lack of which effectively prevents us from achieving any such goods." [92] I think that adultery would effectively prevent me from achieving the good of marriage, but

my judgment that this is so rests on consequentialist rather than ontological considerations. Perhaps that judgment could be generalized
across married couples generally, but I would hesitate to make any
such claim without evidence.[93]

In sum, the dialectical defense of NNL's view of the goods of integrity and marriage is, to put it charitably, underdeveloped. The NNL
theorists have not shown that either marriage or integrity ought to be
conceived in the way that they do. They appeal to settled practice and
belief to vindicate their claims, but practice and belief oppose as much
as they support the NNL view.

The arguments of the NNL theorists are in some ways strange and
difficult to follow, but their importance is greater than is generally recognized. They alone, among defenders of traditional views about the
morality of homosexuality, manage to construct a defense of those
views that does not depend on false factual claims about gay people.
They alone recognize that their task is to identify some valuable characteristic that is present even in infertile heterosexual couples but absent from gay couples.

The failure of the NNL argument is important, because it was the
last intellectually respectable stronghold of the beliefs that homosexual conduct is intrinsically wrong and that marriage is inherently heterosexual. Those beliefs remain politically potent by virtue of being
widely held. In this respect, however, they do not differ from other
widely held beliefs, such as astrology or abduction by aliens.

CHAPTER FIVE

CHOICE OF LAW AND PUBLIC POLICY

Whatever the constitutional or moral merits of the case, there will not soon be a uniform national solution to the gay rights question. For that reason, it is important for lawyers to think about how to deal with plurality. The concluding part of this book, therefore, will address the ways in which the law should deal with the conflict of laws over gay rights, focusing on the most profound topic of disagreement: same-sex marriage.

No state now recognizes same-sex marriage. Here are two predictions. First, this state of affairs will not change in the next few years. Second, it will change eventually. American culture is becoming increasingly accepting of gay relationships, and sooner or later some state will give those relationships legal recognition.

In the meantime, one state has already come to the brink of full recognition of same-sex marriage. Vermont, in response to prodding by its Supreme Court, has now recognized such marriages in all but name, giving same-sex couples in "civil unions" every right that married couples have in that state.[1] Moreover, the Netherlands now gives full legal recognition to same-sex marriages.[2]

The eventual recognition of same-sex marriage and Vermont's new recognition of "civil unions" both present similar questions of interstate recognition. Suppose that a couple is married, or "civilly united," in one state and that they then seek to have their union recognized in a second state. How should courts in the second state respond? The nature of the problem is only slightly affected by Vermont's decision to use a different label for the relationship.

This chapter will address the question of interstate marriage recognition by developing an analogy with the most profound disagreement in American history over marriage recognition, the conflict of laws over interracial marriage. Until 1967, when the Supreme Court invalidated them, many state laws prohibited such marriages.

Like same-sex marriage, interracial marriages involved an exceedingly strong public policy: the Southern courts regarded marriages between blacks and whites as "connections and alliances so unnatural that God and nature seem to forbid them."[3] The statutes prohibiting such marriages were worded at least as strongly as those of the recent state laws against same-sex marriage: they usually declared such marriages void and punished their celebration with criminal penalties. Yet even in this charged context, the courts rejected the blanket rule of nonrecognition. In every case that did not involve cohabitation within the forum, and in some that did, the Southern courts recognized interracial marriages.

Blanket nonrecognition of same-sex marriage, then, would be an extraordinary rule. Its extraordinary character is relevant to the interpretation of the statutes, recently enacted in more than half the states, declaring that those states will not recognize same-sex marriages that are valid in other states. There is no evidence that any of the legislatures that recently acted gave any thought to how extraordinary it would be, and the laws that were enacted are ambiguous and do not compel that interpretation. Even states that have laws expressly prohibiting same-sex marriages (and a fortiori, those that do not) should recognize such marriages at least some of the time, for some purposes.

* * *

Ordinarily, marriages that are valid where they are celebrated are valid everywhere, for all purposes. There is a longstanding exception to this rule, however, in cases where a marriage violates the strong public policy of the forum in which the question arises. Until recently, the importance of this exception had been diminishing. Now, it matters again, because of the controversy over same-sex marriage.

In the 1990s, when the Hawaii Supreme Court seemed to be about to recognize same-sex marriage, there was intensive discussion of the marriage recognition question. Two simple answers were commonly offered. The first, typically presented by gay rights advocates, was that courts everywhere must recognize such marriages, under all circumstances. The second, typically presented by defenders of traditional sexual mores, was that other states need never recognize such marriages for any purpose. Both answers are wrong. The first is easily refuted. Answering the second will be the task of this chapter.

In the following discussion of the conflicts question, I will focus on the recognition of same-sex marriages, where the precedents are clearest. I will consider from time to time whether the analysis is changed in any way by the fact that Vermont has assigned a different label to the same-sex relationships that it recognizes. This difference of label changes the analysis in two respects, which however tend to cancel one another out. First, the policy in favor of recognizing such marriages may be weaker in this case. Second, the recent wave of legislation refusing to recognize same-sex marriages is of doubtful relevance here, since all of those statutes specifically refuse recognition only to same-sex marriages.[4]

Suppose that some state—call it State A—recognizes same-sex marriage. The interstate marriage recognition question may then arise in a variety of contexts. Most typically, a same-sex couple will travel to State A, marry, return to their home state, and there attempt to file a joint tax return, or ask an employer to enroll them as a married couple for health insurance, or move into a neighborhood that is zoned for single families. Such a couple's claim to recognition is, at least in many states, doubtful. There is ample precedent for states refusing to recognize marriages of their own residents who marry elsewhere in order to avoid their home states' marriage restrictions. But even same-sex couples who reside in State A may need to have their status adjudicated in other states. One partner may accrue a wrongful death action elsewhere or die and leave property in another state that the spouse seeks to inherit. While traveling, a partner may become too incapacitated to make her own medical decisions, so that a family member (if there is one recognizable by the forum) must assume that responsibility. One partner may move out of the state, leaving both in doubt as to their marital status. Whether the same-sex marriage will be recognized in each of these contexts depends on whether and when the public policy exception applies.

Traditionally, in choice-of-law cases involving the recognition of marriage, courts have balanced the forum's public policy interest against the interests of other states in effectuating their own marriage laws and the interests of the parties in having their marriages recognized in the forum. The outcome has usually been recognition of the marriage. Although most states' courts have often cited the public policy exception, many have never actually used it to invalidate a marriage.[5] The principal counterexamples are the thirteen states (and the District of Columbia) that have marriage evasion statutes, which declare void marriages of persons who travel elsewhere in order to avoid their home state's marriage restrictions.[6]

Although, until recently, no court ever recognized a same-sex marriage, there was room for doubt in many states as to whether a public policy against such marriages existed that would invalidate them if they were recognized by other states. Absent a clear statutory answer, courts would have to rely on a multitude of factors, such as the existence of laws against homosexual sex, laws against discrimination on the basis of sexual orientation, laws universally validating out-of-state marriages, or marriage evasion laws.[7]

In more than half the states, however, that doubt has now been re-solved. Since a 1993 decision by the Hawaii Supreme Court that for a time made it seem likely that that state would recognize same-sex mar-riages, 34 states (including Hawaii itself) have enacted statutes indi-cating plainly that their public policies forbid recognition of same-sex marriage, and the U.S. Congress has approved and authorized these measures.[8] Other states already had laws on the books to the same effect. Similar efforts have failed in many other states, but they will surely be renewed. These measures have been widely interpreted as dis-placing the balancing effort in favor of a blanket rule of nonrecogni-tion, under which states would "ignore marriage licenses granted to same-sex couples in other states."[9] Under the blanket nonrecognition rule, a state's courts would never recognize any same-sex marriage for any purpose whatsoever.

Lawmakers in these states were preoccupied with the prospect of their own citizens evading their home state's marriage laws by travel-ing to Hawaii, marrying there, and then promptly returning home and demanding recognition of the marriage. Their primary concern was to prevent evasion of their laws by these means. But a blanket rule of non-recognition would sweep far more broadly. It would deny recognition to same-sex marriages in every possible context, regardless of whether the couple resides in State A or elsewhere.

Consider the position of the same-sex couple who make their home in State A. They do not seek to evade any other state's laws. They sim-ply have done what their own state's laws authorize them to do. What is their status to be within the federal system?

The blanket nonrecognition rule would place such a couple in a dif-ficult position. They would lose all the rights arising out of their mar-riage as soon as they crossed the border into any state that had such a rule. Moreover, even if they never left their home state, they would be treated as unmarried if their status should become relevant to litigation that takes place in another state.

The consequences would be harsher than any proponent of non-recognition probably contemplated. To begin with the most extreme case, suppose a lesbian couple is married and raising a child together in State A, and that the child's biological mother takes the child on a weekend trip to the mainland.[10] While there, the mother and child are both seriously injured in an automobile accident. As soon as she learns the news, the other spouse gets on an airplane and soon arrives at the hospital. Under the blanket nonrecognition rule, this is what she would be told: "You may not visit either of these patients, because only fam-ily members may visit patients here, and you are not a family member of either of these people in any respect that our state recognizes. You may not visit or participate in medical decisions for either of them. If the mother dies, you will not have any parental rights in the child. If there is no surviving biological relative, we will regard the child as an orphan and place him in an orphanage."

This chapter will defend the modest claim that, even though many state laws now prohibit same-sex marriage, no state's law requires the described result. These laws state a public policy, but they do not foreclose the case-sensitive balancing of relevant factors and interests characteristic of modern choice-of-law reasoning. Even in novel situations, courts should not depart from ordinary choice-of-law principles in the absence of a clear legislative command that they do so.

Public policy is sometimes said to be an amorphous and unpredictable doctrine. Over time, however, it needn't be. Even the vaguest judicial standard becomes clearer as a body of decided cases comes to encrust its surface. It is possible for a court, when deciding whether to apply public policy, to be guided by past cases in which similar conflicts arose. Most relevantly here, a court can consider a previous case in which there was a forum public policy that was at least as strong as the public policy at issue in the instant case. If, in the previous case, the public policy exception was *not* invoked, then a court should conclude that the exception should not be invoked in the instant case.

*   *   *

The gay rights question, I noted in the introduction, is an instance of a general problem in modern political theory, well stated by John Rawls: "[H]ow is it possible for there to exist over time a just and stable society of free and equal citizens, who remain profoundly divided by reasonable religious, philosophical, and moral doctrines?" [11] The answer that dominated liberal political theory in the 1970s and early 1980s, and that is still offered by Rawls, is that in order to be legitimate in such a pluralistic society, the state must be neutral among controversial conceptions of the good. That prescription would answer the question we are considering, because it seems obviously to forbid discrimination between same-sex and opposite-sex marriages. As a general political theory, however, it has come under heavy criticism, on grounds of both incoherence and normative unattractiveness.

An alternative solution is a federalist one, in which different regions are permitted to arrive at different answers to controversial issues without any region's resolution either being imposed on the others or being subverted by the contrary decisions of other states.[12] But a federalist solution cannot work without a clear division of territorial authority, so that each region's efforts to govern itself are not thwarted by forum-shopping parties. Criminal law is ineffective without extradi-tion. Civil law is ineffective without full faith and credit to judgments.

If it is granted that the state need not be neutral concerning all con-troversial moral matters, and also that there is more than one decent and tolerable comprehensive moral view,[13] then political theory must accept, and work through the implications of, the existence of multiple legitimate governments, at least some of which have laws that reflect moral views that some other governments reasonably reject. Because State A, which has enacted morally controversial (but not morally in-decent) legislation, is legitimate, it would be prima facie wrong for State B to subvert the operation of State A's laws by making itself a safe haven for those who wish to evade those laws. This prima facie duty becomes especially strong if both states are members of a federal sys-tem, which exists in order to subordinate parochial interests to the needs of the whole. In short, the recent turn away from moral neutral-ity toward moral pluralism in political theory makes the devising of sound choice-of-law rules, with respect to controversial moral matters, integral to the project of constructing a political ideal.

This project does not, of course, begin on a blank slate. Choice of law is classically a problem for courts, and their experience can teach political theorists something about how to allocate authority fairly. Al-though much of the impetus for this chapter is the problem in political theory that I have just described, this is a study in law, not philosophy.

As with earlier moral controversies that have divided the country, such as the struggle over slavery, courts will (at least until a national solution is reached) be obligated to devise choice-of-law rules that can fairly divide authority between states that have taken different posi-tions. To the extent that statutory law does not resolve the choice-of-law question—and I will argue that it does not do so in all cases, any-where in the country—the question that they must address is one of precedent: is there any set of cases in which a similar problem arose, and how was the problem resolved then?

No choice-of-law cases have ever arisen in American law concern-ing same-sex marriage, because no state has ever recognized such mar-riages. There have, however, been equally profound moral disagree-ments concerning marriage. They have involved differences in state laws concerning incest (for example, marriages of first cousins), mar-riageable age, remarriage after divorce, and above all, interracial marriage.

The most revealing of these disagreements was the last of these. It involved an exceedingly strong public policy. The statutes prohibiting such marriages were worded at least as strongly as the recent laws against same-sex marriage: they usually declared such marriages void and punished their celebration with criminal penalties.[14] Yet even in this charged context, the courts rejected the blanket rule of nonrecognition. In every case that did not involve cohabitation within the forum, and in some that did, Southern courts recognized interracial marriages.

Nor is nonrecognition of foreign marriages on public policy grounds often found in other countries. Although the issue of same-sex marriage has not yet arisen, and so it is impossible confidently to predict what a court in any country would do if the issue were presented, there appear to be few settled bodies of law anywhere in the world that routinely refuse to give *any* effect to any set of foreign marriages validly contracted elsewhere by foreign domiciliaries.[15]

Blanket nonrecognition of same-sex marriage, then, would be an extraordinary rule. There is no evidence that any of the legislatures that recently acted gave any thought to how extraordinary it would be, and the laws that were enacted are ambiguous and do not compel that interpretation. Even states that have laws expressly prohibiting same-sex marriages (and a fortiori, those that do not) should recognize such marriages at least some of the time, for some purposes.

*   *   *

Any discussion of this issue must take as axiomatic two truths that many gay rights supporters will find uncomfortable. The first of these is that courts are likely to continue to hold that homosexual sexual conduct is not protected by the constitutional right to privacy and that laws discriminating against lesbians and gay men are not presumptively unconstitutional under the Equal Protection Clause of the Fourteenth Amendment. The first axiom, then, is that courts ordinarily will not invalidate laws that facially discriminate against lesbians and gay men. This axiom is necessary in order for the choice-of-law issue to arise at all. If either the privacy or the equal protection arguments are sound, then no state has the right to deny marriage licenses to same-sex couples within its own territory, no variation in state law with respect to this question is constitutionally permissible, and the conflicts problem disappears. The issue would be analogous to the conflict-of-laws problem with respect to interracial marriage, which once generated a significant body of legal doctrine,[16] but which was rendered obsolete when the Supreme Court invalidated all laws against such marriages in 1967.

This first axiom contradicts the previous parts of this book, which argue that the Constitution forbids discrimination against gays and thus requires recognition of same-sex marriage. However, it would be surprising if the federal courts were to impose same-sex marriage on the entire country, and the strength of the constitutional arguments for doing so does not change that fact. The reality is that there is a choice-of-law issue. For purposes of this chapter, then, I shall assume what I am confident is not true.[17]

Much of the argument of this chapter explores the relevance of conflict-of-laws cases involving interracial marriage. I will not pretend that I am not pleased to find that the analogy between the two kinds of prohibition is still not exhausted. Nonetheless, here I do not wish to use the analogy to argue in favor of same-sex marriage, but only to explore how courts have in the past dealt with conflict-of-laws issues involving marriage. Thus, we must also stipulate what courts, in the period under examination, believed: that the Constitution permitted a state to have and enforce a strong public policy against interracial marriages. Same-sex marriage is unique today in the degree of moral passion that it arouses, but there have been other situations in American history when marriages of a certain kind aroused comparable opposition in some quarters. If we are to learn anything from these cases, we must place ourselves in the shoes of the judges who decided them, giving weight to public policies that we either would repudiate or would endorse with far less strength than was once assigned to them.

The most useful such line of cases involves interracial marriage. Such marriages provoked more vehement antipathy than the other kinds of marriage that were permitted in some states and forbidden in others. Moreover, those cases form a fairly consistent pattern from which a set of rules can be drawn. If we suspend, for the sake of the argument, our objections to the substantive laws in question, we may find a certain wisdom in these rules. The Jim Crow judges were horrifyingly wrong about many things, but they did understand the problem of moral pluralism in a federal system, and we can learn something important from the solutions they devised.

The second axiom we must accept is that many states have very strong public policies against same-sex marriage. Whatever doubts may have existed on this score have been resolved in the states that have enacted the statutes just discussed, and courts in at least some other states will probably find such a policy even without an express statutory directive.

It seems to be widely assumed that if these two axioms are accepted, then the conclusion inevitably follows that same-sex marriages will never be recognized, for any purpose, outside of State A. This chapter challenges that assumption. Even given the two axioms, there are strong reasons why states should not invariably withhold recognition from same-sex marriages that have taken place in sister states. These reasons are not constitutional commands. I will make no constitutional arguments of any kind in this chapter. I am discussing what the courts *should* do according to settled choice-of-law principles, not what the Constitution *requires* them to do. Even if state courts are entirely unfettered by the Constitution in this area, a blanket rule of nonrecognition would be a radical departure from pre-existing choice-of-law principles and should not be adopted.

The reason why this is so can be summarized in two counter-axioms. The first is that the Constitution is not the only constraint on state officials' ability to withhold recognition from marriages they dislike. They will also be constrained by their own states' laws, including (absent a statute that is plainly to the contrary) their established choice-of-law rules. The second counter-axiom is that, even if there is a legitimate public policy against same-sex marriage, that public policy must, in any given case, be weighed against the policies in favor of validating marriages and according comity to the laws of sister states.

* * *

This chapter will now describe the public policy exception's history and the rationales that have been offered. Next, it examines the way public policy has been relied upon in cases involving marriage, in which conflicts of law have arisen with respect to nonage, incest, polygamy, and interracial marriage—the most pertinent historical analogue to the present deep moral disagreement over the morality of same-sex marriage. The chapter then goes on to examine the state statutes prohibiting same-sex marriage that have recently been enacted, and concludes that none of them supports a blanket rule of nonrecognition. This conclusion is unaffected by the federal Defense of Marriage Act, which has no impact on pre-existing choice-of-law rules. Finally, I survey a number of possible choice-of-law rules that would recognize and seek to balance the competing individual and state interests. Under any such rule, I conclude, courts should at least sometimes recognize extraterritorial same-sex marriages, their strong public policies to the contrary notwithstanding. The conclusion considers the effect of any defensible choice-of-law regime on the ongoing symbolic struggle over the meaning of marriage.

THE PUBLIC POLICY EXCEPTION
TO CHOICE-OF-LAW RULES
The Exception's History

The public policy exception is not unique to marriage law. It is invoked wherever a court has to decide an issue of conflict of laws—that is to say, any issue in which a court must decide "whether or not and, if so, in what way, the answer to a legal question will be affected because the elements of the problem have contacts with more than one jurisdiction."[18] Public policy has been invoked in cases involving property, trusts, contracts, and torts—any area in which a court may have to choose between applying the law of one or another state. "Invoking the concept of 'public policy,' a court can refuse to enforce, as contrary to its own notions of justice and fairness, a rule found in the state designated by the forum's choice-of-law rule."[19] In a situation in which a state would ordinarily apply another forum's law, in other words, the public policy doctrine permits the state nonetheless to prefer its own law.

Perhaps because the public policy doctrine has the potential to displace all other choice-of-law rules, it is not often invoked. Modern commentators warn against its too-frequent use. In Judge Cardozo's classic formulation, courts should not refuse to entertain a foreign cause of action unless application of the foreign law "would violate some fundamental principle of justice, some prevalent conception of good morals, some deep-rooted tradition of the common weal."[20]

The public policy exception has thus been cabined and to that extent has become less hostile to differing foreign law. In another respect, however, it has evolved in a direction that has a greater potential to encroach on foreign law. In early uses of the doctrine, the court would simply close the forum to the claim, rather than reaching the merits, thus leaving the plaintiff (at least theoretically) free to search for another forum in which to pursue his claim. In one case, the Supreme Court went so far as to hold that it would be unconstitutional for a state to invoke its public policy by denying effect to a defense based on an obnoxious foreign law.[21] Today, on the other hand,

> courts that rely on public policy seldom stop at the jurisdictional threshold, but rather make the occasion an excuse to apply forum law. This is invariably true in the marriage cases; rather than merely refuse to apply the place of celebration rule, courts routinely apply forum law and declare the suspect marriages invalid.[22]

With respect to marriage, little may have changed. Since marriage itself is not a legal cause of action, the question of a marriage's validity
invariably arises incidentally to some other legal question. Usually, at
least before the twentieth century, it would arise in connection with a
dispute over the disposition of a decedent's estate. In such a case, dismissing the cause was not an option; the court was going to distribute
the estate no matter what. If the disputed marriage was deemed valid,
one claimant would inherit; if invalid, the money would go to someone
else.

As a matter of logic, the doctrine can only exist in a jurisdiction that
has choice-of-law rules that, at least under certain circumstances, require it to apply some law other than its own. If a forum never applied
any law but its own, there would be no use for a public policy doctrine.
Thus, the doctrine grows in importance with the development of clear,
predictable conflicts rules (such as the rule that marriages that are valid
where celebrated are valid everywhere). Since the doctrine is an exception, it can only exist in the teeth of a contrary general rule, and that
general rule must be such as to sometimes yield unpalatable solutions.

> Obviously, a mechanism that blindly selects the appropriate law by seiz-
> ing upon some contact that a person, a thing or a transaction has with
> a given territory opens the door to undesirable foreign rules. To prevent
> miscarriages of justice, the mechanism requires a bouncer who throws
> out the most objectionable of those that enter.[23]

Rationales for the Doctrine

What sense does the public policy doctrine make? For much of the
twentieth century, it has been the subject of vigorous attack, particularly with respect to cases in which the foreign law was that of another
state. The principal objection is that the doctrine was needlessly
parochial. Beach thought that, among states whose "differences relate
to minor morals of expediency, and to debatable questions of internal
policy," a declaration that another state's laws were repugnant con-
noted "an intolerable affectation of superior virtue."[24]

Two defenses were offered in response to this objection. The first
was that the public policy doctrine is in practice typically used, not in
order to assert the forum's control over a situation entirely foreign to
its concerns, but only to vindicate the state's own legitimate interests.
In effect, " 'public policy' is one way to avoid the application of a choice
of law rule which the forum wishes to avoid. The objection of the forum, thus, is not to the content of the foreign law but to its own choice
of law rule."[25] Call this the "forum interest" rationale.

The second defense of the public policy doctrine is that some foreign laws are so repugnant that they ought not to be enforced. It has been argued that courts should not "exhibit to the citizens of the state an example pernicious and detestable." [26] Call this the "odious statutes" rationale. This defense of the doctrine is frankly parochial: your law is so bad, and our law is so much better, that we will disregard yours at every opportunity. The odious statutes rationale thus has the character of a sort of declaration of judicial war on the foreign state. It indicates, in effect, that the foreign law will be treated as no law at all, because it ought not to exist at all. Parties are invited to come to the forum with their claims, for the obnoxious foreign law (which presumably operates adversely to those claims) will be ignored and, to that extent, undermined here. Such declarations are sometimes justified. For example, despite a New York court's conclusion to the contrary, it should not have been a defense to a lawsuit for breach of contract that the plaintiff was a Jew and so the defendant was authorized by Nazi Germany's laws to break its agreement with him.[27]

If one relies exclusively on the forum interest rationale, it is possible to make a sympathetic case for the application of the public policy rule to marriages. Any choice-of-law rule implies certain premises about political legitimacy. The premises that states would rely on here seem fairly unproblematic: each state is entitled to govern those who dwell within its territory, and no state is entitled to rule the world. "Each state as a sovereign has a rightful and legitimate concern in the marital status of persons domiciled within its borders." [28]

Since each state regulates marriages within its borders, no state ought to have to defer automatically to marriages of its own domiciliaries in another state, because those are marriages in which the foreign state has no legitimate interest. If a state determines, for instance, that its residents must be eighteen years old in order to marry, one may reasonably think that this policy, if it is worth enforcing at all, ought not to be evaded by the insipid device of driving across the border and spending an hour in another state that allows the marriage of twelve-year-olds.

If it is claimed that any particular state's marriage restrictions unduly infringe the liberty of its citizens, then the restriction ought to be discarded wholesale for that reason, not evaded piecemeal by tricks. If same-sex couples are entitled to marry, that right should not be conditional on the ability to afford airplane tickets to some distant state, however much this might help tourism there! If there is to be a national right to same-sex marriage, it should be because no state has the power to deny such marriages, regardless of the actions of other states.

The odious statutes rationale for the exception is more far-reaching, because it extends to transactions with which the forum has no connection other than the accident of being the place of trial. Reliance upon it is an anomaly in a federal system. A state may legitimately assert its right to govern itself as it sees fit; it may occasionally refuse to enforce the law of foreign tyrannies; but it may not legitimately denounce and attempt to impede other states' efforts to govern themselves. Moreover, as federal law has increasingly constrained the states during the twentieth century, the likelihood that any state's laws will be beyond the pale of civilized policy becomes ever smaller. The public policy rule, at least as justified by the condemnatory rationale, "is a relic carried over from international law without reflection on the changes in interstate relations wrought by the Constitution."[29]

Moreover, any application of the strong public policy rule that is justified by the odious statutes rationale invites forum-shopping, because it implies that the forum state will impose its own rule even if another state has a greater interest in regulating the transaction and so would appropriately look to its own law. As Douglas Laycock has observed, any choice-of-law rule that permits the forum to prefer its own law, just because it is its own, is irreconcilable with basic principles of federalism.[30] In a federal system, no state can have a legitimate interest in deliberately subverting the legitimate operation of the laws of other states. A forum preference rule is also "inconsistent with the rule of law, because [under such a regime] no person can know the law that governs his conduct until after his case has been decided."[31]

Uncertainty in the area of marriage is about as intolerable as it is in any area of the law. "If there is one thing that the people are entitled to expect from their lawmakers, it is rules of law that will enable individuals to tell whether they are married and, if so, to whom."[32] Therefore, any choice-of-law principle, to be acceptable, must set forth a uniform rule that can be followed by all states that apply the law. Because the odious statutes rationale for the public policy rule makes uniformity impossible, it can have no legitimate place in interstate choice-of-law decisions, such as whether to recognize a marriage that is valid in another state.

MARRIAGE AND THE PUBLIC POLICY EXCEPTION

The Modern Trend Toward Recognition

In the specific context of marriage, the public policy exception's scope of application has been shrinking for some time. Today, the "overwhelming tendency" is to validate marriages.[33]

Polygamy and Incest in the Conflict of Laws

One reason for the withering away of the public policy exception in this subfield of conflict of laws is a growing respect for the settled expectations of couples who, under color of some state's law, regard themselves as married. Another important factor, however, is the disappearance of major moral divisions among the states over marriage. The public policy exception has been invoked primarily in three contexts:[34] polygamy, incest, and miscegenation. The first two were misnomers to some extent.

The only jurisdictions in which polygamy was ever legally valid in the United States were certain Native American reservations, and when those practices were questioned in litigation, the attitude of state courts was uniformly one of "casual tolerance."[35] No state ever legalized polygamy. It was, of course, a common practice among the Mormons for a long time, but this practice was never recognized as part of the positive law of any jurisdiction, so no conflict-of-laws problem ever arose in connection with it. Most "polygamy" cases involved subsequent marriages of parties who had obtained divorces, at a time when divorced persons were often forbidden to remarry. (Such restrictions were most often imposed on a former spouse who, the court had found, had committed adultery.) Those restrictions have now become obsolete, but while they were in effect courts were divided about the effect of remarriages in other states, with the weight of authority tending to favor recognition of the second marriage. Finally, cases occasionally arose involving polygamous or potentially polygamous marriages contracted abroad. With few exceptions, courts recognized these marriages. The blanket rule of nonrecognition never prevailed with respect to polygamous marriages.

Similarly, no state ever violated the core instances of the incest taboo by legalizing parent-child or sibling marriages; the incest cases involved marriages between first cousins, aunts and nephews, uncles and nieces, or even more remote relations. Although earlier cases tended to invalidate such marriages, later ones have tended to uphold them. Even the most hostile of the earlier cases, which sustained criminal prosecution of a party to a forbidden marriage, relied primarily on the fact that the prohibited sexual conduct had occurred on the soil of the forum and reasoned that the forum therefore had a sufficient reason to look to its own criminal law.[36]

Finally, interracial marriage aroused the strongest passions in the courts, whose "opinions can be arranged along a discomfort continuum, with polygamy being the least offensive, incest falling in the middle and miscegenation giving courts the greatest amount of consternation."[37] In 1967, the Supreme Court declared unconstitutional every miscegenation prohibition in the country, thereby eliminating any conflict of laws with respect to that issue.[38] Since that time, there has not been any comparably severe moral conflict among the states with respect to marriage. Until now.

Miscegenation in the Conflict of Laws

The divide between states that permitted and those that forbade marriage between whites and blacks is the closest historical analogue to the radical moral disagreement over same-sex marriage that will shortly divide the states. For this reason, the miscegenation cases deserve particularly close examination. Miscegenation prohibitions were in force as early as the 1660s, but only after the Civil War did they begin to function as a central sanction in the system of white supremacy. At one time or another, forty-one American colonies and states enacted them.[39]

The miscegenation taboo was held in the Southern states with great tenacity; it was close to the psychological core of racism.[40] "Although such marriages were infrequent throughout most of U.S. history, an enormous amount of time and energy was nonetheless spent in trying to prevent them from taking place."[41] When they defended the prohibition, Southern courts were at least as passionate in their denunciations as modern opponents of same-sex marriage:

> The purity of public morals, the moral and physical development of both races, and the highest advancement of our cherished southern civilization, under which two distinct races are to work out and accomplish the destiny to which the Almighty has assigned them on this continent— all require that they should be kept distinct and separate, and that connections and alliances so unnatural that God and nature seem to forbid them, should be prohibited by positive law, and be subject to no evasion.[42]

The Southern states typically went far beyond the recent legislation prohibiting same-sex marriage, by making interracial marriage a felony. And often it was specifically *marriage,* and not merely interracial sex, that was criminalized. In some states, it was necessary to prove cohabitation in order to convict for miscegenation; in others, the prosecutor was required to prove an actual marriage. One conviction was reversed because, although the ceremony had taken place, the officiating notary's commission had expired![43]

Today, on the other hand, even the states most strongly opposed to same-sex marriage no longer seek to punish as criminals those who engage in homosexual sex. The laws against consensual sodomy that remain on the books are almost never enforced. No state has criminalized same-sex marriage per se. It would, in short, be hard to argue that the Southern states' public policy against miscegenation was *less* strong than modern public policies against same-sex marriage.

Yet even in this charged context, the Southern states did not make a blunderbuss of their own public policy. Their decisions concerning the validity of interracial marriages were surprisingly fact-dependent. They did not utterly disregard the interests of the parties to the forbidden marriages or of the states that had recognized their marriages, but weighed these against the countervailing interests of the forum. Where the forum's interests were attenuated, Southern courts sometimes upheld marriages between blacks and whites.

Three classes of choice-of-law problems arose involving interracial marriages. The first were cases in which parties had traveled out of their home state for the express purpose of evading that state's prohibition of their marriages and thereafter immediately returned home. Despite some early Northern authority to the contrary, Southern courts always invalidated these marriages. Second were cases in which the parties had not intended to evade the law, but had contracted a marriage valid where they lived, and subsequently moved to a state where interracial marriages were prohibited. These were the most difficult cases, and the Southern authorities were evenly divided on how to deal with them. Finally, there were cases in which the parties had never lived within the state, but in which the marriage was relevant to litigation conducted there. Typically, after the death of one spouse, the other sought to inherit property that was located within the forum state. In these cases, the courts invariably recognized the marriages.

MARRIAGES INTENDED TO EVADE THE FORUM'S RESTRICTIONS
The earliest case involving an attempt to evade a prohibition on interracial marriage, *Medway v. Needham*,[44] arose in Massachusetts in 1819. A mulatto man and a white woman, both domiciled in Massachusetts, had gone to Rhode Island, where interracial marriage was legal, in order to evade their home state's prohibition on their marriage. The court upheld the marriage, emphasizing, as modern authorities do, the importance of certainty and uniformity with respect to the existence of a marriage. A contrary rule would involve "extreme inconveniences and cruelty";[45] the rule it adopted "must be founded on

principles of policy, with a view to prevent the disastrous consequences to the issue of such marriages, as well as to avoid the public mischief, which would result from the loose state, in which people so situated would live." [46]

The leading American treatise on conflict of laws defended the result in *Medway*,[47] but it was criticized by others,[48] was never followed in any miscegenation case, and was later overruled by a marriage evasion statute.[49] The principal counter-argument was that states had a right to govern their own residents.

NONEVASIVE MARRIAGES OF COUPLES PRESENTLY IN THE FORUM   This anti-evasion principle was applied, however, only in cases where the parties were domiciliaries of the forum at the time of marriage. In cases where they had been domiciled elsewhere at the time of the marriage, and even in one case where they had left the forum before the marriage, intending to reside elsewhere, and after marrying had decided to return to the forum, the marriage was held valid.

One obvious difficulty with drawing the lines in this way was that a marriage would be valid or not depending on whether the parties, at the time of the marriage, intended to return to the domicile that prohibited their marriage. The difficulties of determining such intent led Joseph Story to endorse a blanket rule validating all such marriages. It is, he wrote,

> far better to support marriages celebrated in a foreign country as valid, when in conformity with the laws of that country, although the rule may produce some minor inconveniences, than, by introducing distinctions as to the designs and objects and motives of the parties, to shake the general confidence in such marriages, to subject the innocent issue to constant doubts as to their own legitimacy, and to leave the parents themselves to cut adrift from their solemn obligations when they may become discontented with their lot.[50]

An even weightier objection was that any validating rule, either Minor's or Story's, would mean that the Southern states would have to tolerate some interracial cohabitation within their borders after all. Only two state statutes spoke to the issue, and elsewhere only two cases arose in which this result was threatened when an interracial couple moved to the forum state. Each pair of authorities reached opposite results.

A 1906 Louisiana statute provided that where the parties were formerly domiciled in Louisiana, in order for their marriage elsewhere to be exempt from criminal prosecution, the parties must have acquired a domicile in the state where the marriage was validly celebrated.[51] It is unclear whether this implied formal recognition of the marriage, but it certainly meant that the couple could cohabit in the state with impunity. The 1879 Texas Penal Code, on the other hand, provided that

> [i]f any white person and negro shall knowingly intermarry with each other within this state, *or having so intermarried, in or out of the state, shall continue to live together as man and wife within this state,* they shall be punished by confinement in the penitentiary for a term not less than two nor more than five years.[52]

The case law was equally divided. In *State v. Ross,*[53] a white citizen of North Carolina, which prohibited interracial marriage, traveled in May 1873 to South Carolina, where she married a black South Carolina resident. At that time, South Carolina did not prohibit interracial marriage. In August of the same year, they both moved to North Carolina, where they were tried for fornication and adultery. A divided state supreme court held that the South Carolina marriage was a valid defense to the charge.

The court rejected the state's claim that the female defendant had sought to evade the law, because it had not proven that, at the time of the marriage, she had intended to return to North Carolina.

> It is difficult to see how in going to South Carolina to marry a negro, without an intent to return with him to this State, she could evade or intend to evade the laws of this State. Our laws have no extra territorial operation, and do not attempt to prohibit the marriage in South Carolina of blacks and whites domiciled in that State.[54]

The court conceded that interracial marriages were "revolting to us and to all persons, who, by reason of living in States where the two races are nearly equal in numbers, have an experience of the consequences of matrimonial connections between them."[55] This was not, however, "the common sentiment of the civilized and Christian world."[56]

> The general rule is admitted that a marriage between citizens of a foreign State contracted in that State and valid by its laws is valid everywhere where the parties might migrate, although not contracted with the rites required by the law of the country into which they come and between persons disqualified by such law from intermarrying.[57]

Because of the strong common interest in uniformity, marriages not deemed odious to all had to be given extraterritorial recognition by all.

"Upon this question above all others it is desirable . . . that there should not be one law in Maine and another in Texas, but that the same law shall prevail at least throughout the United States."[58] Because the civilized world was not united in rejecting interracial marriages, North Carolina had a duty to join the rest of civilization in enforcing the common rule. "The law of nations is a part of the law of North Carolina. We are under obligations of comity to our sister States."[59]

Two judges dissented, insisting on the forum state's right to govern within its territory. "If such a marriage solemnized here between our own people is declared void, why should comity require the evil to be imported from another State? Why is not the relation severed the instant they set foot upon our soil?"[60] If this consequence is inconvenient to some, "individuals who have formed relations which are obnoxious to our laws can find their comfort in staying away from us."[61] In coming to North Carolina and asking that their marriage be recognized, the dissent argued, the defendants were asking for more than that to which North Carolina's own citizens were entitled.

> It is courteous for neighbors to visit, and it is handsome to allow the visitor family privileges and even give him the favorite seat; but if he bring his pet rattlesnake or his pet bear or spitz dog, famous for hydrophobia, he must leave them outside the door. And if he bring smallpox the door may be shut against him.[62]

The *Ross* dissenters' position prevailed in *State v. Bell*,[63] in which a white man and a black woman married in Mississippi, where they then resided,[64] and later moved to Tennessee, where the husband was arrested and tried. He pleaded the Mississippi marriage as a defense. The state supreme court rejected the defense, complaining that under it

> we might have in Tennessee the father living with his daughter, the son with the mother, the brother with the sister, in lawful wedlock, because they had formed such relations in a state or country where they were not prohibited. The Turk or Mohammedan, with his numerous wives, may establish his harem at the doors of the capitol, and we are without remedy. Yet none of these are more revolting, more to be avoided, or more unnatural than the case before us.[65]

There are a few other miscegenation cases that are pertinent, even though they do not squarely reach the question presented in *Bell*. A federal district court attempted to adjudicate between these competing visions of comity in *Ex parte Kinney*,[66] in which a convict in a marriage evasion case sought a writ of habeas corpus in federal court, alleging that his federal rights had been violated. *Kinney* is the only miscegenation case that contains any discussion of constitutional limitations deriving from federalism (rather than from the Equal Protection Clause of the Fourteenth Amendment).

The defendant and his partner had traveled from Virginia to the District of Columbia, married there, and then returned to Virginia, where they were convicted of miscegenation and each sentenced to five years in prison at hard labor.[67] Kinney claimed that the Constitution held "that a marriage lawful in the District of Columbia is lawful everywhere in the United States."[68] The court rejected the claim, holding that the marriage was a fraud on the laws of Virginia.[69] It took a hard line on the question that had lately divided the high courts of North Carolina and Tennessee, declaring that Kinney's claim would be rejected even in a closer case, involving "citizens of another state, lawfully married in that domicile, afterward migrating thence in good faith into this state."[70]

But the court also declared that Virginia could not enforce its law against nondomiciliaries, nor exclude altogether interracial couples domiciled in the District of Columbia. "That such a citizen would have a right of transit with his wife through Virginia, and of temporary stoppage, and of carrying on any business here not requiring residence, may be conceded, because these are privileges following a citizen of the United States. . . ."[71] Thus, the only federal authority to reach the issue held that, even conceding a state's right to outlaw interracial marriages, that state was obligated to make reasonable accommodation of those states that held different views on the miscegenation question.

There were also a few cases in which the interracial couple had married in the forum state before the statutory prohibition of miscegenation was adopted. In these cases, the marriage was invariably recognized. The most fully reasoned of these cases deemed it dispositive that the parties in the case before it were entitled to marry when they did. "They did not then bring into this state an institution disfavored by a declared policy. They remained where they were domiciled, as many others did, and had a right to do. The law of their domicile was changed."[72] Thus, the policy of preserving existing marriages overrode the policy against intermarriage. "[A]n act designed to wipe out, by the wholesale, legal, existing marriages between members of the white and black races would be almost profligate in its tendency. . . ."[73]

These were the hard cases for the courts interpreting the antimiscegenation statutes. When the couple had traveled abroad with the intention of evading the forum's restrictions, the case was easy. And when the couple remained in another state, and the validity of their marriage happened to come into issue in litigation in the forum, the case was equally easy.

COUPLES WHO NEVER RESIDED IN THE FORUM   Other cases espoused a principle similar to that adopted by the majority in *Ross*, but in each of them the interracial couples had not cohabited in the state, seeking instead recognition of some incident of their marriage in the state. Courts routinely upheld the marriages in these cases. They reasoned that, because the purpose of the law was to prevent interracial cohabitation, there would be no harm in recognizing the marriage after the death of one partner and consequently allowing the surviving spouse or (thereby legitimated) children to inherit the decedent's property. All deemed it dispositive that their states' laws were not intended to have any extraterritorial application.[74]

The blanket rule of nonrecognition, then, is very nearly unheard of in the United States. (It is rarely heard of anywhere.) The reporter of the Restatement (Second) of Conflict of Laws states that "[s]o far as is known, no marriages have been held invalid . . . except by application of the law of a State where at least one of the spouses was domiciled at the time of marriage and where both made their home thereafter."[75]

PUBLIC POLICY AND SAME-SEX MARRIAGE

Thus far, I have said nothing specifically about same-sex marriage. As noted at the beginning, in order for there to be any conflict-of-laws issue at all here, it must be stipulated that the Constitution permits states to refuse to license same-sex marriages.[76] What follows?

A Persistent Tension

The basic problem that is presented when states disagree radically about the proper scope of marriage is that the choice of law involves a tension among three strong sets of demands, which the courts typically attempt to balance. First, states want to determine for themselves the precise contours of their marriage prohibitions. The importance of this interest has become attenuated in recent years, but the same-sex marriage issue has shown that many states—indeed, every state legislature that has spoken—still take it very seriously. Second, individuals want to be certain of their status. This interest is far more salient now than it was at the time of the miscegenation cases, because citizens are far more mobile than they once were. With the advent of the automobile and the airplane, many people cross state lines every day, often on their way to and from their jobs. It would be ridiculous to have people's marital status blink on and off like a strobe light as they jet across the country. Third, states have an interest in regulating the marital relationships of their own domiciliaries. It is as important for State A to be able to say that its citizens *can* enter into same-sex marriages as it is for State Z to be able to say that its citizens *cannot* do so.

How should courts balance these interests? In recent years, as we have seen, the "overwhelming tendency" has been toward recognition, and courts addressing marriage recognition questions "typically are more concerned with personal than with governmental interests." [77] This, however, is probably at least in part an artifact of the diminishing importance of the public policies involved. Some states have statutes voiding marriages of domiciliaries who marry elsewhere in order to avoid the forum's restrictions, but these statutes say nothing about the marriages of nondomiciliaries and immigrants into the forum. On the other hand, for a forum to say that it will simply never recognize, for any purposes, a marriage that is against its state's policy would be a declaration of anathema upon states with a different rule, and an invitation to litigants to avoid the other state's rule by bringing their suits in the forum state. This rule could only be justified by relying on the odious statutes rationale for the public policy exception, the rationale that the foreign state's law ought not to exist. As we have seen, laws with this basis have no place in a federal system. Even the Southern courts addressing miscegenation never went so far.

The New State Statutes

Nonetheless, 34 states now have statutes indicating that they do not permit same-sex marriages. Even if the common law courts in these states would recognize same-sex marriages in some circumstances, they must consider whether this decision has been preempted by the legislature. It turns out, however, that almost all of these statutes are so vague about their intended scope that courts retain considerable discretion to decide whether they apply to nondomiciliaries.

Some of these laws' provisions state that marriage licenses may not be issued to persons of the same sex, which says nothing about the effect of marriages celebrated elsewhere. Statements that such marriages are "void" or "prohibited" or both are ambiguous and can be read either to invalidate, or not to reach, extraterritorial marriages. Some specify that such marriages are invalid within the jurisdiction, which leaves open the status of couples living outside the state, or deem such marriages contrary to the state's public policy, which does not indicate whether that public policy is so strong that the state will attempt to apply it to transactions, in or out of the state, involving nondomicil-iaries. Maine makes it pretty clear that its prohibition does not apply to transients, stating that a foreign marriage that would not be valid if performed in Maine "is not recognized in this State and is considered void if the parties take up residence in this State."[78]

To make matters more complicated, even the strongest language used in these laws has a history. Similar wording was ubiquitous in the miscegenation statutes, which usually declared interracial marriages "void."[79] The cases described earlier, which held that the miscegenation laws did not reach extraterritorial marriages not involving cohabitation in the state,[80] all involved statutes using this term. If such language did not bar that result in those cases, neither should it here.[81]

Finally, there is the problem of what these statutes mean for recognition of Vermont civil unions. Two considerations here point in opposite directions. On the one hand, these statutes almost all refer to recognition of *"marriages"* between persons of the same sex. Since Vermont does not recognize same-sex *marriages*, it is arguable that these statutes have no application to recognition of Vermont civil unions.[82] On the other hand, these statutes clearly indicate a policy of nonrecognition of same-sex relationships, and it could be argued that that policy is unchanged by the label. What makes the puzzle insoluble, and the doctrine indeterminate, is that it is very clear that the label matters. Opposition to legal recognition of same-sex relationships is far weaker than opposition to giving those relationships the label of marriage. So it is unclear whether the statutes are or are not an obstacle to full recognition of Vermont civil unions. I would suggest that in these cases, these considerations cancel one another out, and that the analysis goes through in much the same way that it would if the label "marriage" were used.

In almost every state, then, judges have a free hand to craft sensible conflicts rules. This conclusion is not affected by the federal Defense of Marriage Act ("DOMA"). I will argue in the next chapter that DOMA is unconstitutional, but even if it is assumed to be valid, it does not instruct the states on how to decide these conflicts cases. DOMA purports to redefine states' constitutional obligations toward the acts of other states. It therefore is not relevant to our subject, which is how courts ought to interpret their *own* choice-of-law rules. None of the arguments that I have made in this chapter relies upon constitutional limitations. Certainly, no such limitations were perceived by the courts in any of the cases discussed so far, yet they rejected the blanket rule of nonrecognition. DOMA's stated purpose is to leave the states free to decide this policy issue for themselves; it does not purport to bring about any change in state law.

There is, to be sure, some evidence that DOMA invites state courts to disregard a non-collusive sister state judgment just because the rendering court decided that a same-sex marriage existed. If this is correct, then Congress has endorsed the second rationale for the public policy exception,[83] which denies effect to a foreign law, not because the forum has a greater legitimate interest in the transaction, but because the foreign law is substantively condemned. I argued earlier that, in a federal system, the states can have no legitimate authority thus to pronounce anathema on each other's laws, partly because such use of the public policy exception makes uniform results impossible.[84] There is no legitimate reason for any state court to engage in this kind of interstate warfare.

In short, DOMA should have no effect whatsoever upon state courts' deliberations on the same-sex marriage recognition question in any individual case.

BALANCING THE INTERESTS

The simple, blanket rule of nonrecognition is excessively crude. It is insufficiently attentive to the legitimate interests of the parties to same-sex marriages and of their domicile state. More complex rules are unavoidable.

What would a better rule look like? Between the extreme ones that I have already considered and rejected, one may discern several possibilities. Each of these would attempt to strike a balance between the individual and state interests involved, rather than simply disregarding any of them. None relies on the second rationale for the public policy exception, which turns on the forum's distaste for the substantive foreign law.

One possibility is for a court to hold that same-sex marriage simply cannot exist within its borders, so that a bearer of that status under the laws of a sister state cannot carry those laws with him, for any purpose, into the territory of the forum state. A second is for a court to follow the Second Restatement rule (and some of the miscegenation cases!) by holding that a marriage valid under the law of the most interested state at the time of the marriage is thereafter valid everywhere, even if the parties later move to a state where that marriage could not have been celebrated. Third, a court could hold that the legal right of two people to be married to each other is to be determined on the basis of the law of the common domicile from time to time. Fourth, a court could say that the interests of the different jurisdictions are to be balanced on a case-by-case basis in order to determine which of them has a greater interest in determining the existence or nonexistence of the marriage with respect to the incident of marriage that is at issue in the litigation. Finally, a court could use the Second Restatement's approach to determine whether a valid marriage exists, but use the domicile state's law to determine what incidents of marriage the couple may enjoy.

A Status That Cannot Exist in the Forum

The approach that would be least hospitable to recognition of same-sex marriage would accord maximal force to the state's legitimate interests in self-governance. Part of the reason for the complexity of debates about choice of law, Mark Gergen has observed, is that they often implicitly turn "on whether one thinks that state power should be ordered on a territorial or a personal basis. In a territorial order, states have power over events within their borders. In a personal order they have power over events involving their citizens." [85] The principal rationale for nonrecognition of marriages, we have seen, has invoked the personal order: states can control the capacity of their citizens wherever those citizens go, so that those citizens cannot evade the state's prohibitions by brief forays outside its borders. A territorial view is, however, equally available: states can decide what statuses may exist within their borders.

The principal authority supporting the idea that a state can declare that a status cannot exist within its borders is *Lemmon v. People*.[86] In 1852, a slave owner was in transit from Virginia to Texas with his slaves, and stopped in New York, planning to remain only long enough to secure passage to New Orleans.[87] While staying in a hotel, they were discovered by a free black, who petitioned for a writ of habeas corpus.

The New York Court of Appeals held that a slave from Virginia became free the instant he set foot on New York soil, because slavery could not exist in New York. As a concurring judge in the court of appeals put it, "It is the *status*, the unjust and unnatural relation, which the policy of the State aims to suppress, and her policy fails, at least in part, if the *status* be upheld at all." [88]

Supporters of a blanket nonrecognition rule could, perhaps, invoke *Lemmon* as a precedent. Just as slavery could not exist in New York, it is argued, a state can legitimately decide that same-sex marriage simply cannot exist within its borders. A member of such a marriage becomes a single person the instant he sets foot within the borders of such a state.

This argument could support a uniform choice-of-law rule, to be recognized everywhere, that members of same-sex marriages are legally single whenever they are outside State A, temporarily or permanently. In our drunk-driver hypothetical considered earlier, if the accident were to occur in Georgia, the surviving spouse could not sue for wrongful death anywhere. Even if State A courts could obtain jurisdiction over the case—supposing, for instance, that the driver was another State A resident who only happened to be visiting Georgia at the time of the accident—judgment must go to the defendant, because the marriage did not exist in Georgia, where the accident occurred. If, however, the accident had occurred in State A, then State A's law would determine the validity of the marriage, and the wrongful death suit would have to be permitted even if the suit happened to be filed in a Georgia court.

If formulated at the level of abstraction necessary to cover both slavery and same-sex marriage, this idea has absurd implications. The difficulty is clearest when we consider the possibility that one party to a marriage will seek to evade his obligations simply by going outside the state that recognizes the marriage. If the *Lemmon* rule is pushed to its logical limit, then by stepping across a border, a married person becomes single, free of all marital obligations, able to remarry without bothering to get a divorce, and entitled, at least under the law of the new domicile, to dispose of the marital property without accounting for the proceeds. The prospect of a person having two marriages in different states, each of which may have children whose rights are not recognized by the other state, is a daunting one.

Finally, although it is morally impossible to reject the result in *Lemmon,* it is far from clear that its reasoning, which effectively made interstate migration with their property impossible for many slaveholders, makes sense in a federal system. Slavery was sanctioned and protected in the original Constitution. The obstacle to interstate commerce that New York imposed was far more severe than the imposition of domestic trucking regulations on interstate transport, which the Supreme Court has invalidated when they interfered with the needs of the interstate system. Had the Civil War not intervened, *Lemmon* would probably have been overruled. At a minimum, New York might have been required to respect the slave property of transients.[89]

If we wholeheartedly endorse *Lemmon* today, it is because we no longer believe that there was a genuine conflict of valid laws and therefore no longer perceive a true federalism problem. We are unwilling to concede that Lemmon was entitled to his slaves *anywhere.* This is a poor precedent on which to rely in a controversy in which it is conceded, even by opponents of same-sex marriage, that State A is entitled to recognize such marriages. (It is revealing that DOMA makes no attempt directly to interfere with any state's internal laws.) But if State A residents are entitled to enter into same-sex marriages, then it makes little sense to say that those marriages can never be recognized in any legal controversy that arises outside State A's borders.

The same analysis applies to the Vermont "civil union"—a status that exists nowhere outside Vermont. If Vermont legitimately has the power to recognize such relationships for its own domiciliaries—and no one denies that it does—then those relationships ought to be recognized by other states.

Settling It Once and for All

A solution that would settle the status of a marriage once and for all is that of the Restatement (Second), in which a marriage valid where celebrated is valid everywhere "unless it violates the strong public policy of another state which had the most significant relationship to the spouses and the marriage at the time of the marriage."[90] The Restatement (Second) is the basis of choice of law in approximately half the states.[91] As noted already, this solution was unsatisfactory to some Southern courts, because it meant that they would have to allow some interracial cohabitation within their borders. In the present context, this approach would mean that same-sex couples could not marry on a weekend trip to State A and expect their marriage to be recognized in Georgia, but they could move to State A, marry while domiciled there, and later return to Georgia and demand recognition.

While this approach honors state interests as much as is possible while avoiding redeterminations of a marriage's validity, some states are likely to insist that they need more than this if they are to vindicate their domestic policies. Those policies will be the same regardless of where the marriages in question came into existence. If their own domiciliaries are forbidden to live in same-sex marriages, then the same constraint can sensibly be imposed on those who voluntarily immigrate.

There is, nonetheless, an argument that can be made for this approach even in those states with declared public policies against same-sex marriage. As already noted, the Jim Crow courts were evenly split on the question whether interracial marriages must be recognized in immigration situations. Since that time, the presumption in favor of recognizing marriages has plainly become stronger than it was in the 1800s. This strengthened presumption, one might argue, serves as a tiebreaker in the face of evenly divided nineteenth-century authority. This cannot be a conclusive argument, because there is an equally plausible alternate explanation for the shift in authority: the weakening, throughout the twentieth century, of public policies against certain kinds of marriage. One can argue that the presumption in favor of marriage has grown stronger, but one can with equal plausibility explain the same body of law by saying that the countervailing policies became weaker, until the advent of same-sex marriage changed all that. I know of no conclusive argument for one rather than the other of these interpretations. At best, the argument considered in this paragraph permits, rather than requires, a court to recognize a same-sex marriage in an immigration situation.

Domicile-Based Rules

Douglas Laycock has suggested that a clean solution to the question of a marriage's existence would be to rely, in all cases, on the law of the parties' domicile.[92] This solution preserves states' ability to govern the status of their own domiciliaries, while entitling citizens to travel without constant, confusing changes in their legal status. If both same-sex spouses move to another state, their marriage would cease (or, perhaps, become dormant; it is unclear whether it should spring back to life when one or both of them move back to State A). So long as they make their home in State A, however, they would have to be recognized as married everywhere and for all purposes.

This solution is not without its problems. "Domicile" is a category with fuzzy boundaries of its own; it is not always clear whether a person has changed domicile. And it is not clear how Laycock would address cases, increasingly common, in which the spouses reside in different states. Clear-cut, codified rules of domicile would help. For example, one could deem the situs of the marriage to be the last place (if any) where the parties lived together for a year.

This approach would also, as a practical matter, call for some procedure for formally nullifying a same-sex marriage when one or both of the parties have left the state recognizing it. If a member of a same-sex couple leaves State A and later wants to marry a person of the opposite sex in Louisiana, she should be required to secure a formal declaration that the first marriage no longer exists. Otherwise, the marital status of the spouse who remains in State A would be doubtful. (And, once more, this analysis applies without modification to Vermont "civil unions.")

Finally, if the marriage just dissolves on moving to a new state, some court somewhere must be able to divide the property, adjudicate custody of any children, and so forth. Perhaps the former domicile ought to retain continuing jurisdiction for that purpose.

A domicile-based solution accommodates states' interests in not having their domestic institutions governed by another state's laws. It generates predictable, non-arbitrary results. It offers a federalist solution to a profound moral disagreement.

Different Incidents, Different Outcomes

Another approach would be to allow the choice of law in any particular case to depend on which incident of marriage is at issue. Scoles and Hay observe that "the significance of the status and its relevance arises in conflict of laws litigation almost exclusively concerning questions regarding the incidents of marriage, such as succession or claim to property, or a claim for support, or a claim for damages in tort."[93] Moreover, "in recent choice of law cases, the courts have begun to recognize that the enjoyment of different incidents of marriage involves different policies."[94] As I have already rehearsed in detail,[95] this approach was anticipated by some of the miscegenation cases. One can read in this way even the most hostile of the miscegenation cases, *State v. Bell,* in which a couple was imprisoned for moving into the forum state.[96] One way of thinking about this case is to say that the marriage ceased to exist when they entered the forum. But Goodrich, writing in 1927, when the miscegenation prohibition was alive and healthy, would concede only that "[c]ertain incidents of the marriage relationship may be refused recognition if they involve a violation of public policy or good morals of the law of the forum."[97] On this account, even the couple that was imprisoned remained married; they simply were not permitted the incident of cohabitation in certain states. The reasoning supporting these decisions seems readily transferable to the case of same-sex spouses. It is also applicable to Vermont "civil unions." If the facts of a case do not warrant the withholding of the incidents of foreign marriages, they do not warrant denying the incidents of civil unions, either.

The trouble with this approach is its inherent uncertainty. It is hard for parties to anticipate how their enjoyment of any particular incident of their marriage will be weighed against countervailing policies.

Barbara Cox has argued that it would be unacceptably burdensome to require same-sex couples to "relitigate their marital status repeatedly as they request recognition of their marriage for each incident."[98] Deborah Henson has pointed out, on the other hand, that treating each incident separately may result in recognition of more same-sex marriages, for more purposes, than would occur if courts had to decide marriage recognition issues wholesale.[99] A public policy is less likely to be offended by limited recognition of a marriage, for limited purposes, than by a judicial declaration that the marriage is valid for all purposes. Nonetheless, the inevitable consequence of this approach, as one of its most prominent proponents conceded, is "a situation where a marriage may be good for the purposes of one issue and yet invalid for the purposes of another." [100]

Cox and Henson are both right. If the argument of this chapter is correct, then ordinary choice-of-law analysis should continue to govern these issues. The separate-incidents argument should remain available to litigators, while the other approaches will be of interest primarily to legislators, although state supreme court judges may wish to craft more predictable rules if legislators do not act.

The strongest case for the incidents approach focuses on a puzzle that has arisen repeatedly in our analysis. If a certain kind of marriage is prohibited in the forum, is a person, who has contracted a marriage of that kind (or a "civil union") elsewhere, a single person in the forum, and so free to contract a new marriage with someone else? The fullest consideration of this problem appears in *Baindail v. Baindail,*[101] an English case in which an English woman discovered that her husband had previously contracted a Hindu marriage in India—"a fact in his personal history," the court dryly noted, "which he did not think it necessary to reveal." [102] When she sought to annul the marriage, he cited several cases that seemed to indicate that potentially polygamous marriages were not regarded as marriages at all by English law, and argued that he was therefore legally a single man at the time of his English marriage. The court conceded that this was "a question which is not covered by authority," [103] but found conclusive the prospect that, if it adopted the husband's argument, "this English lady would find herself compelled in India [should he choose to return there] either to leave her husband or to share him with his Indian wife." [104] Under these circumstances, "effect must be given to common sense and decency." [105] The annulment was granted. *Baindail* was one of the cases that began the erosion of Britain's blanket rule of nonrecognition for potentially polygamous marriages.

The difficulty raised by same-sex marriage is, of course, precisely that reasonable people disagree about what common sense and decency require. Nonetheless, it can perhaps be agreed that the licensing of polygamy in the United States is something that no one intends. And if that is correct, then every state must recognize same-sex marriages at least as an impediment to the contracting of new marriages. Public policy should never treat marriages, valid in another state, as absolute nullities.

A Synthesis

It may be possible to synthesize the different approaches in a way that preserves the strengths of each while avoiding their weaknesses. The *Lemmon* approach, we have seen, recognizes the importance of territorial boundaries, but produces arbitrary and unpredictable results that give no weight to the interests of the states involved. The Restatement (Second) prevents the marriage validity question from being repeatedly reopened, but arguably gives inadequate weight to the public policies of states that do not want same-sex couples cohabiting as married within their borders. Laycock's approach produces clear rules for the most part, which give due weight to each state's interests, but does not adequately account for the need to formally terminate marriages. And the incidents approach balances the relevant issues in a way that takes full account of the equities in each case, but seems ad hoc and unpredictable.

The solution, I suggest, is to recast Laycock as a systematizer of incidents, and the Restatement as determining merely which marriages are valid ab initio.

With respect to whether a marriage exists at all or is void for all purposes, the Restatement's rule makes sense: a marriage valid where celebrated is valid everywhere, unless it violates the strong public policy (which means in practice, the marriage evasion statute) of the state where the parties are domiciled before and immediately after the marriage. Absent the operation of this exception, a marriage exists and, until formal divorce or annulment, is an impediment to any subsequent marriage by either of the parties, regardless of any later change of domicile by either.

Each state's own public policies will determine whether its own domiciliaries (including immigrants) who have entered into same-sex marriages may enjoy the incidents of those marriages, such as a homestead exemption, the right to file a joint state tax return, or the ability to compel an unwilling employer to insure one's spouse. If a couple is domiciled within a state, wholesale denial of benefits may make sense. It is hard to see how a state could grant even one incident to its domiciliaries without opening the door to granting them all. A state might even hold that an immigrant from a state that permits same-sex marriage, who is married there to a person of the same sex, can, after establishing a new domicile in the forum state, obtain an annulment on the grounds that the marriage is voidable.[106] Even with transients, states may—it is uncertain, and probably doesn't matter much—prohibit sodomy within their borders.[107] Otherwise, however, Laycock is right: if a State A resident visiting Michigan is killed by a drunk driver there, the surviving same-sex spouse should have the right to file a wrongful death suit. Unless the couple resides within its borders, no state has a sufficient interest in an extraterritorially valid same-sex marriage to deny it recognition.

CONCLUSION

My conclusion, that state courts should recognize the same-sex marriages (or "civil unions") of foreign domiciliaries who are transient within their borders, may seem like pretty small beer. Most gay Americans who are in enduring, committed relationships and who wish to marry do not live in Vermont and will not move there. But this underestimates the value for gays of having same-sex marriages legally recognized, at least for certain purposes, in every state. An important message is sent when courts nullify *all* same-sex marriages, even those in which their states have no legitimate interest. An equally important message is sent when they refrain from doing that.[108]

Even if one agrees that one state should not legislate for all, there are limits to this principle. Simply by existing and being known, an institution has extraterritorial impact. The First Amendment destroys states' ability to preserve their local mores by preventing information about rival ways of life from penetrating their borders. If such rival ways of life are successfully being lived elsewhere, domiciliaries are going to learn about it. And that may change the way they think about how things are run locally.

Merely by existing publicly, gay couples challenge and delegitimize a world view in which heterosexuality is the only legitimate sexual option for human beings. It has been the burden of this chapter to show that married same-sex couples should have their marriages recognized throughout the United States, at least when they are domiciled in a state that celebrates same-sex marriages. The pressure this must place on local institutions is no less than that placed upon slavery by the presence of free blacks in the antebellum South[109] or interracial couples there after the Civil War. In both cases, the Southern states worked hard to expunge that presence, only to be frustrated at least in part by their obligations in the federal system.

There is a reason why some states want to withhold recognition even from same-sex couples who live outside their borders. An important symbolic point is at stake. For the same reason, symbolism will matter if it is held that courts must recognize same-sex marriages under some circumstances.[110] Perhaps Georgia can keep some couples out, but it should not keep them, in all circumstances, from asserting their marital rights in its courts. To that limited extent, same-sex marriage must become a social fact in every state in the country. Small victories can plant the seeds of big ones.

CHAPTER SIX

DUMB AND DOMA

Why the Defense of Marriage Act Is Unconstitutional

The recently enacted and widely publicized Defense of Marriage Act ("DOMA"), which passed both houses of Congress by huge margins[1] and was quietly signed by President Clinton,[2] has two provisions. One of these defines marriage, for federal purposes, as exclusively heterosexual. When same-sex marriages are eventually recognized,[3] this provision's impact on same-sex couples is likely to be harsh, since at a stroke it deprives them of all the federal benefits to which other married couples are entitled. Its constitutionality however seems difficult to challenge. The other provision authorizes individual states to ignore same-sex marriages when they are performed in other states. In this chapter, I argue, looking back to the *Romer* case discussed in chapter 1, that this second provision injures the targeted class of persons so broadly and indiscriminately that it gives rise to an inference of unconstitutional intent. This inference contaminates the first section as well, and so it invalidates the entire act.

DOMA'S DEFINITIONAL PROVISION

When the bill was being debated, most attention focused on the choice-of-law provision of DOMA. The definitional provision, however, was far more important. It provides:

> In determining the meaning of any Act of Congress, or of any ruling, regulation, or interpretation of the various administrative bureaus and agencies of the United States, the word "marriage" means only a legal union between one man and one woman as husband and wife and the word "spouse" refers only to a person of the opposite sex who is a husband or wife.[4]

Given the broad range of federal laws to which marital status is relevant, the consequences of DOMA are far-reaching. Same-sex spouses would be unable to file joint tax returns. Same-sex spouses' debts incurred under divorce decrees or separation agreements would be dischargeable in bankruptcy.[5] Same-sex spouses of federal employees would be excluded from the Federal Employees Health Benefits

Program,[6] the Federal Employees Group Life Insurance program,[7] and the Federal Employees Compensation Act, which compensates the widow or widower of an employee killed in the performance of duty.[8] Same-sex spouses would be the only surviving widows and widowers who would not have automatic ownership rights in a copyrighted work after the author's death.[9] Same-sex spouses would lack federal protection against enforcement of due-on-sale clauses, which allow a lender to declare the entire balance due and payable if mortgaged property is transferred and which could compel the loss of the family home if the holder of the mortgage died and the spouse inherited the property.[10] Same-sex spouses would be denied the benefit of the Family and Medical Leave Act of 1993, which provides for up to twelve weeks per year of unpaid leave to employees for, among other purposes, "care for the spouse."[11] Same-sex spouses would similarly be unable to receive benefits under the Social Security Act's Old Age, Survivors, and Disability Insurance Program.[12] Same-sex spouses would be denied preferential treatment under immigration law and would, therefore, be the only legally married spouses of American citizens who could face deportation.[13]

The definitional provision of DOMA may be unwise, inhumane, and insulting, but its constitutionality seems, on first blush, to be secure from doubt. Congress obviously has the power to define the terms of the U.S. Code. The only way to challenge this provision is to claim that it is impermissibly discriminatory. All discrimination claims allege the abuse of a power that the actor concededly possesses. Congress could not define "marriage" to mean only a legal union between persons of the same race.[14] But the constitutional significance of discrimination against *gays* is uncertain. As I noted in chapter 1, the federal courts have been unwilling to give heightened scrutiny to laws that target gays, and the Supreme Court has not directly confronted the question. On one occasion, however, the Court did invalidate a law that singled out gays for disadvantage. Any equal protection challenge to DOMA must rely heavily on *Romer v. Evans*.

DOMA's definitional provision and the amendment invalidated in *Romer* have telling similarities. Like the Colorado amendment, this provision "identifies persons by a single trait [membership in a same-sex marriage] and then denies them protection across the board."[15] Congress does not seem to have given any specific consideration to the broad range of federal policies to which spousal status is relevant or to have made any effort to justify the numerous specific disabilities that the statute imposed. For the first time in American history, DOMA would create a set of second-class marriages, valid under state law but void for all federal purposes. The exclusion of a class of valid state marriages from all federal recognition is "unprecedented in our jurisprudence."[16] DOMA's "general announcement that [the lawful civil marriages of] gays and lesbians shall not have any particular protections from the law,"[17] its critics have argued, demonstrates its lack of any legitimate purpose and compels the inference that, like Amendment 2, it rests on a bare desire to harm a politically unpopular group.[18]

A defender of the statute could reply, however, that the disability it imposes, though broad, is proportionate to the situation that called it forth: Hawaii's then-imminent (or so it seemed) recognition of same-sex marriages. DOMA's definitions of "marriage" and "spouse," the House committee report observed, "merely restate[ ] the current understanding of what those terms mean for purposes of federal law."[19] When Congress used the term "marriage" in the U.S. Code, it never imagined that this term would include same-sex couples.[20] Hawaii's adoption of same-sex marriage "would radically alter a basic premise upon which the presumption of adoption [for federal purposes] of state domestic relations law was based—namely, the essential fungibility of the concepts of 'marriage' from one state to another."[21] This provision of DOMA, then, "merely reaffirm[s] what is already known, what is already in place."[22] It is hard to see how a law that simply declares the status quo can be unconstitutionally discriminatory.

The *Romer* analogy does not devastate DOMA because there are significant disanalogies as well. Unlike Amendment 2, DOMA does not "outrun and belie any legitimate justifications that may be claimed for it."[23] Amendment 2's license to discriminate against gays was so broadly worded that it seemed to the Court likely to mandate some unconstitutional applications. That fact bespoke a bare desire to harm gays. There is, on the other hand, no fundamental right to file a joint tax return or to receive social security benefits.

The discrimination against same-sex couples may be unprecedented, a defender of DOMA could say, but so is the situation that called the law forth. If there is any positive value to the tradition of restricting marriage to one man and one woman, then this positive value provides a rational basis for DOMA. One cannot confidently infer, simply by considering the definitional provision on its face, that its purpose is a desire to harm the group. That *might* be the purpose, but an innocent explanation is available. The Court has often been prone to credit innocent explanations of statutes, even those that harm constitutionally protected groups.[24] In order for the law to be invalidated, there has to be some reason to disbelieve that explanation.

The statute's targeting of gays and the uniqueness of the disability imposed provide some of the needed evidence of invidious purpose. "[L]aws singling out a certain class of citizens for disfavored legal status are rare,"[25] and "'[d]iscriminations of an unusual character especially suggest careful consideration to determine whether they are obnoxious to the constitutional provision.'"[26] But where is this "careful consideration" to lead? *Romer* relied—how heavily?—on the fact that no innocent explanation of the statute seemed even facially plausible. The Court's opinion does not indicate what should be done if the state is able to proffer such an innocent explanation. An equal protection challenge to the definitional provision of DOMA, standing alone, would be a hard case.

This difficulty is resolved, however, if we read the rest of the statute.

DOMA'S CHOICE-OF-LAW PROVISION

DOMA's other provision sets forth the following rule to govern state choice-of-law cases:

> No state, territory, or possession of the United States, or Indian tribe, shall be required to give effect to any public act, record, or judicial proceeding of any other State, territory, possession, or tribe respecting a relationship between persons of the same sex that is treated as a marriage under the laws of such other State, territory, possession, or tribe, or a right or claim arising from such relationship.[27]

This is a strange provision. The problems it purports to address do not exist. It effectuates almost no change in preexisting law. To the extent that it does change the law, it does so in capricious and indefensible ways. Even if Congress has the power to enact a law of this sort, this provision would still be unconstitutional because of the discriminatory way in which the power has been exercised.

It is the choice-of-law provision, and not the definitional provision, that is unrelated to any legitimate governmental interest and thus fails the *Romer* test. This conclusion invalidates *both* parts of DOMA. Because the invidious intent that is inferrable under *Romer* infects both provisions of the law, the entire statute is unconstitutional.

DOMA was a response to widespread speculation that, once same-sex marriages were recognized in Hawaii, other states would be required to recognize them, too. This was a misapprehension of existing law.

The Full Faith and Credit Clause of the Constitution, which is the primary source of whatever obligation states have to recognize each other's laws, provides:

> Full Faith and Credit shall be given in each State to the public Acts, Records, and judicial Proceedings of every other State. And Congress may by General Laws prescribe the Manner in which such Acts, Records and Proceedings shall be proved, and the Effect thereof.[28]

As I noted in chapter 5, American law has presumed for a long time that marriages valid where celebrated are valid everywhere. This, however, is a common law rule regarding conflicts rather than an interpretation of full faith and credit. The rule has an exception that is equally ancient: a marriage will not be recognized when it violates the strong public policy of the forum in which the question arises. In the United States, public policy has often been invoked to deny recognition to incestuous, underage, or interracial marriages. Unless their restriction violated some substantive constitutional prohibition (as, it was eventually held, the prohibition of interracial marriage did), states have never been constitutionally prevented from withholding recognition from foreign marriages where those marriages violated their own strong public policies. Whether any particular marriage need be recognized is, then, primarily a question of state rather than federal law.[29]

Choice-of-Law Rules

The Full Faith and Credit Clause, as it is now interpreted by the Supreme Court, is not much of a constraint on states' power to fashion choice-of-law rules. The Court has held that full faith and credit does not impose any limitation on a state's choice of law distinct from the limitation of fundamental fairness imposed by the Fourteenth Amendment's requirement of due process.[30] Even if a case is properly before a court, that court may violate the parties' rights by applying its own law to the case. In order to have jurisdiction over the parties, either the defendant must be served with process somewhere within the forum's territory or the forum must have "minimum contacts . . . such that the maintenance of the suit does not offend 'traditional notions of fair play and substantial justice.'"[31] In order for a forum to be able to apply its own law, there must be "'a significant contact, or significant aggregation of contacts, creating state interests, such that [a state's] choice of its law is neither arbitrary nor fundamentally unfair.'"[32] Cases sometimes arise in which the forum has jurisdiction over the parties, but no significant contact with the transaction.[33]

This constraint will rarely be relevant in litigation. Where it is not, DOMA will not be relevant, either. One must strain a bit to imagine situations in which the significant-contacts standard requires a state to recognize a foreign marriage, but the exercise is worth undertaking, since only by imagining such unusual (but possible) cases can one discern whatever effect DOMA has on existing law. Consider, then, two hypothetical cases: [34]

> A, who lives and works in a state that recognizes same-sex marriages, is insured by a group health insurance plan that is paid for by A's employer. The insurance policy specifies that coverage will be provided to the "spouse" of the named insured. A's same-sex spouse, B, becomes seriously ill, requiring expensive treatment. The insurance company would prefer not to pay for the treatments, even though they are plainly required by the terms of the policy. While B is on an airplane flying over Georgia on its way to another state, a representative of the insurance company serves B with a summons to appear in a declaratory judgment action that the insurer has filed in a Georgia court.[35] In its pleadings, the insurer claims that, since Georgia law declares same-sex marriages "void" and "prohibited" and "contractual rights granted by virtue of" such marriages are "unenforceable in the courts of this state," [36] the court should apply Georgia law and declare that A and B were never validly married, and that the insurer therefore has no contractual liability to B. (If the Georgia court agrees with the insurer's claim,[37] a court in A's home state would have to give full faith and credit to its judgment, which, because it does not "treat" the relationship between A and B "as a marriage under the laws of" Georgia, is unaffected by DOMA.)[38]

> During C's long marriage to D, a person of the same sex, during which they have both always lived in a state that recognizes same-sex marriages, C has amassed substantial wealth from his business, while D has cared for their children at home. C now wants to become single again, but would prefer that D not receive any share of the property that C has accumulated during the marriage. While both are on an airplane flying over Georgia, C serves D with a summons to appear in a declaratory judgment action that C has filed in a Georgia court. And so forth.

In each of these cases, the application of Georgia law would violate due process. Georgia had no contact with the parties or the transaction before the filing of the suit. There is no legitimate reason for applying Georgia's substantive law to the case. Each case presents what proponents of the interest-analysis approach to conflict of laws call a "false conflict," because only one state has a legitimate interest in having its law applied. The results that DOMA thus licenses are indefensible; at any rate, there is no evidence that the proponents of DOMA would try to defend them. The authors of the law do not appear to have given any thought to these possibilities. Whatever their subjective intent was, however, the plain language of the statute covers these situations and mandates these consequences.[39]

Both of these are unusual cases, but it is only in such unusual cases that DOMA's choice-of-law provision can have any effect on preexisting law. The due process constraint will not often arise in litigation. Where it does, however, Congress cannot make it go away. Due process is as much of a limitation on Congress as it is on the states. Even if Congress has plenary authority to define the scope of full faith and credit, it cannot exercise that authority in ways that violate the due process rights of individuals.

When states devise choice-of-law rules, therefore, the only constraint imposed upon them by the Full Faith and Credit Clause is one that Congress cannot remove. Any change in the meaning of full faith and credit that DOMA brings about is necessarily unconstitutional.

In order to say that DOMA was usefully addressing any choice-of-law issue, its proponents were obliged to treat the most speculative claims about full faith and credit made by gay rights advocates as though they were likely to be adopted by a court. In its report accompanying DOMA, the House Judiciary Committee cited at length a memo by Evan Wolfson, Director of the Marriage Project for the Lambda Legal Defense and Education Fund and co-counsel for the plaintiffs in the *Baehr* case. Wolfson argued that states have an obligation to recognize a sister-state marriage under each prong of the Full Faith and Credit Clause: marriage is a "public Act" because it occurs pursuant to a statutory scheme and is performed by a public official; the marriage certificate is a "Record" that a marriage has been validly contracted; in at least those sixteen states where judicial officials perform the ceremony, marriage is a "judicial Proceeding."[40] This is a clever argument, but no authority supports it, and it is most unlikely to be accepted by any court in the foreseeable future, particularly in light of the remarkably weak interpretation of full faith and credit that has prevailed in recent decades. The Supreme Court has very nearly given the states carte blanche to disregard other states' laws that are not embodied in judgments. Wolfson's memo and similar scholarly claims hardly establish a need for congressional action. In order for DOMA to have any effect at all with respect to these claims, there must (improbably) be a court that is persuaded by Wolfson's innovative interpretation of the self-executing force of the Full Faith and Credit Clause, but that also believes that Congress has unlimited power to abridge the robust rights created by the Clause thus understood.

Recognition of Judgments

There is, on the other hand, one way in which DOMA would plainly alter preexisting law. The Supreme Court has enforced the Full Faith and Credit Clause only weakly with respect to laws, but has enforced it stringently with respect to judgments. It has been settled for nearly a century that no state may invoke its public policy in order to withhold enforcement of a final judgment issued by the courts of another state.[41] The rule that states must enforce sister-state judgments is best understood as an expression of the "strong and pervasive policy in all legal systems to limit repetitive litigation of claims and issues."[42]

DOMA's declaration that a state need not even give effect to a "judicial proceeding" respecting a same-sex marriage implies, however, that other states may ignore *any* judgment in which the prevailing party has pled the existence of a same-sex marriage. In the two hypothetical cases discussed above, a judgment by a court against the insurer or an award of marital property to the less wealthy spouse might not be enforceable outside the state that recognizes same-sex marriages. If a drunk driver runs down and kills a pedestrian in that state, and the victim happens to have been married to a person of the same sex, and the surviving spouse wins a wrongful death suit, the driver could flee with his money to a state that does not recognize same-sex marriage. Under DOMA, courts in other states would have no obligation to enforce the judgment.

To make matters more complicated, federal law, as amended by DOMA, withdraws full faith and credit only from judgments in which the rendering court *recognizes* a same-sex marriage, while continuing to require full faith and credit for judgments in which the rendering court *denies* recognition.[43] Only the former is a "judicial proceeding of any other State . . . respecting a relationship between persons of the same sex that is treated as a marriage under the laws of such other State."[44] Thus, a court's decision will or will not be entitled to full faith and credit, depending on whether it reaches a result that Congress likes. The asymmetry here is reminiscent of that created by the invalidated law in *Romer,* which withdrew antidiscrimination protection from gays while preserving it for heterosexuals.

In the hypothetical wrongful death case just analyzed, if the defendant filed a counterclaim for a declaratory judgment and relitigated the liability question in the new forum,[45] and the court held that no wrongful death suit could lie because no marriage ever existed, *that* judgment would be entitled to full faith and credit everywhere—*even in the state that recognizes same-sex marriages.* The defendant would then be free to return home and put his money back in the bank there, secure in the knowledge that federal law would protect his assets from seizure by his victim's survivors.

If, on the other hand, the new forum state refused to collude in this evasion and reconfirmed the judgment, that second judgment, too, would under DOMA not be entitled to full faith and credit, because that second judgment too would have recognized the existence of a same-sex marriage. The defendant would then be free to relitigate the question anew in a third forum, and a fourth, and so on. When at last he found a court that would cooperate with his scheme, the judgment issued by *that* forum would then be entitled to full faith and credit throughout the United States![46]

I do not suggest that any member of Congress intended these surprising results. Once again, the drafters of DOMA appear to have been blind to the statute's effects on the targeted class. Like the drafters of the law the Court struck down in *Romer,* they were apparently so eager to prevent undeserved (or so they thought) benefits from being conferred on gays that they did not even pause to think about the breadth of the disability they were imposing.[47]

In writing the provision to cover judgments as well as choice-of-law decisions, Congress does not seem to have contemplated any genuinely adversarial proceeding, even though this is the only kind of proceeding that can generate a judgment entitled to full faith and credit. Some gay rights advocates had suggested that a couple traveling to Hawaii to marry should also get a declaratory judgment of the marriage's validity.[48] The House Committee report, citing these writers, noted that "it is possible that homosexual couples could obtain a judicial judgment memorializing their 'marriage,' and then proceed to base their claim of sister-state recognition on that judicial record."[49] The report therefore states plainly that DOMA applies to "judicial orders."[50] Again, Congress conjured up a bogey without substance. In a forum with a strong public policy against recognizing same-sex marriage, a court would surely (and correctly) hold that the domicile state is not bound by a collusive judgment to which it was not a party.[51]

In genuinely adversarial cases, such as our hypotheticals involving the insurance company or the drunk driver, state courts would be unlikely to indulge the litigants claiming the nonexistence of the same-sex marriages. It is most unlikely that any court would be inclined, even with Congressional authorization, to disregard a non-collusive sister-state judgment just because the rendering court decided that a same-sex marriage existed.[52]

DOMA'S PERVASIVE EQUAL PROTECTION PROBLEM

Earlier in the chapter, I reviewed the difficulties of relying on *Romer v. Evans* in an attack on the definitional provision of DOMA. When one mounts a similar attack on the choice-of-law provision, these difficulties vanish.[53] In this section, I argue that no innocent explanation of DOMA's choice-of-law provision can be persuasive.

The choice-of-law provision of DOMA, like the definitional provision, "identifies persons by a single trait [membership in a same-sex marriage] and then denies them protection across the board."[54] But it is hard to explain *this* provision's breadth in terms of the narrow situation it seeks to address. The choice-of-law provision goes well beyond anything necessary to "ensure[ ] that each State can define for itself the concept of marriage and not be bound by decisions made by other States."[55] It permits states to disregard the marriages of same-sex couples under any circumstances, even when the forum state has so little contact with the couples that it would be unconstitutional for it to apply its own marriage law to them. The *Romer* Court thought it relevant that the Colorado amendment's "disqualification of a class of persons from the right to seek specific protection from the law [was] unprecedented in our jurisprudence."[56] Similarly, no group whose marriages were prohibited by some states—not married first cousins, not members of polygamous marriages, not even interracial couples, whose marriages were punishable as felonies in the Jim Crow states— has ever had its marriages, validly recognized in one jurisdiction, subjected to the degree of ostracism by others that DOMA licenses.[57]

Unlike the definitional section, the choice-of-law section's operation cannot plausibly be described as a measured response to the situation that called it forth. As we have seen, the results it authorizes are ones no one could have intended. Its broad sweep "divorce[s it] from any factual context from which we could discern a relationship to legitimate state interests."[58] Like Amendment 2, the effects of the choice-of-law provision "outrun and belie any legitimate justifications that may be claimed for it."[59] Like Amendment 2, "its sheer breadth is so discontinuous with the reasons offered for it that the [law] seems inexplicable by anything but animus toward the class that it affects."[60]

One conceivable way to save a law that has no constitutionally permissible effects is to construe it to be merely declaratory of existing doctrine.[61] Like the definitional provision, one could say, the choice-of-law provision merely preserves the status quo. Such a construction would forestall all the strange effects we have discussed. It is consistent with an understanding of the environment in which DOMA was passed, in which the press fecklessly repeated lurid claims that full faith and credit law would automatically obligate every state to recognize same-sex marriages for all purposes. Congress, on this account, performed a useful function by restating, in the most prominent possible way, what already was the law: that for many purposes, states have no obligation to recognize marriages that are contrary to their public policies.[62] This is an excessively charitable construction of DOMA, but excessively charitable constructions are part of the business of courts when this is necessary to save a statute from unconstitutionality.[63]

This maneuver fails. DOMA's choice-of-law provision is poorly drafted, but its language is too plain (and, with respect to judgments, too clearly supported by the legislative history) to be construed away. That plain language, we have seen, produces results that are so weird that it is not possible to show that they are rationally related to any permissible state purpose. The only end to which this provision has any rational relation is the bare desire to harm same-sex couples—to authorize state courts to ignore sister-state judgments if and only if those judgments vindicate the marital interests of those couples.

What does this imply about the other provision of DOMA, which merely defines marriage?

For an answer, we must consider what an inference of unconstitutional purpose means as a general matter. In his dissent in *Romer,* Justice Scalia argued that the facial challenge to Amendment 2 ought to fail under *United States v. Salerno,*[64] because the amendment was "unquestionably" constitutional in at least some applications.[65] *Salerno* holds that a facial challenge to legislation can succeed only if the challenger shows "that no set of circumstances exists under which the Act would be valid."[66] Under *Salerno,* "a facial challenge to a statute will fail if a statute has *any* constitutional application."[67] There was no question that some of the applications of Amendment 2 were constitutional. Yet the Court's facial invalidation of the law meant that it could not be enforced under any circumstances. Why did the Court strike it down *in toto*?

Richard Duncan, in his explanation of *Romer,* cites Michael Dorf's observation that if a statute has an "'impermissible purpose, courts cannot save it by severing its unconstitutional applications. The invalid legislative purpose pervades all of the provision's applications.'"[68]

This, Duncan thinks, is why the *Salerno* rule did not save the amendment. Having found that the law reflected a bare desire to harm gays, the Court properly inferred that no application of the amendment could be permissible.

Duncan nonetheless thinks that *Romer* was wrongly decided because the draconian or unconstitutional applications that worried the Court were unlikely ever to occur and, in any event, were not the primary effect of the law. At oral argument, the justices wondered whether the amendment would authorize libraries to refuse to lend books to gays or hospitals to deny gays access to kidney dialysis.[69] Although the amendment's literal language might have authorized such discrimination, such scenarios were unlikely and might have been cured by a narrow interpretation of the amendment. Duncan tellingly cites Justice Kennedy's observation, in another context, that courts should not invalidate laws "on a facial challenge based upon a worst-case analysis that may never occur." [70]

I think that *Romer* is correctly decided, but will not engage Professor Duncan on that ground here.[71] (Like it or not, *Romer* is now part of established doctrine.) I merely point out how much weaker his arguments would be if someone made them on behalf of DOMA. Amendment 2 would probably never have brought about the parade of horribles envisioned by the Court, and it would have permitted those with conscientious religious objections to homosexual conduct to avoid associating with those who engage in such conduct.[72] The latter is unquestionably a constitutional end. The choice-of-law provision of DOMA, on the contrary, has no effects that are not arbitrary and indefensible. It does not change the law in *any* constitutionally permissible way. Even more than Amendment 2, the "sheer breadth"[73] of DOMA "outrun[s] and belie[s] any legitimate justifications that may be claimed for it." [74]

The constitutional defects of DOMA's choice-of-law provision put its definitional provision in a different light. The bill's proponents argued that the definitional provision merely preserves the status quo. That provision, however, accomplishes its end by doing something unprecedented. Same-sex marriages are assigned a legal pariah status that has never before existed in American history. Of all the married couples in the country, only the marriages of same-sex couples will not be recognized by the federal government—ever, for any purpose, no matter how much they may resemble, for relevant purposes, all other married couples. (If two federal employees are killed in the line of duty, is the same-sex spouse of one less deserving of compensation than the opposite-sex spouse of the other?) If impermissible animus pervades the choice-of-law provision of DOMA, the same animus infects the definitional section, in which the federal government "deem[s] a class of persons a stranger to its laws."[75] In the context of the bill as a whole, the innocent explanation of the definitional provision loses credibility.

Ordinarily, Dorf observes, "if the purpose of one provision of a statute is invalid, but other provisions serve valid legislative purposes, then the invalid portion may be severed subject only to conventional severability constraints."[76] Conventional severability principles would certainly call for preserving the definitional provision of DOMA, even if the choice-of-law provision were invalidated.[77] As we saw earlier, however, there is already some doubt as to whether the definitional provision itself serves valid legislative purposes.[78] It is no accident that the two provisions of DOMA happen to be in the same bill. This was not an omnibus budget reconciliation act. If there is no way to escape the inference that the purpose of DOMA's choice-of-law provision was to harm the affected group, then this inference ought to extend to the definitional provision, which targets the same group and injures it even more severely than the choice-of-law provision does.

In a recent case in which it was faced with a similar situation, the Court readily inferred that an innocent-sounding statute was invalid because of the invidious legislative scheme of which it was a part. In chapter 1, I discussed *Church of Lukumi Babalu Aye v. Hialeah*,[79] in which the Court struck down four ordinances that a city had enacted with the avowed purpose of preventing a Santeria church from practicing animal sacrifice. One of those laws, you will recall, was facially neutral toward the targeted religious group, but the Court invalidated it anyway. *Lukumi* makes clear that an impermissible purpose invalidates an entire legislative scheme, even the colorably innocent-sounding and severable parts, if those parts inflict unusual burdens on the same class that is targeted by the clearly discriminatory ones. Perhaps, standing alone, the definitional section of DOMA could be given an innocent explanation. In context, however, that explanation cannot be credited. The definitional section functions in the same way as the choice-of-law section, to inflict indiscriminate harm on married same-sex couples.

I also noted in chapter 1 that *Lukumi* holds (what is inferrable from *Romer* as well) that the invidious purpose that invalidates a statute is that which appears on the face of law, not the unexpressed intentions of the legislators. DOMA is unconstitutional because of its invidious purpose. I possess no knowledge of, and am making no claim about, any legislator's or staff member's subjective state of mind. Members of Congress may be guilty of nothing worse than sloppy draftsmanship.

But the purpose of DOMA that appears plainly on its face, the only end to which the statute is suited, is a bare desire to harm a politically unpopular group. That purpose is unconstitutional.

CONCLUSION

Both provisions of DOMA, therefore, are facially invalid. If and when same-sex couples are allowed to marry in any state, they should be deemed to be entitled to the same treatment as all other married couples under federal law.

This conclusion has an important further implication. *Romer*'s long-term importance is contested. Either *Romer* turns solely on the peculiar way in which Amendment 2's language singled out gays for special disadvantage, in which case it depended on unusual facts that are unlikely to be repeated, or it is the *Sweatt v. Painter* of gay rights law, a precursor to a constitutional revolution on behalf of a hitherto oppressed class. Which it turns out to be will depend on how the Court decides the doctrinal question, which it has never addressed, of whether sexual orientation should be deemed a suspect classification calling for heightened scrutiny.

Whether a classification should be deemed suspect depends, at least in part, on the motivation that the Court thinks is likely to underlie it. "Racial classifications that disadvantage minorities are 'suspect,'" writes John Hart Ely, "because we suspect that they are the product of racially prejudiced thinking of a sort we understand the Fourteenth Amendment to have been centrally concerned with eradicating."[80] Repeated instances of unjustified disadvantage strengthen the case for the kind of generalized suspicion that is embodied in the suspect classification doctrine.[81]

Every time another law is enacted that singles out gays for disadvantage and is inexplicable except by reference to a bare desire to harm them, the case for general judicial protection of gays against legislative discrimination becomes stronger. For this reason, the drafters of DOMA have harmed their own cause. Their law was denounced as unnecessary and mean-spirited, but it is more than that. It is dumb. Its authors have furnished ammunition to their enemies.

THE LIMITATIONS OF
THE COURTS

On December 20, 1999, the Vermont Supreme Court ruled that gay couples were entitled, under the state constitution, to the same legal rights as married heterosexual couples.[1] Its decree was an unusual one. The court refused to order the state to issue the marriage licenses that the plaintiffs sought. Instead, it told the legislature that it did not have to legalize same-sex marriage so long as it gave gay couples the same rights.

The legislature complied with remarkable speed. Four months later, Vermont enacted its "civil unions" law, which gave same-sex couples all of the rights of married couples except for the name of "marriage." Parties to civil unions in Vermont have rights of marital property, workers' compensation benefits, family leave benefits, homestead rights, and all of the other entitlements of married couples. And the new status is a commitment as serious as marriage. Unlike other jurisdictions' "domestic partnerships," which can be dissolved at will by either of the parties, Vermont's civil unions can only be terminated by divorce proceedings.[2]

The Vermont law is a triumph of judicially driven social reform. And the decision's success is no accident. The judges were not only thinking about the law. They were also thinking about politics.

One of the most remarkable things about *Baker v. State* was how nakedly the court's political calculations were displayed in the opinion. The court explained that it would not order "a sudden change in the marriage laws," because this could have "disruptive and unforeseen consequences."[3] Judges often worry about the political reaction to their decisions, but they usually don't admit it. The Vermont court was prodded to candor by the objections of one of its own judges. All the judges agreed that the same-sex couples had stated a valid claim of discrimination, but one of them, Justice Denise Johnson, thought that the court should immediately decree that the couples receive the marriage licenses they had asked for. The court's "novel and truncated remedy," she complained, "abdicates this court's constitutional duty to redress violations of constitutional rights."[4] The majority opinion, written by Chief Justice Jeffrey Amestoy, responded that her claim was "insulated from reality."[5] Amestoy noted that his decision had given more protection to same-sex relationships than any other high court decision, with the "instructive exception"[6] of Hawaii. Hawaii's supreme court decided in 1993 that the state would probably have to recognize same-sex marriages, only to be overruled by a constitutional amendment enacted by referendum. Amestoy cited that amendment, as well as a similar one that Alaska adopted after a lower court in that state had ordered recognition of a same-sex marriage. Both amendments passed by overwhelming margins. Amestoy's implication was clear: if we don't want to arouse the same kind of reaction here, we had better be careful. Johnson was unimpressed. "If the people of Vermont wish to overturn a constitutionally based decision, as happened in Alaska and Hawaii, they may do so," she wrote. "The possibility that they may do so, however, should not, in my view, deprive these plaintiffs of the remedy to which they are entitled."[7]

The debate between the justices brings to light a very old question about the role of courts in American government. America's written constitutions, state and federal, give courts a degree of political power that is rarely found elsewhere in the world. Should their political role affect the way in which they decide cases? We expect responsible leaders to think about the consequences of their decisions when they act. Should courts do this, too? Or should they merely say what the law is and let others worry about what follows?

The second view is Johnson's, and it has a long and distinguished pedigree. Perhaps its most notable ancestor is Justice Robert Jackson's dissent in *Korematsu v. United States,*[8] a 1944 case in which the U.S. Supreme Court upheld the internment of Japanese-American citizens in concentration camps during World War II. That decision, which is today universally acknowledged to be a disastrous mistake,[9] held that laws that curtailed the rights of a single racial group were "suspect" but that the internment was justified by military necessity, since there was no way to tell which (if any) Japanese-Americans might be planning espionage or sabotage. Among the several dissenting opinions, Jackson's was the subtlest, because he recognized that the judiciary cannot reliably appraise military decisions, which often rest on secret information and unprovable assumptions. Jackson thought that a court should not enforce an unconstitutional order even if that order was justified by military necessity. If courts allowed themselves to worry about consequences, he explained, then they would have no alternative but to bow to the military's claims, and the approval of racial discrimination would thereafter contaminate constitutional law in peacetime. The courts should just do their job, and let the military be the military.[10]

Jackson's logic has a deep appeal, because he understood the limitations of the judiciary while offering it a way to perform its distinctive role despite those limitations. His approach provided a principled basis for resisting the plausible arguments for internment, arguments that overwhelmed such great civil libertarians as Justice Hugo Black, who wrote the Court's opinion in *Korematsu*. But Jackson left important questions unanswered about the Supreme Court's authority. Somebody has to worry about the balance between military necessity and civil liberties. If the court makes clear that it isn't worrying about that, then why should the authorities—who, after all, have a war to fight— obey a court's order to empty the camps? The other dissenters were less modest about the judiciary's competence. They looked at the sparse evidence of necessity and concluded that Japanese-Americans posed no real threat to anybody and that the internment was the product of racist hysteria. They were right.

Justice Johnson claimed that the Vermont court should have issued the marriage licenses because that is "the most straightforward and effective remedy." [11] Outcomes were not her concern. Even if it were ultimately overruled by a constitutional amendment, the court would have done its job. If the Vermont constitution requires same-sex marriage, she thought, the court should say so. If the electorate disagrees and overrules the court, then the court will thereafter simply be interpreting a changed document. Johnson's view implies that the court should not *care* what the law is; its job is simply to report whatever it reads in the legal texts—texts that are written by others.

Amestoy implicitly relies on a different and more persuasive view of the judicial role, one in which the courts have a responsibility, not merely to state the law accurately, but to bring about certain results. On this account, courts are valuable because they enforce constitutional principles that are themselves valuable. The courts ought not to act in ways that weaken those principles, even if legal procedures, such as those for enacting constitutional amendments, are scrupulously followed when this weakening takes place.

On this account, the court is itself a sort of political entity. We might call it the party of principle. The term "party of principle" is an oxymoron, of course. Principles are supposed to stand above the factional struggles in which parties engage. But the oxymoron captures the paradoxical situation of courts facing resistance to constitutional rights. Judges must be politicians for the sake of the things that should be beyond politics. [12]

There are two dangers in regarding courts as the party of principle. The first is that this may produce too idealized a view of the courts.

The record of courts in upholding constitutional principle is decidedly mixed. Courts in America have given their approval to egregious violations of rights. The World War II internments have already been mentioned. Other instances include the kidnapping of free blacks into slavery,[13] the extension of slavery into the territories,[14] the second-class citizenship of women,[15] and racial segregation in the South.[16]

The second danger is that of understating the responsibilities of the other branches of government. Worrying about the interplay of principle and consequence is not the peculiar business of the courts. Think of the debate over intervention in Kosovo or the question of how trade with China or Cuba will affect human rights in those countries.

But certain principles *are* the special concern of courts. These are the principles of constitutional law—the basic rules that restrain government. Constitutional law is a peculiar sort of law. Law usually constrains individuals, either in their dealings with one another or when they violate the public order. Constitutional law, however, attempts to use law to constrain the exercise of political power. Constraining the exercise of power is itself a political act. Since law here attempts to do something that is fundamentally different from everything else it tries to do, courts deciding constitutional issues must ride two horses at once. They must follow legal procedures and think like lawyers, but they must also engage in the sort of prudential calculations that we normally expect of politicians.

A smart statesman knows when to act and when to wait. The power of courts has severe limitations. As Alexander Hamilton pointed out more than two centuries ago, courts control neither the sword nor the purse. Courts cannot resolve controversial political issues by decree. *Roe v. Wade*[17] legalized abortion, but abortions remain nearly impossible to get in many parts of the United States, and the decision aroused a powerful pro-life movement. The Court's most politically ambitious decision, *Dred Scott v. Sandford*,[18] was a disaster. The 1857 case tried to settle the issue of slavery in the territories by holding that slaveholders had a constitutional right to take their "property" anywhere they wanted; the Civil War soon followed.

If same-sex marriage really is required by high principle—and Amestoy and Johnson both agreed that it is—then it is no light thing to act in a way that makes it less rather than more likely that such marriages will in fact be recognized and remain so. That is the deep flaw in Johnson's position. With same-sex marriage, the courts are unusually far ahead of public opinion. "Public opinion may change," writes Richard Posner, chief judge for the U.S. Court of Appeals for the Seventh Circuit, "but at present it is too firmly against same-sex marriage for the courts to act."[19] He suggests "allowing the matter to simmer for a while before the heavy artillery of constitutional rightsmaking is trundled out."[20] His warning is sound, but it understates what courts can do. Perhaps a judicial command won't work, but a judicial nudge can accomplish a lot. The Vermont court's limited remedy produced the most far-reaching domestic partnership law in the nation. It is the most that gays can possibly hope for, at least in the next few years.[21]

Amestoy thus had the better of the prudential argument. He appears to be a wise statesman. Unfortunately, his opinion in *Baker* is a poor piece of judicial craftsmanship.

I have said nothing yet about the reasons the court gave for its decision. Those reasons matter. As the courts have become increasingly hospitable to claims of unfair discrimination against gays, conservative commentators and politicians have become fond of denouncing these decisions as judicial activism, with little basis in the law. These commentators have rarely bothered to examine the courts' reasoning. Until they do that, their claims cannot be taken seriously. The claim that the same-sex marriage issue is properly one for the legislature assumes that the courts have had no legal basis for their decisions. By the same token, though, if the courts are going to intervene in this controversial area, they had better do a good job of explaining why. As the party of principle, a court ought to state forthrightly what principle it is upholding.

Amestoy's majority opinion relies on the peculiar "common benefits clause" of the Vermont constitution, which says that "government is, or ought to be, instituted for the common benefit, protection, and security of the people, nation, or community, and not for the particular emolument or advantage of any single person, family, or set of persons, who are a part only of that community."[22] (Since the decision relied on the state constitution, it couldn't be appealed to the U.S. Supreme Court.) The court interpreted this provision to require "the elimination of artificial governmental preferments and advantages."[23] In practice, this interpretation would mean that the state would have to show an "appropriate and overriding public interest" in order to justify "statutory exclusions from public benefits and protections."[24] To justify its policy, the state had cited its interests in promoting ties between biological parents and children, in providing good role models for children, in minimizing the legal complications of surrogacy contracts and sperm donors, and in discouraging marriages of convenience. The court observed that the discrimination against gay couples did not seem to promote any of these interests.

The state's justifications for its policy were weak, but so was the court's rationale for holding the state to such a heavy burden of justification. All laws classify, and in some cases, those classifications are bound to be arbitrary. Twelve-year-olds can't get driving licenses anywhere in the United States, and twenty-year-olds can get them everywhere, even though some twelve-year-olds drive better than some twenty-year-olds. The court's rule means that any law that classifies—which means in practice, any law at all—will be struck down unless the court thinks the classification is reasonable. As another of the Vermont judges noted, this approach practically constitutes the courts as a third house of the legislature, approving or disapproving laws depending on whether they seem to the court to make sense.[25]

The U.S. Supreme Court experimented with this kind of rule in the early twentieth century, when it undertook to review the reasonableness of any law that interfered with individual liberty in any way. Among the laws that it struck down as unreasonable were minimum wage laws, maximum hours laws, and laws restricting the use of child labor.[26] This period culminated in the Court's struggle in the 1930s with President Franklin Roosevelt over the constitutionality of the New Deal, a struggle that culminated in the Court's embarrassed retreat after Roosevelt won reelection by an overwhelming margin and threatened to pack the Court with sympathetic judges. Since then, the Court has abandoned the task of reviewing the reasonableness of most laws, amid general agreement that this is not a suitable task for judges. Instead, the Court only engages in this kind of searching review when a law infringes on a fundamental right or discriminates on the basis of race, sex, or other "suspect" classifications. With a few aberrations, it had been clear before *Baker* that Vermont followed a similar rule when interpreting its own constitution. Almost no lawyers, academics, or judges think that it would make sense to return to the pre-New Deal rules. It is odd that the Vermont court chose the same-sex marriage case as the occasion for resurrecting this doctrine, which has nothing to do with the distinctive claims of gays.

What else could the court have said? One of the judges wanted to say that sexual orientation is a suspect classification—an argument considered in chapter 1, above. Amestoy dismissed this claim, though without argument; he merely noted that it had been rejected by other courts. On the other hand, he concluded his opinion with the ringing statement that "to acknowledge plaintiffs as Vermonters who seek nothing more, nor less, than legal protection and security for their avowed commitment to an intimate and lasting human relationship is simply, when all is said and done, an acknowledgement of our common humanity." [27] He thereby acknowledged that gays, unlike most citizens, have their humanity subjected to question on a regular basis. This is the core reason for giving gays precisely the special protection that Amestoy denied them.

The other argument, adopted by Justice Johnson, is that discrimination against gays is "a straightforward case of sex discrimination." [28] Amestoy expressly rejected this argument as well. He reasoned that "the marriage laws are facially neutral" since they "prohibit men and women equally from marrying a person of the same sex." [29] Johnson correctly responded that Amestoy's reasoning implied that "a statute that required courts to give custody of male children to fathers and female children to mothers would not be sex discrimination." [30]

Why did the court expressly reject strong arguments and embrace a weaker one instead? Perhaps the stronger arguments were *too* strong, given the limited remedy that the court meant to give. (This would explain why other courts have also evaded these arguments.) If either of them were accepted, it would be hard to resist the politically untenable conclusion that the same-sex couples ought to get their marriage licenses.

The mushy rationale that the Vermont court adopted provided maximum flexibility. This has obvious attractions. And it did provide an occasion for the court to march through the state's reasons for denying gay couples the right to marry and expose them for the sophistries that they were. These advantages are, however, purchased at some cost to the court's distinctive character as the party of principle, because the court's rationale stands for no principle at all. [31]

Prudence may sometimes dictate that courts obscure the very principles that they are defending. The most impressive precedent is *Brown v. Board of Education*, [32] which declared in 1954 that racially segregated schools were unconstitutional. *Brown* is commonly remembered today, inaccurately, as holding that segregation was wrong because it treated blacks unequally, and as rejecting Southern whites' mantra of "separate but equal" as the vicious lie that it was. Every year, my students in Constitutional Law are shocked and disappointed when they read the weak opinion that Chief Justice Earl Warren actually wrote. Warren's reasoning was that (1) education is very important; (2) segregation makes black children feel inferior; (3) low self-esteem impairs a child's ability to learn; therefore (4) "separate but equal" has no place in public education. Each step of this alleged causal sequence is dubious. Suppose (it is not a fanciful supposition) that black children didn't naively accept the message of segregation, but rather regarded the segregators as disgusting racists whose views deserved no respect whatsoever? What if the absence of white children does not itself harm black children? Is segregation then harmless and constitutional?

But Warren, who had been governor of California and a candidate for vice president before he was appointed to the Court, knew something about politics. He understood how vulnerable the Court was in taking on segregation, and he did not think it prudent to offend the South by too vigorous a denunciation of its oppressive social system. Warren also understood the importance of delivering a unanimous decision, and a more forthright opinion would probably have lost the vote of Justice Stanley Reed, a Southerner who, shortly before the case was decided, expressed shock at the notion of bringing his wife to a restaurant where blacks were allowed to dine.[33] *Brown* was cautiously written and cautious in its result. It did not order the immediate desegregation of the Southern schools. The Court only pushed ahead a decade later, after Lyndon Johnson mobilized the political branches in support of integration.

The Warren Court's wariness was plainest when a case came up, a year after *Brown,* involving a Virginia statute prohibiting interracial marriage, which was one of the most emotionally charged racial issues of the time. The Court simply refused to hear the case and did not invalidate the Southern laws against interracial marriage until 1967. One of the judges reportedly said, coming out of the conference, that "one bombshell at a time is enough." [34]

But the comparison with *Brown* also reveals what's wrong with *Baker. Brown* did no damage to the law. *Brown* did not endorse poorly reasoned decisions by other courts and reject the claims of the very group it was protecting. *Baker's* attack on the sex-discrimination argument embraces the very principle of "separate but equal" that *Brown* rejected. The claim that the marriage laws treat both sexes equally resembles the one that the Southern states made for their prohibition of interracial marriage: it's true that blacks can't marry whites, they explained, but whites likewise can't marry blacks, so there's no discrimination.[35]

Brown did not embrace arguments that were sound but impolitic, but neither did it foreclose them. And when the Court avoided hearing the interracial marriage case, it said nothing at all.

Precisely because Amestoy's opinion is one of the landmark decisions on behalf of gays, it will have unusual authority. The technical defects on which I have been dwelling are important, because they threaten to have a destructive effect on legal doctrine. If gays' equality arguments were rejected even in Vermont, other courts may say, why should we accept them?

Amestoy did not need to use every legal argument in the tool box, and he was wise to avoid using some of them. But there is no excuse for damaging the tools that he elected not to use.

Amestoy's imperfect opinion invites comparison with the other recent judicial attempt to vindicate the rights of same-sex couples. Eleven days before the Vermont decision, in *Baehr v. Miike,*[36] the Hawaii Supreme Court ended years of litigation by rejecting the claims of three same-sex couples who had sought the right to marry. The press has treated Vermont as a qualified victory for gays, while Hawaii is thought a costly failure. Yet in the long run the Hawaii case may offer gays as much as Vermont has.

Gays lost a lot in Hawaii. In 1993, they scored a big win when the court adopted the sex-discrimination argument, implying that gays would have a right to marry in that state. But the prospect of same-sex couples marrying in Hawaii and then attempting to get their marriages recognized in other states produced a major backlash. Thirty-four states enacted laws stating that they would not recognize same-sex marriages. Congress passed the Defense of Marriage Act, which declared those laws constitutional and provided that same-sex marriages would not be recognized by federal law for any purpose.[37] And in the end, Hawaii's voters amended its constitution to bar gay marriages.[38] The amendment was ambiguous enough that the court could still have issued licenses to the three couples, but in the end it declined to do that.

The fate of Hawaii's decision may be taken by some as a vindication of Professor Gerald Rosenberg's well-known claim that courts cannot bring about significant social change. Rosenberg's book *The Hollow Hope*[39] usefully deflates conventional wisdom about the power of courts. He shows how little *Brown v. Board of Education* accomplished until the elected branches decided to throw their weight on the side of desegregation. He chronicles other judicial failures in the areas of abortion, the environment, reapportionment, and criminal law. Hawaii may be understood as yet another instance of failed judicial social engineering.

Yet Hawaii can be understood a different way. Politics is not just about who wins political fights. It is also about what issues make it onto the agenda in the first place, or even get thought of as worth having an argument about.[40] And when the issue is looked at from that angle, Hawaii was a triumph for gays.

In 1993, when the Hawaii Supreme Court first acted, same-sex marriage was virtually unthinkable as a political proposition. Yet

American culture had changed in fundamental ways that were making it less hostile to gays' claims. The homosexuality taboo, as noted in chapter 3, is largely about preserving traditional meanings of masculinity and femininity. As women have moved into the workforce in ever greater numbers, Americans have become less anxious about preserving the hierarchy of the sexes. The widespread acceptance of contraception has also changed the meaning of sex. When heterosexuals routinely have sex that isn't procreative, it becomes hard to see what's wrong with homosexual sex. And, of course, gays themselves have become an increasingly normal presence in American society. Those who first came out of the closet in the 1950s were extraordinarily courageous. It is not nearly so hard to be openly gay today.

None of these changes, however, were enough to put same-sex marriage on the political agenda. The marriage issue is one that some gays feel very strongly about, but it makes many heterosexuals so uncomfortable that they just want the issue to go away. It is unsurprising that no legislature (not even Vermont's) has seriously considered it.

This is where courts come in. The distinctive advantage of courts as political players is that it doesn't take political consensus (or the machinations of a powerful interest) to get them to consider an issue. All it takes is one person with a claim of right that makes sense to the judges.

The Hawaii Supreme Court's decision put the issue of same-sex marriage on the national agenda as it had never been before. Articles debating the pros and cons of the issue began to appear in newspapers and magazines all over the country. Legislation to prevent recognition of same-sex marriage was enacted in 34 states, but it died in many others.[41] Millions of people have now read sympathetic news stories about gay people in stable, loving relationships who appear morally indistinguishable from themselves. Increasingly, "domestic partnerships," which would give same-sex couples all or most of the same benefits accorded to heterosexual married couples and which were once regarded as a politically extreme proposal, have emerged as the moderate compromise solution to the same-sex marriage question. Two-thirds of Americans think that same-sex marriage will be legalized in the next century.[42] It is hard to imagine how the success in Vermont could have happened without the previous "failure" in Hawaii. It is already possible to anticipate the day when same-sex marriage will be uninteresting, in the way that interracial marriage has nearly become. This is a massive cultural shift, and it is hard to imagine its taking place without the debate that the litigation stirred up. Before Hawaii, the marriage issue was well settled, in a way that was not a bit friendly to gays.

The implementation of controversial judicial decisions that seek to bring about significant social change can also create new social facts that themselves help to change popular mores. The claim that the moral authority of courts helps to reshape popular mores has been powerfully challenged by Rosenberg, who has shown that most citizens don't even know what courts are doing.[43] There is, however, another avenue by which courts can bring about significant social reform[44] by means of such reshaping. Court orders can create social facts, and social facts create values. When *Loving v. Virginia* was decided, the overwhelming majority of Americans were opposed to interracial marriage. In 1958, 96 percent of whites surveyed by the Gallup poll disapproved of intermarriage. In 1963, the National Opinion Research Center found that 62 percent of respondents supported laws against interracial marriage.[45] A Gallup poll taken in 1968, the year after the *Loving* decision, found that only 20 percent of Americans approved of interracial marriage, while 72 percent disapproved.[46] In the same year, 56 percent still supported laws against intermarriage. Opinions shifted, but they did so slowly. In 1978, 34 percent approved and 66 percent disapproved of interracial marriage. In 1983, 39 percent approved and 61 percent disapproved. By 1991, 51 percent approved and 49 percent disapproved, and 20 percent still believed that such marriages should be illegal. By 1997, 67 percent approved and 33 percent disapproved.[47] In the 1998 election, nearly 40 percent of South Carolina voters voted against deleting a provision in the state constitution that prohibited interracial marriage.[48] Despite the stubbornness of these attitudes, after *Loving* interracial marriages became more common,[49] and their very existence has tended to legitimate them. A similar point can be made about the abortion decisions. *Roe v. Wade* brought abortion into the mainstream. Some supporters of abortion rights have argued that the pro-choice movement was hurt by its demobilization after its unexpected victory in *Roe*.[50] Even if they are right, this has been compensated for, at least to some extent, by the creation of a generation of women who took their right to abortion for granted. Most nonlawyers do not read *U.S. Reports,* but they do read the Yellow Pages, and it makes a good deal of difference whether there are any listings under "Abortion." In neither of these cases can causation be proven, but in both cases the Court eliminated a legal obstacle to an activity, which then increased. The claim of causation is very plausible. With same-sex marriage, too, there is probably a lot of pent-up demand.[51] Most nonlawyers won't read appellate choice-of-law decisions, but if same-sex couples can sometimes successfully plead their marriages in local courts, the public is likely to hear about it.

Hawaii also offers an important legal precedent. The court's decision there endorsed the sex-discrimination argument—the first court in the country to do so—and instructed the trial court to give the marriage licenses to the couples unless the state could show that this would harm some "compelling state interest"—the same burden that courts impose on laws that discriminate by race, and one that is nearly impossible to satisfy. (Like the Vermont decision, Hawaii's was based on the state constitution and raised no federal issues, so it, too, could not be appealed to the U.S. Supreme Court.) The amendment to the state constitution left open the possibility that the court might order the same remedy that Vermont did, since the amendment only bars same-sex *marriage,* and does not mention the accompanying legal rights. It might still be discriminatory to deny same-sex couples those rights. The sex-discrimination argument that Hawaii has kept alive also has important implications for federal constitutional law, since the U.S. Supreme Court has held that classifications based on sex require an "exceedingly persuasive justification" [52] in order to be upheld. *Baehr* is a dagger pointed at all the laws that discriminate against gays, including the recent wave of anti–gay marriage statutes. The backlash against *Baehr* makes it likely that courts will not take up the invitation soon. But, as noted earlier, the culture is shifting.

In 280 B.C., after a costly victory against the Romans, King Pyrrhus of Epirus famously declared, "one more such victory and we are lost." After the Hawaii litigation, the gay rights movement may well be entitled to say, one more such defeat and we will have won.

Without Hawaii, it is hard to imagine that the Vermont court would have been bold enough to go even as far as it did. Things that were unthinkable a decade ago are now very thinkable, and may eventually be inevitable. When—it is probably no longer necessary to write "if"—same-sex marriage is recognized in America, we will look back and see that Hawaii is where it began. Even in the most dangerous political minefields, there is room for judicial leadership.

The faults of the Vermont opinion may perhaps be regarded as venial ones. No one but lawyers reads judicial opinions anyway. So long as it reached the right result, who cares what the court said? But if courts matter in American politics, then legal reasoning matters, too. Lawyers do read judicial decisions, and those decisions are more likely to last if the lawyers are convinced by what they read. More generally, the rule of law is valuable in itself, and it requires that judges give sound reasons for the results that they reach. Legal craft isn't everything, but it isn't nothing, either. In a constitutional regime, judges need to be both good lawyers *and* good politicians.

In short, two cheers for Vermont! The Vermont court crafted its remedy in a way that was finely calibrated to vindicate the parties' rights to the greatest extent possible consistent with the political limitations under which it labored. On the other hand, in those areas where it could not say the right thing, it would be better if the court had said nothing at all.

* * *

I have been focusing on the judges and their role in reshaping society. But where does that leave the rest of us? Most readers of this book are not judges. Even if we figure out how courts ought to decide cases, we will not be the ones doing the deciding. What are the rest of us to do?

The limitations of the judiciary invite reflection about what this book is fundamentally up to. We turned from rights-based arguments because judges will not and should not directly confront the widespread opposition to same-sex marriage. We moved beyond legislative arguments because lawmakers are not (yet!) ready to abandon ancient prejudices. We turned to choice-of-law questions because, as this book is written, those are the ones that are still unsettled. The latter part of this book thus has the most immediate practical importance. But the first part is of greater ultimate significance. Claims of right are not only addressed to the courts. It is often assumed that the role of law professors is to kibitz the courts, to whisper into the judges' ears and tell them what to do. This is a cramped vision of the mission of an intellectual. Law professors have no more authority in public discourse than other citizens, but they also have no less. This book's task has been primarily to develop the most persuasive moral and legal arguments about the legal status of gay people.

Political actors need clearly defined goals. Lawmakers (and in a democracy all citizens are lawmakers to some extent) need to know what sort of laws are desirable. Lawyers and judges need to know what the law, properly understood, requires. This book has attempted to address these questions.

What no book can do is to say what strategies are appropriate in concrete circumstances. In the decade following *Brown v. Board of Education,* the Supreme Court repeatedly avoided adjudicating the constitutionality of laws against interracial marriage, and it did not invalidate those laws until 1967. Leading scholars criticized this evasion, but Alexander Bickel thought it "wise" for the court to withhold judgment at a time when the Court "was subject to scurrilous attack by men who predicted that integration of the schools would lead directly to 'mongrelization of the race' and that this was the result the Court had really willed." [53] Bickel thought that the Fourteenth Amendment's guarantee of equality "cannot in our society constitute a hard and fast rule of action for universal immediate execution. That is nothing to be proud of. It is a disagreeable fact, and it cannot be wished away." [54]

The abstract principles defended herein cannot be immediately implemented in the world. Resistance is a fact of life; it must be taken into account even when deciding what to demand of one's own political leaders. On the other hand, principled arguments do have a role to play in practical politics. The most important thing that has happened to the status of gays in American society in recent decades is the spread of the suspicion that their treatment as subhuman, as outcasts within society, is morally wrong. It is because that suspicion continues to spread that the transformation of gays' legal status has begun to seem inevitable. Sometimes, at least in the long run, abstract argument is the most effective instrument of politics.

NOTES

1. All this is extensively documented in William N. Eskridge Jr., Gaylaw: Dismantling the Apartheid of the Closet (1999). (Since Eskridge's book was published, Arizona repealed its sodomy statute.)

2. John Rawls, Political Liberalism 4 (1993).

3. New books and articles on gay rights proliferate like dandelions on a spring lawn. A February 2000 search of articles listed under "sexual orientation discrimination" in the Index of Legal Periodicals found 96 articles written on the subject from 1989 to 1994. From 1995 to the date of the search, there were 540 articles. The trend in publication of books is similar but less pronounced. A February 2000 search of the WORLDCAT database found 169 books on "gay rights" from 1989 to 1994, 256 from 1995 to date, and 32 books on "sexual orientation discrimination" from 1989 to 1994 and 40 from 1995 to date. In contrast, as recently as the mid-1970s, there was virtually no legal literature on the status of gay people. See Rhonda R. Rivera, Our Straight-Laced Judges: Twenty Years Later, 50 Hastings L.J. 1179, 1180–81 (1999).

4. Romer v. Evans, 517 U.S. 620, 652–53 (1996) (Scalia, J., dissenting). A survey by Lynn Wardle found that "between 1990 and June 1995, only one of seventy-two articles, notes, comments, or essays focusing primarily on same-sex marriage (only 1.4%) fully defended the heterosexuality requirement for marriage (though lit did so on religious, rather than legal, grounds)." Lynn D. Wardle, A Critical Analysis of Constitutional Claims for Same-Sex Marriage, 1996 B.Y.U. L. Rev. 1, 18–19. See also Thomas Grey, Eros, Civilization, and the Burger Court, 43 Law & Contemp. Probs. 83, 99–100 (1980) (almost all scholarly literature on the privacy cases between 1965 and 1979 construed them as constitutionalizing sexual libertarianism).

5. This part of the consensus is weakening. In recent years, there has been mounting dissent from this idea, but the privacy-based argument still has many defenders.

6. I use the terms "homosexuality" and "homosexual" (the latter as an adjective) to refer to sexual conduct between persons of the same sex. I recognize that this term has the unfortunate connotation that such sexual conduct is a different species of behavior from heterosexual sex. One of the aims of this book is to combat that idea, but before one can fight it one needs to be able to name it, and there is no other word in the English language that refers to this category of behavior. I do not use the word as a noun to refer to persons. There are persons who identify themselves in terms of their unorthodox sexual orientation. These include lesbians, gay men, bisexuals, and transgendered persons. Rather than refer to these people by the clumsy acronym "LGBT," I simply refer to them as "gays."

7. A Newsweek poll in March 2000 found that 83 percent of Americans thought that gays deserved job protection, up from 56 percent in a 1977 survey.

Health insurance for gay partners was supported by 58 percent, and 54 percent thought that partners should get Social Security benefits. Only 34 percent thought there should be legally sanctioned same-sex marriages. John Leland, Shades of Gay, Newsweek, March 20, 2000, p. 46. An Associated Press poll two months later produced nearly identical results. The poll found that 51 percent were opposed to allowing gay couples to marry, while 34 percent approved. On the other hand, at least half of Americans support the rights of gays to receive health insurance (53 percent), Social Security benefits (50 percent), and inheritance (56 percent) from their partners. Will Lester, Poll: Americans Back Some Gay Rights, Associated Press, May 31, 2000.

CHAPTER ONE

1. 478 U.S. 186 (1986).

2. 517 U.S. 620 (1996).

3. Id. at 632 (Scalia, J., dissenting).

4. For a catalogue of the various scholarly views of the opinion, see Andrew Koppelman, *Romer v. Evans* and Invidious Intent, 6 Wm. & Mary Bill of Rights J. 89, 90–92 (1997).

5. See Lynn A. Baker, The Missing Pages of the Majority Opinion in *Romer v. Evans,* 68 U. Colo. L. Rev. 387 (1997).

6. The full text of the amendment follows:

No Protected Status Based on Homosexual, Lesbian, or Bisexual Orientation. Neither the State of Colorado, through any of its branches or departments, nor any of its agencies, political subdivisions, municipalities or school districts, shall enact, adopt or enforce any statute, regulation, ordinance or policy whereby homosexual, lesbian or bisexual orientation, conduct, practices or relationships shall constitute or otherwise be the basis of or entitle any person or class of persons to have or claim any minority status, quota preferences, protected status or claim of discrimination. This Section of the Constitution shall be in all respects self-executing.

Colo. Const. art. 11, § 306, cited in *Romer,* 517 U.S. at 624.

7. 517 U.S. at 632.

8. Id. at 633, quoting Louisville Gas & Elec. Co. v. Coleman, 277 U.S. 32, 37–38 (1928). It appears that "careful consideration" is a synonym for heightened scrutiny.

9. Id. at 635.

10. Id. at 629.

11. Id. at 635.

12. Id. at 630.

13. Id.

14. Id. at 635.

15. Id.

16. Id. at 634, emphasis in original, quoting Department of Agriculture v. Moreno, 413 U.S. 528, 534 (1973).

17. Id. at 636 (Scalia, J., dissenting).

18. Id. at 645.

19. Id. at 644.

20. Id. at 652.

21. City of Cleburne v. Cleburne Living Ctr., 473 U.S. 432, 440 (1985).

22. Korematsu v. United States, 323 U.S. 214, 216 (1944).

23. *Cleburne,* 473 U.S. at 440.

24. Id.

25. Mills v. Habluetzel, 456 U.S. 91, 99 (1982).

26. See Owen Fiss, Groups and the Equal Protection Clause, in Equality and Preferential Treatment 84–123 (Marshall Cohen, Thomas Nagel, and Thomas Scanlon eds., 1977). It is sometimes argued that this approach to Fourteenth Amendment interpretation is a mistake and is inconsistent with the Amendment's underlying purposes. See Andrew Koppelman, Antidiscrimination Law and Social Equality 57–114 (1996). I won't try in this chapter to adjudicate this dispute, but rather will take as given the process-based approach that now prevails. *Romer,* I shall argue, can be defended without going beyond that approach.

27. United States v. Carolene Prods. Co., 304 U.S. 144, 152 n.4 (1938).

28. Washington v. Davis, 426 U.S. 229, 240 (1976).

29. John Hart Ely, Democracy and Distrust: A Theory of Judicial Review 145 (1980).

30. For a long time, confusion reigned as to whether motive mattered at all in determinations of the constitutionality of a law. The Supreme Court has often stated that legislative motive is not subject to judicial review, but it has also handed down many important decisions that can be explained only in terms of motive. Theodore Eisenberg, Disparate Impact and Illicit Motive: Theories of Constitutional Adjudication, 52 N.Y.U. L. Rev. 36, 106–10 (1977). Washington v. Davis may have ended this confusion, at least to the extent of declaring conclusively that motivation is relevant. See 426 U.S. at 238–39.

31. Ely, Democracy and Distrust at 145.

32. Id. at 243 n.11.

33. Id. at 146.

34. Alexander Bickel, The Least Dangerous Branch 16–17 (2d ed. 1986).

35. Ely, Democracy and Distrust at 87.

36. Id., footnote omitted.

37. Id. at 76.

38. Id. at 223 n.33.

39. See Koppelman, Antidiscrimination Law and Social Equality at 18 n.22.

40. The two theories are set out in detail in Walter F. Murphy, James E. Fleming, and Sotirios A. Barber, American Constitutional Interpretation 41–53 (2d ed. 1995).

41. Walter F. Murphy, Merlin's Memory: The Past and Future Imperfect of the Once and Future Polity, in Responding to Imperfection: The Theory and Practice of Constitutional Amendment 163, 178 (Sanford Levinson ed., 1995).

42. Id. at 179, footnotes omitted.

43. Id. at 178–79, footnotes omitted.

44. Id. at 180.

45. Walter F. Murphy, Consent and Constitutional Change, in Human Rights and Constitutional Law: Essays in Honour of Brian Walsh 143 (James O'Reilly ed., 1992).

46. Id.

47. Jeremy Waldron, The Irrelevance of Moral Objectivity, in Natural Law Theory: Contemporary Essays 158 (Robert P. George ed., 1992); see esp. id. at 180–82.

48. David Strauss, Discriminatory Intent and the Taming of *Brown,* 56 U. Chi. L. Rev. 935, 985 (1989).

49. Personnel Adm'r v. Feeney, 442 U.S. 256, 272 (1979). It should be noted, however, that this statement is immediately preceded by the following: "Certain classifications . . . in themselves supply a reason to infer antipathy. Race is the paradigm." Id.

50. Ely, Democracy and Distrust at 138.

51. John Hart Ely, Legislative and Administrative Motivation in Constitutional Law, 79 Yale L.J. 1205, 1278 (1970).

52. Daniel R. Ortiz, The Myth of Intent in Equal Protection, 41 Stan. L. Rev. 1105, 1115 (1989), emphases in original.

53. Id. at 1116.

54. Personnel Adm'r v. Feeney, 442 U.S. 256, 279 (1979).

55. In addition to the Supreme Court cases cited above, in which no plaintiff ever prevailed, see, e.g., Price v. Austin Indep. Sch. Dist., 945 F.2d 1307, 1319 (5th Cir. 1991); Lee v. Lee County Bd. of Educ., 639 F.2d 1243, 1268 (5th Cir. 1981); Mihalcik v. Lensink, 732 F. Supp. 299, 302 (D. Conn. 1990); Larry P. v. Riles, 495 F. Supp. 926, 975–76 (N.D. Cal. 1979); Harris v. White, 479 F. Supp. 996, 1001–6 (D. Mass. 1979); Debra P. v. Turlington, 474 F. Supp. 244, 254–57 (M.D. Fla. 1979), aff'd, 644 F.2d 347 (5th Cir. 1981) (each citing and following *Feeney*).

56. Strauss, Discriminatory Intent and the Taming of *Brown* at 963.

57. "Some of them may have sincerely desired only to promote social stability and the harmonious development of both races. Some may have sincerely believed that segregation aided blacks. Or they may have recognized its harmful effects but considered them a regrettable byproduct of a system that was best for society as a whole." Id. at 964.

58. Id. at 939.

59. Id.

60. I have offered a similar criticism of the Court's equal protection doctrine in Antidiscrimination Law and Social Equality 103–11.

61. Kenneth L. Karst, The Costs of Motive-Centered Inquiry, 15 San Diego L. Rev. 1163, 1164–65 (1978).

62. Strauss, Discriminatory Intent and the Taming of *Brown* at 957.

63. Edwards v. Aguillard, 482 U.S. 578, 636 (1987) (Scalia, J., dissenting).

64. 508 U.S. 520 (1993).

65. Id. at 541–42.

66. Id. at 534.

67. Hialeah Ordinance 87-72, quoted in id. at 528; see id. at 555–57 for the full text.

68. Id. at 545.

69. See, e.g., New Orleans v. Dukes, 427 U.S. 297 (1976); Railway Express Agency v. New York, 336 U.S. 106 (1949).

70. 508 U.S. at 539–40.

71. See id. at 540.

72. Amendment 2 is an illustration. 813,966 voted for the amendment, while 710,151 voted against it. See Evans v. Romer, 854 P.2d 1270, 1272 (Colo. 1993).

73. Hunter v. Erickson, 393 U.S. 385 (1969); Reitman v. Mulkey, 387 U.S. 369 (1967); Washington v. Seattle Sch. Dist. No. 1, 458 U.S. 457 (1982).

74. Equality Found. of Greater Cincinnati v. City of Cincinnati, 54 F.3d 261, 270 n.9 (6th Cir. 1995), *vacated and remanded on other grounds,* 518 U.S. 1001 (1996).

75. See, e.g., Richard F. Duncan, Who Wants to Stop the Church: Homosexual Rights Legislation, Public Policy, and Religious Freedom, 69 Notre Dame L. Rev. 393, 401–11 (1994).

76. See Andrew Sullivan, Virtually Normal 157 (1995). But see William N. Eskridge Jr., Gaylaw: Dismantling the Apartheid of the Closet 231–38 (1999).

77. Such an apparatus has been and continues to be deployed within the United States military, which routinely engages in illegal wiretaps and searches, days-long interrogations, denial of access to counsel, groundless threats of severe penalties for noncooperation, incessant demands for names of other gays, coerced or forged confessions, and intimidation of witnesses. See generally Samuel A. Marcosson, A Price Too High: Enforcing the Ban on Gays and Lesbians in the Military and the Inevitability of Intrusiveness, 64 UMKC L. Rev. 59 (1995). These practices are, however, so anomalous in American society that spokespersons for the military have found it necessary to deny that they exist. See Andrew Koppelman, Gaze in the Military: A Response to Professor Woodruff, 64 UMKC L. Rev. 179, 186 n.41 (1995).

78. *Hardwick,* 478 U.S. at 196.

79. *Romer,* 517 U.S. at 633.

80. John D'Emilio and Estelle B. Freedman, Intimate Matters: A History of Sexuality in America 293 (1988).

81. See id.; John D'Emilio, The Homosexual Menace: The Politics of Sexuality in Cold War America, in Making Trouble: Essays on Gay History, Politics, and the University 57–73 (1992). The most thorough study to date of the legal status of gays in the decade and a half after World War II is William N. Eskridge Jr., Gaylaw: Challenging the Apartheid of the Closet 57–97 (1999).

82. Committee on Expenditures in Executive Departments, Employment of Homosexuals and Other Sex Perverts in Government, U.S. Senate, 81st Cong., 2d Sess., S. Doc. 81-241, at 4 (1950).

83. Allied Stores v. Bowers, 358 U.S. 522, 528 (1959).

84. Laurence Tribe, American Constitutional Law 1443 (2d ed. 1988).

85. *Romer,* 517 U.S. at 646 (Scalia, J., dissenting).

86. See, e.g., Richard F. Duncan, Who Wants to Stop the Church: Homosexual Rights Legislation, Public Policy, and Religious Freedom, 69 Notre Dame L. Rev. 393, 397–98 (1994).

87. Ronald Dworkin, Sex, Death, and the Courts, N.Y. Rev. Books, Aug. 8, 1996, at 49.

88. See, e.g., Ronald Dworkin, Taking Rights Seriously 272–77 (1977).

89. John Finnis, Legal Enforcement of "Duties to Oneself": Kant v. Neo-Kantians, 87 Colum. L. Rev. 433, 437 (1987).

90. Ely, Democracy and Distrust at 256 n.92.

91. Brown v. Board of Educ., 347 U.S. 483, 495 (1954).

92. Charles L. Black Jr., The Lawfulness of the Segregation Decisions, 69 Yale L.J. 421, 427 (1960).

93. Id.

94. Kendall Thomas, Beyond the Privacy Principle, 92 Colum. L. Rev. 1431, 1464 (1992).

95. Id. at 1463–64 n.125, citing National Gay Task Force, Anti-Gay/Lesbian Victimization 24 (June 1984).

96. Id. at 1464, quoting Peter Finn and Taylor McNeil, The Response of the Criminal Justice System to Bias Crime: An Exploratory Review 2 (1987).

97. Id. at 1465.

98. Quoted in id. at 1463.

99. Quoted in id. at 1466.

100. Gordon W. Allport, The Nature of Prejudice 49 (1954).

101. Id. at 57.

102. Id. at 59.

103. Id. at 14.

104. Kenneth Sherrill, The Political Power of Lesbians, Gays, and Bisexuals, PS 469, 470 (1996).

105. Id.

106. Richard Mohr, A More Perfect Union: Why Straight America Must Stand Up for Gay Rights 61–62 (1994).

107. Quoted in Jules Witcover, Marathon: The Pursuit of the Presidency, 1972–1976, at 603 (1978).

108. See supra text accompanying note 82.

109. Colorado For Family Values, Equal Rights—Not Special Rights! (1992), reprinted in Robert F. Nagel, Playing Defense, 6 Wm. & Mary Bill of Rts. J. 167, 192–99 (1997). See generally Gregory M. Herek, Myths About Sexual Orientation: A Lawyer's Guide to Social Science Research, 1 L. & Sexuality 133 (1991) (cataloguing common, demonstrably false stereotypes).

110. Ely, Democracy and Distrust at 157.

111. Id.

112. Id.

113. 393 U.S. 385 (1969).

114. In an earlier version of this chapter, I also enumerated "imposition of religious beliefs" among the impermissible motives that underlay Amendment 2. See Andrew Koppelman, *Romer v. Evans* and Invidious Intent at 130–31. I am now persuaded that this was a mistake. Religious motivation alone cannot invalidate an otherwise valid statute, provided that the statute does not itself endorse any particular religious view. See Andrew Koppelman, Secular Purpose, 88 Va. L. Rev. (forthcoming 2002).

115. 517 U.S. at 644 (Scalia, J., dissenting).

116. 388 U.S. 1 (1967).

117. Id. at 11.

118. Brief of Appellee, Loving v. Virginia (No. 395) at 41.

119. Brief for Appellants, Loving v. Virginia (No. 395), at 37.

120. 388 U.S. at 11.

121. Id., quoting Hirabayashi v. United States, 320 U.S. 81, 100 (1943).

122. Id.

123. Id. at 12 n.11 ("[W]e find the racial classifications in these statutes repugnant to the Fourteenth Amendment, even assuming an even-handed state purpose to protect the 'integrity' of all races.").

124. Village of Arlington Heights v. Metropolitan Hous. Dev. Corp., 429 U.S. 252, 265–66 (1977).

125. Richard F. Duncan, Wigstock and the Kulturkampf: Supreme Court Storytelling, the Culture War, and *Romer v. Evans*, 72 Notre Dame L. Rev. 345 (1997).

126. Romer v. Evans, U.S. Supreme Court Official Transcript, 1995 WL 605822 (U.S. Oral Arg. Oct. 10, 1995).

127. Ohio v. Akron Ctr. for Reproductive Health, 497 U.S. 502, 514 (1990), quoted in Duncan, Wigstock at 354.

128. Duncan, Wigstock at 354.

129. A poll conducted a month after the vote by an independent survey firm on behalf of the Denver Post and KCNC-TV showed that 81 percent of voters surveyed agreed with the statement that "Except for their choice of sexual partners, homosexuals are not really different from anyone else." Only 6 percent agreed that "A homosexual is more likely to sexually molest children than a person who is heterosexual." Only 13 percent agreed that "Homosexual behavior should be against the law, even if it occurs between consenting adults." Talmey-Drake Research & Strategy, Inc., December 1992 Issues Poll. Indeed, it appears that most Colorado voters supported the idea that people should not be denied a job or housing based on sexual orientation. Amendment 2's proponents evidently succeeded in inducing voters to believe that Amendment 2 was principally about affirmative action, which many opposed. See Evan Gerstmann, The Constitutional Underclass: Gays, Lesbians, and the Failure of Class-Based Equal Protection 99–110 (1999). It is not unusual for voters to be confused about the referenda they are voting upon. Nor is it unusual for proponents and opponents of ballot measures to deliberately compound voters' confusion. See Julian N. Eule, Judicial Review of Direct Democracy, 99 Yale L.J. 1503, 1515–18 (1990).

130. Letter from Michael Dorf to Andrew Koppelman, November 6, 1996. Our correspondence was prompted by Professor Dorf's fine article, Facial Challenges to State and Federal Statutes, 46 Stan. L. Rev. 235 (1994).

131. These limitations have long been emphasized by Justice Scalia, who thinks that it is almost never appropriate for courts to rely on extrinsic evidence of legislators' meaning. See William N. Eskridge Jr., The New Textualism, 37 UCLA L. Rev. 621, 650–56 (1990).

132. 517 U.S. at 632.

133. Akhil Amar, Attainder and Amendment 2: *Romer's* Rightness, 95 Mich. L. Rev. 203, 224 (1996).

134. The amendment would then read (the new words are emphasized):

No Protected Status Based on *Sexual* Orientation. Neither the State of Colorado, through any of its branches or departments, nor any of its agencies, political subdivisions, municipalities or school districts, shall enact, adopt or enforce any statute, regulation, ordinance or policy whereby *sexual* orientation, conduct, practices or relationships shall constitute or otherwise be the basis of or entitle any person or class of persons to have or claim any minority status, quota preferences, protected status or claim of discrimination. This Section of the Constitution shall be in all respects self-executing.

135. 530 U.S. 640 (2000).

136. Brief for Petitioner, Boy Scouts of America v. Dale, 2000 WL 228616, at 47.

137. *Dale*, 530 U.S. at 653.

138. See Steven D. Smith, Symbols, Perceptions, and Doctrinal Illusions: Establishment Neutrality and the "No Endorsement" Test, 86 Mich. L. Rev. 266 (1987).

139. "All Things Considered" on National Public Radio, June 28, 2000, available in LEXIS, News Library, NPR file.

140. The weaknesses of the *Dale* opinion are explored in more detail in Andrew Koppelman, Signs of the Times: *Dale v. Boy Scouts of America* and the Changing Meaning of Nondiscrimination, 23 Cardozo L. Rev. (forthcoming 2002).

141. Black, The Lawfulness of the Segregation Decisions, at 430.

142. There are other members of the set in addition to Amendment 2. Shortly after *Romer*, the Court vacated and remanded a decision upholding an amendment to the Cincinnati Charter, the wording of which was nearly identical to that of the Colorado amendment. See Equality Found. of Greater Cincinnati v. City of Cincinnati, 54 F.3d 261 (6th Cir. 1995), *vacated and remanded on other grounds*, 518 U.S. 1001 (1996), *reaffirmed on remand*, 128 F.3d 289 (1997), *cert. denied*, 525 U.S. 943 (1998). The Court in the end denied certiorari, but it is difficult to distinguish the Cincinnati amendment from that invalidated in *Romer*. Rhonda Rivera has noted that the Supreme Court's action has left this area of the law in confusion.

> What was this denial supposed to mean? States cannot pass laws solely based on animus, but cities can? Was the Supreme Court resorting to its former days of not taking gay cases unless absolutely forced to? Who knows?

Rhonda R. Rivera, Our Straight-Laced Judges: Twenty Years Later, 50 Hastings L.J. 1179, 1190 (1999). Another likely member of the set is the recent Defense of Marriage Act, which is as indiscriminate as Amendment 2 in the injury it inflicts on gays and as difficult to defend in the details of its applications. See chapter 6.

143. 478 U.S. 186 (1986).

144. Jeffrey Rosen, The Agonizer, New Yorker, Nov. 11, 1996, at 82, 90. "I'm not going to comment," he told his interviewer. "It will be interesting to see how *Romer* is understood." Id.

145. See 517 U.S. at 641 (Scalia, J., dissenting), citing Padula v. Webster, 822 F.2d 97, 103 (D.C. Cir. 1987) See also Equality Found. of Greater Cincinnati, Inc. v. City of Cincinnati, 54 F.3d 261, 266 (6th Cir. 1995); High Tech Gays v. Defense Ind. Sec. Clearance Office, 895 F.2d 563, 571–74 (9th Cir.), *reh'g and reh'g en banc denied*, 909 F.2d 375 (9th Cir. 1990); ben-Shalom v. Marsh, 881 F.2d 454, 464–66 (7th Cir. 1989), *cert. denied*, 494 U.S. 1004 (1990); Woodward v. United States, 871 F.2d 1068, 1076 (Fed. Cir. 1989), *cert. denied*, 494 U.S. 1003 (1990). This reasoning was rejected in Watkins v. United States Army, 847 F.2d 1329, 1345–49 (9th Cir. 1988), *aff'd on other grounds*, 875 F.2d 699 (9th Cir. 1989) (en banc), *cert. denied*, 498 U.S. 957 (1990); Jantz v. Muci, 759 F. Supp. 1543, 1546–47 (D. Kan. 1991), *rev'd on other grounds*, 976 F.2d 623 (10th Cir. 1992); Dean v. District of Columbia, 653 A.2d 307, 340–44 (D.C. 1995) (Ferren, J., concurring in part and dissenting in part); and implicitly in Baehr v. Lewin, 852 P.2d 44, 57 (Haw. 1993), which rejected a privacy challenge to a statute disallowing same-sex marriages while sustaining an equal protection challenge to that same statute.

146. See Bowers v. Hardwick, 478 U.S. 186, 196 n.8 (1986).

147. The point has been explained in detail, with more patience than I could muster, in Cass R. Sunstein, Sexual Orientation and the Constitution: A Note on the Relationship Between Due Process and Equal Protection, 55 U. Chi. L. Rev. 1161 (1988). The contradictions in *Padula*'s reasoning are richly explored in Janet E. Halley, The Politics of the Closet: Towards Equal Protection for Gay, Lesbian, and Bisexual Identity, 36 UCLA L. Rev. 915, 948–50 (1989).

148. See *Hardwick*, 478 U.S. at 196.

149. 478 U.S. at 191–92.

150. In fact, the Court did hold such statutes unconstitutional. See McLaughlin v. Florida, 379 U.S. 184 (1964) (invalidating a Florida statute that prohibited cohabitation of a "white person" and a "negro"). It would have been unfortunate

if such a privacy case had arisen. It would have been still more unfortunate if the Court, faced with a prosecution of an interracial couple under a statute prohibiting fornication simpliciter, had behaved in the way it did in *Hardwick* by announcing that the question before it was whether there was a right to "interracial fornication," and had expressly reserved the issue of whether "monoracial fornication" was protected. Nonetheless, such ill-advised dicta could not have posed any obstacle to the later invalidation of the statute on equal protection grounds.

151. Or perhaps the number is nine if one counts Maryland and Oklahoma, which have judicially invalidated their sodomy laws as applied to heterosexual sex, while expressing no opinion as to those laws' validity with respect to heterosexual sex. See chapter 3, note 16.

152. See Andrew Koppelman, Note, The Miscegenation Analogy: Sodomy Law as Sex Discrimination, 98 Yale L.J. 145, 149–53 (1988).

153. City of Cleburne v. Cleburne Living Ctr., 473 U.S. 432, 440 (1985).

154. Id. at 441.

155. 473 U.S. 432 (1985).

156. Id. at 450.

157. Id. at 446.

158. Id. at 443.

159. See id. at 444.

160. Id. at 445.

161. Id. at 446.

CHAPTER TWO

1. This way of putting it dates back to the 1957 report of the Wolfenden Committee, which reconsidered the law of sexual crimes in England. The committee concluded that private consensual homosexual acts should be decriminalized, because "There must remain a realm of private morality and immorality which is, in brief and crude terms, not the law's business." Quoted in H. L. A. Hart, Law, Liberty, and Morality 14–15 (1963).

2. For two somewhat overlapping lists of such commentators, see David J. Garrow, Liberty and Sexuality: The Right to Privacy and the Making of *Roe v. Wade* 902 n.97 (1994); and Earl M. Maltz, The Court, the Academy, and the Constitution: A Comment on *Bowers v. Hardwick* and Its Critics, 1989 BYU L. Rev. 59, 60 n.4.

3. Loving v. Virginia, 388 U.S. 1 (1967); Zablocki v. Redhail, 434 U.S. 374 (1978); Turner v. Safley, 482 U.S. 78 (1987).

4. Boddie v. Connecticut, 401 U.S. 371 (1971).

5. Griswold v. Connecticut, 381 U.S. 479 (1965); Eisenstadt v. Baird, 405 U.S. 438 (1972); Carey v. Population Servs., 431 U.S. 678 (1977).

6. Moore v. East Cleveland, 431 U.S. 494 (1977).

7. Roe v. Wade, 410 U.S. 113 (1973).

8. See Diana Hassel, The Use of Criminal Sodomy Laws in Civil Litigation, 79 Tex. L. Rev. 813 (2001).

9. 381 U.S. 479 (1965).

10. Id. at 484.

11. Id.

12. Id.

13. Id. at 485.

14. Id. This schematic summary of the Court's reasoning is adapted from Harry H. Wellington, Interpreting the Constitution: The Supreme Court and the Process of Adjudication 45–46 (1990).

15. *Griswold,* 381 U.S. at 508 (Black, J., dissenting).

16. Id. at 482–83 (opinion of the Court).

17. 357 U.S. 449 (1958).

18. Id. at 462.

19. *Griswold,* 381 U.S. at 486.

20. Id.

21. 198 U.S. 45 (1905).

22. *Griswold,* 381 U.S. at 482.

23. Id. at 515 (Black, J., dissenting). Justice Stewart, the other dissenter, also thought that the decision was indistinguishable from *Lochner.* See id. at 528 (Stewart, J., dissenting).

24. Id. at 488–98 (Goldberg, J., concurring).

25. Id. at 503–6 (White, J., concurring).

26. Id. at 501 (Harlan, J., concurring).

27. Poe v. Ullman, 367 U.S. 497, 543 (1961) (Harlan, J., dissenting from dismissal on jurisdictional grounds); quoted in Planned Parenthood of Southeastern Pennsylvania v. Casey, 505 U.S. 833, 848 (1992).

28. Robert Bork, Neutral Principles and Some First Amendment Problems, 47 Ind. L.J. 1, 8 (1971).

29. Laurence Tribe, American Constitutional Law 778 (2d ed. 1988).

30. See David J. Garrow, Liberty and Sexuality: The Right to Privacy and the Making of *Roe v. Wade* 668–70 (1994).

31. Id. at 671.

32. See id. at 672 (describing Senate Judiciary Committee testimony of Anthony Kennedy); 684 (describing Senate Judiciary Committee testimony of David Souter); Hearings on Nomination of Judge Clarence Thomas before the Senate Comm. on the Judiciary, 102d Cong. 127 (1991); Hearings on Nomination of Judge Ruth Bader Ginsburg before the Senate Comm. on the Judiciary, 103d Cong. 185 (1993); Hearings on Nomination of Judge Stephen G. Breyer before the Senate Comm. on the Judiciary, 103d Cong. 268–69 (1994).

33. Garrow, Liberty and Sexuality at 905 n.101, citing National Law Journal, Feb. 26, 1990, pp. 1, 36–37. In contrast, only 41 percent of the 805 respondents could name even one member of the Supreme Court.

34. Bruce Ackerman, Robert Bork's Grand Inquisition, 99 Yale L.J. 1419, 1431 (1990).

35. Robert Bork, The Tempting of America 7 (1990).

36. Id. at 49; see also id. at 143, 160.

37. Id. at 95; see also letter of Robert Bork to Hon. Joseph R. Biden Jr., Chairman, Senate Committee on the Judiciary, Oct. 1, 1987, in Hearings on Nomination of Robert Bork to be Associate Justice of the Supreme Court of the United States, v. 3 at 3903 ("it cannot realistically be said that failure to invalidate the Connecticut law would have had any material effect on the ability of married couples to use contraceptives in the privacy of their homes."). Bork emphasizes the difficulty of arranging a test case, see The Tempting of America at 95, but neglects to mention one of the chronic sources of difficulty: "recruiting a willing doctor, even from among the [Planned Parenthood] league's leading supporters, proved seemingly impossible

because of how a case that would imaginably risk any sort of conviction might thereby place the physician's license to practice medicine in danger." Garrow, Liberty and Sexuality at 60.

38. For details, see Garrow, Liberty and Sexuality.

39. Robert H. Bork, The Tempting of America: The Political Seduction of the Law 83–84 (1990), footnote omitted.

40. This is the problem with Richard Posner's pragmatic defense of *Griswold,* which frankly locates the ground of judicial action "in instinct rather than analysis." Richard Posner, Overcoming Law 192 (1995).

41. See Garrow, Liberty and Sexuality at 256–57.

42. See id. at 217–18, 228–29. That opposition had earlier been quite energetic, as when one Sunday in 1939 a resolution calling for criminal prosecution of any birth control clinic was read from the pulpit of every Catholic church in the Waterbury area. See id. at 5.

43. A 1964 survey "found that 78 percent of Catholic respondents—as compared with 82 percent of Protestants, and only 53 percent of Catholics just two years earlier—now agreed that 'birth control information should be available to anyone who wants it.'" Id. at 229.

44. See id. at 235, 251.

45. 60 U.S. (19 How.) 393 (1857).

46. See Commonwealth v. Bonadio, 415 A.2d 47 (Pa. 1980); Commonwealth v. Wasson, 842 S.W.2d 487 (Ky. 1992); Powell v. State, 510 S.E.2d 18 (Ga. 1998); State v. Pilcher, 242 N.W.2d 348 (Iowa 1976); Gryczan v. State, 942 P.2d 112 (Mont. 1997); People v. Onofre, 415 N.E.2d 936 (N.Y. 1980); Post v. State, 715 P.2d 1105 (Okla. Crim. App. 1986); Campbell v. Sundquist, 926 S.W.2d 250 (Tenn. App. 1996); National Coalition for Gay and Lesbian Equality v. Minister of Justice, 1998 (12) B.C.L.R. 1517 (South Africa Constitutional Court). In an unreported decision, an Arkansas trial court has invalidated the state's sex-specific sodomy law on both privacy and sex discrimination grounds. See http://www.lambdalegal.org/sections/library/decisions/picadodecision.pdf. The decision will surely be appealed.

47. See, e.g., Posner, Overcoming Law at 194.

48. See John C. Jeffries Jr., Justice Lewis F. Powell Jr. 518–30 (1994).

49. Robert Bork, Neutral Principles and Some First Amendment Problems, 47 Ind. L.J. 1, 7 (1971).

50. Dronenburg v. Zech, 741 F.2d 1388, 1392 (D.C. Cir. 1984) (Bork, J.).

51. Id.

52. See, e.g., Bruce Ackerman, Liberating Abstraction, 59 U. Chi. L. Rev. 317 (1992).

53. Bork, The Tempting of America at 99–100.

54. John Stuart Mill, On Liberty 68 (1859; Gertrude Himmelfarb ed., Penguin 1974).

55. See Commonwealth v. Bonadio, 415 A.2d 47 (Pa. 1980); Commonwealth v. Wasson, 842 S.W.2d 487 (Ky. 1992).

56. This is not to dismiss the very powerful arguments that have been made against the present regime of drug prohibition. See, e.g., Ethan A. Nadelmann, Thinking Seriously About Alternatives to Drug Prohibition, 121 Daedalus 85 (1992). It is simply to note that those arguments, to the extent that they are persuasive, are prudential rather than principled ones. It may be that drug prohibition

is not worth its social costs, but that is not the same as saying that cocaine dealers have a fundamental right to purvey (or consumers a fundamental right to purchase) their wares, whatever the consequences.

57. Gerard V. Bradley, Remaking the Constitution: A Critical Reexamination of the *Bowers v. Hardwick* Dissent, 25 Wake Forest L. Rev. 501, 540 (1990).

58. This objection applies to any attempt to derive privacy rights from liberal political theory. See, e.g., Vincent J. Samar, The Right to Privacy: Gays, Lesbians, and the Constitution (1991); David A. J. Richards, Sex, Drugs, Death, and the Law: An Essay on Human Rights and Overcriminalization 29–83 (1982).

59. See, e.g., Romer v. Evans, 517 U.S. 620, 644–45 (1996) (Scalia, J., dissenting); Lynn D. Wardle, A Critical Analysis of Constitutional Claims for Same-Sex Marriage, 1996 BYU L. Rev. 1, 58–62; John Finnis, Liberalism and Natural Law Theory, 45 Mercer L. Rev. 687, 697–98 (1994).

60. See Robert P. George, Making Men Moral: Civil Liberties and Public Morality 110–28 (1993).

61. See Michael H. v. Gerald D., 491 U.S. 110, 127 n.6 (1989) (opinion of Scalia, J., joined by Rehnquist, C.J.); Bork, The Tempting of America 150 (1990).

62. See Laurence H. Tribe and Michael C. Dorf, On Reading the Constitution 97–117 (1991); J. M. Balkin, Tradition, Betrayal, and the Politics of Deconstruction, 11 Cardozo L. Rev. 1613, 1615–16 (1994).

63. Kendall Thomas, Beyond the Privacy Principle, 92 Colum. L. Rev.1431, 1443–48 (1992).

64. Bowers v. Hardwick, 478 U.S. 186, 206 (1986) (Blackmun, J., dissenting).

65. Id.

66. Bork, Neutral Principles at 7. For this reason, Bradley concludes that the zonal argument is a placeholder for the decisional one. See Bradley, Remaking the Constitution at 512–16.

67. See Carol Steiker, Note, The Constitutional Status of Sexual Orientation: Homosexuality as a Suspect Classification, 98 Harv. L. Rev. 1285, 1288–92 (1985).

68. Thomas, Beyond the Privacy Principle at 1455.

69. Id. at 1446.

70. Bowers v. Hardwick, 478 U.S. 186, 206 (1986) (Blackmun, J., dissenting).

71. Id. at 205–6.

72. Id. at 204.

73. Id. at 205.

74. Richards, Sex, Drugs, Death, and the Law at 41.

75. United States v. Seeger, 380 U.S. 163, 180, 187 (1965).

76. Morris Kaplan, Sexual Justice: Democratic Citizenship and the Politics of Desire 20 (1997).

77. Id.

78. Calder v. Bull, 3 U.S. (3 Dall.) 386, 399 (1798) (opinion of Iredell, J.).

79. Jed Rubenfeld, The Right of Privacy, 102 Harv. L. Rev. 737, 761 (1989).

80. See generally, e.g., Alasdair MacIntyre, After Virtue: A Study in Moral Theory (2d ed. 1984); Michael Sandel, Liberalism and the Limits of Justice (1982).

81. Rubenfeld, Right of Privacy at 763.

82. Id. at 765.

83. Id. at 780.

84. Peter Berger has noted the contrast between the old concept of honor, according to which the individual's identity is most fully expressed by his social role,

and the modern concept of dignity, which implies that identity is independent of institutional roles and which tends to identify the true self with the naked body expressing itself sexually. The comparative value of these two concepts of individual worth is difficult to assess. See Peter L. Berger, On the Obsolescence of the Concept of Honour, in Liberalism and its Critics 149–58 (Michael Sandel ed., 1984).

85. Robert McCloskey, Economic Due Process and the Supreme Court: An Exhumation and Reburial, 1962 Sup. Ct. Rev. 34, 46, citing Kotch v. Pilot Comm'rs, 339 U.S. 552 (1947), in which the Court upheld just such a nepotistic system.

86. West Virginia State Bd. of Educ. v. Barnette, 319 U.S. 624, 639–40 (1943) (majority opinion by Jackson, J.), quoted in Bruce Ackerman, Liberating Abstraction, 59 U. Chi. L. Rev. 317, 328, and passim (1992).

87. Bruce Ackerman, Constitutional Politics/Constitutional Law, 99 Yale L.J. 453, 539–40 (1989).

88. Id. at 544.

89. See Leigh B. Bienen, Defining Incest, 92 Nw. U.L. Rev. 1501 (1998); Richard A. Posner and Katharine B. Silbaugh, A Guide to America's Sex Laws 129–42 (1996).

90. See *Hardwick,* 478 U.S. at 195–96.

91. Id. at 209–10 n.4 (Blackmun, J., dissenting).

92. This idea, I must point out immediately, does not entail anything at all about the status of homosexual conduct and certainly does not entail that same-sex intimacy is an expression of sexuality that is worthless or harmful.

93. This point is developed at length in Harry M. Clor, Public Morality and Liberal Society (1996).

94. The absence of any coherent derivation of the right compounds the difficulty of delimiting it. See Earl M. Maltz, Constitutional Protection for the Right to Marry: A Dissenting View, 60 Geo. Wash. L. Rev. 949 (1992).

95. See, e.g., Lynn D. Wardle, A Critical Analysis of Constitutional Claims for Same-Sex Marriage, 1996 BYU L. Rev. 1, 28–39.

96. See, e.g., William N. Eskridge Jr., Gaylaw: Challenging the Apartheid of the Closet 152–56 (1999); Laurence Tribe, American Constitutional Law, § 15-21, at 1421–35 (2d ed. 1988); Thomas B. Stoddard, Bowers v. Hardwick: Precedent by Personal Predilection, 54 U. Chi. L. Rev. 648 (1987).

97. Cass R. Sunstein, Sexual Orientation and the Constitution: A Note on the Relationship Between Due Process and Equal Protection, 55 U. Chi. L. Rev. 1161, 1173–74 (1988).

98. The concurring justices indicated that the right to privacy did not cover such things as adultery and homosexuality. See id. at 498–99 (Goldberg, J., concurring) (citing Poe v. Ullman, 367 U.S. 497, 553 (1961) (Harlan, J., dissenting)); id. at 500 (Harlan, J., concurring in the judgment) (citing his own dissent in *Poe*).

99. 405 U.S. 438 (1972).

100. See id. at 448.

101. Roe v. Wade, 410 U.S. 113, 154 (1973).

102. Compare Moore v. City of East Cleveland, 431 U.S. 494, 505–6 (1977) (finding unconstitutional an ordinance that prohibited a woman from residing with her two grandsons, who were first cousins rather than siblings), with Village of Belle Terre v. Boraas, 416 U.S. 1, 9 (1974) (upholding an ordinance that prohibited persons unrelated by blood, marriage, or adoption from living together).

103. See Thomas C. Grey, Eros, Civilization, and the Burger Court, 43 L. & Contemp. Probs. 83, 90 (1980); see also Robert A. Burt, The Constitution of the

Family, 1979 Sup. Ct. Rev. 329. (I have not cited all the evidence that these writers compile, so the skeptical reader should consult them.) The right to an abortion may also be derivable from a right to bodily integrity, which may entail a right not to have one's body conscripted for the state's purposes. See Andrew Koppelman, Forced Labor: A Thirteenth Amendment Defense of Abortion, 84 Nw. U.L. Rev. 480 (1990). A prohibition on conduct does not violate that right when the prohibition does not itself imply a command to do anything in particular.

104. Laurence H. Tribe and Michael C. Dorf, On Reading the Constitution 59 (1991).

105. Id.

106. Id. at 60.

107. *Hardwick,* 478 U.S. at 194.

108. Rubenfeld, The Right of Privacy at 747.

109. *Hardwick,* 478 U.S. at 191.

110. Id. at 200 (Blackmun, J., dissenting).

111. Quoted in id. at 188 n. 1 (opinion of the Court).

112. See Garrow, Liberty and Sexuality at 667.

113. *Hardwick,* 478 U.S. at 190.

114. Id. at 196.

115. Id. at 194.

116. See Anne B. Goldstein, History, Homosexuality, and Political Values: Searching for the Hidden Determinants of *Bowers v. Hardwick,* 97 Yale L.J. 1073, 1082–86 (1988). The Court's bad history does not, however, itself entail that *Hardwick* was wrongly decided. An activity need not have been criminalized in the reign of Henry VIII, or in 1866, in order for the legislature to have discretion to criminalize it today. For a contrary view, see Eskridge, Gaylaw at 149–73.

117. See Rowland v. Mad River Sch. Dist., 470 U.S. 1009 (1985) (Brennan, J., joined by Marshall, J., dissenting from denial of certiorari).

118. See Andrew Koppelman, Forced Labor: A Thirteenth Amendment Defense of Abortion, 84 Nw. U.L. Rev. 480 (1990).

119. See Andrew Koppelman, Antidiscrimination Law and Social Equality 57–114 (1996).

120. See id.; see also id. at 29–31.

CHAPTER THREE

1. Ross Sneyd, Vermont's High Court Hears Gay Marriage Arguments, Associated Press, Nov. 18, 1998. Judge Johnson ended up making essentially the same argument in her separate opinion when the case was decided. See Baker v. State, 744 A.2d 864, 904–7 (Vt. 1999) (Johnson, J., concurring in part and dissenting in part).

2. As are some government officials. The U.S. Department of Justice has announced that it will interpret federal prohibitions of sex discrimination to prohibit anti-gay discrimination when such discrimination involves gender stereotyping. See Lou Chibbaro Jr., Policy Targets Bias: DOJ to Use Gender Bias Laws to Pursue Some Gay Cases, Washington Blade, Nov. 20, 1998. (I am grateful to Marcia Kuntz for bringing this article to my attention.) The policy is admirable but incoherent insofar as it attempts to exclude from the scope of the prohibition a supposed category of discrimination against gays that does *not* involve gender stereotyping.

3. David Orgon Coolidge attempts to drive a wedge between legal and popular discourse by arguing that the analogy to the miscegenation cases "is a complex argument more suited to legal conferences than to radio and television propaganda," but the argument is in fact fairly straightforward and easily grasped. David Orgon Coolidge, Playing the *Loving* Card: Same-Sex Marriage and the Politics of Analogy, 12 BYU J. Pub. L. 201, 217 (1998).

4. Sylvia A. Law, Homosexuality and the Social Meaning of Gender, 1988 Wis. L. Rev. 187; Andrew Koppelman, Note, The Miscegenation Analogy: Sodomy Law as Sex Discrimination, 98 Yale L.J. 145 (1988). I have since repeated this argument numerous times. See, e.g., Andrew Koppelman, Why Discrimination Against Lesbians and Gay Men Is Sex Discrimination, 69 N.Y.U. L. Rev. 197 (1994); Andrew Koppelman, Antidiscrimination Law and Social Equality 146–76 (1996); Andrew Koppelman, Three Arguments for Gay Rights, 95 Mich. L. Rev. 1636, 1661–66 (1997); Andrew Koppelman, Why Gay Legal History Matters, 113 Harv. L. Rev. 2035, 2051–55 (2000). The argument was first developed, so far as I am aware, in the early 1970s. During this period, opponents of the proposed Equal Rights Amendment argued that a prohibition of sex-based classifications would necessarily entail the legalization of same-sex marriage. See Note, The Legality of Homosexual Marriage, 82 Yale L.J. 573, 583–88 (1973) (collecting sources). At the same time, some feminist writers were arguing that the prohibition of homosexuality functioned socially to reinforce the subordination of women. See, e.g., Amazon Expedition: A Lesbian Feminist Anthology (Phyllis Birkby et al. eds., 1973); Ti-Grace Atkinson, Amazon Odyssey (1974); For Lesbians Only: A Separatist Anthology (Sarah L. Hoagland & Julia Penelope eds., 1988); Jill Johnston, Lesbian Nation: The Feminist Solution (1973); Anne Koedt, Lesbianism and Feminism, in Radical Feminism 246 (Anne Koedt et al. eds., 1973); Radicalesbians, The Woman Identified Woman, in Radical Feminism 240. See generally Alice Echols, Daring to Be Bad: Radical Feminism in America, 1967–75, at 210–41 (1989); Toby Marotta, The Politics of Homosexuality 229–303 (1981). Unknown to me or (evidently) Professor Law, the argument had been made anew in England a few years before we wrote. See David Pannick, Sex Discrimination Law 197–207 (1985).

5. Compare Kenneth L. Karst, The Freedom of Intimate Association, 89 Yale L.J. 624, 684 (1980) (dismissing the sex discrimination argument as "makeweight"), with Kenneth L. Karst, The Pursuit of Manhood and the Desegregation of the Armed Forces, 38 UCLA L. Rev. 499 (1991) (tracing connections between heterosexism and ideology of masculinity); compare William N. Eskridge Jr., A History of Same-Sex Marriage, 79 Va. L. Rev. 1419, 1510 (1993) ("[j]udges may find it difficult to understand how denying two gay men the right to marry is driven by an ideology that oppresses straight women"), with William N. Eskridge Jr., The Case for Same-Sex Marriage 153–72 (1996) (expounding and endorsing the sex discrimination argument); William N. Eskridge Jr., Gaylaw: Challenging the Apartheid of the Closet 218–28 (1999) (same).

6. I do not here cite and engage all of the voluminous literature, but much of it is addressed in detail in Andrew Koppelman, Defending the Sex Discrimination Argument for Lesbian and Gay Rights: A Reply to Edward Stein, 49 UCLA L. Rev. 519 (2002).

7. One objection has sometimes been raised that does not fall under any of these headings. Those who object to any claim for same-sex marriage sometimes ask whether gays' claim does not logically entail a right to polygamy. Whether it

does or not depends on what kind of claim is being made. As William Eskridge has observed, this objection cannot be made against the sex discrimination argument. "Denying a woman-woman couple a marriage license is discrimination because of sex, a quasi-suspect classification. Denying a man-woman-woman trio a marriage license is discrimination because of numerosity or marital status (if the first two are already married and want to add the third), neither being a suspect classification. . . ." Eskridge, Gaylaw at 281.

8. The only final appellate decision that fully adopts the argument and remains good law is Baehr v. Lewin, 852 P.2d 44 (Haw. 1993). Even in that case, the argument was initially only accepted by two out of five judges; a supplementary opinion after a change of personnel made it effectively a majority opinion. See *Baehr,* 852 P.2d at 74; Koppelman, Why Discrimination Against Lesbians and Gay Men Is Sex Discrimination at 204–5. The argument was accepted by a three-judge panel of an intermediate appellate court in Lawrence & Garner v. State of Texas, June 8, 2000, http://www.lambdalegal.org/cgi-bin/pages/documents/record?record=639 (reversed by *en banc* nine-judge court, 41 S.W.3d 349 (Tex. App. 2001)) (law banning same-sex sodomy), and by the Scottish Employment Appeal Tribunal in MacDonald v. Ministry of Defence, [2000] Industrial Relations Law Reports 748 (appeal heard by Scottish Court of Session, Inner House, in February 2001) (dismissal from military employment). In an unreported decision, an Arkansas trial court has invalidated the state's sex-specific sodomy law on both privacy and sex discrimination grounds. See Picado v. Jegley, Ark. Circuit Court, March 23, 2001, http://www.lambdalegal.org/sections/library/decisions/picadodecision.pdf. The decision will surely be appealed. The argument was intimated, but its implications were not fully articulated, in Nabozny v. Podlesny, 92 F.3d 446 (7th Cir. 1996), a case involving a state school's failure to protect an openly gay student from a campaign of violent harassment. The Court noted that the school tolerated the violence "because both the perpetrators and the victim were males," and found it "impossible to believe that a female lodging a similar complaint would have received the same response." Id. at 454–55. The only other case adopting it was decided by a lower state court and has since been excluded from the official reports. See Engel v. Worthington, 23 Cal. Rptr. 2d 329 (Ct. App. 1993) (holding that refusal of a photographer at a high school reunion to publish a photograph of a same-sex couple violated state civil rights act's prohibition of sex discrimination), *review denied and opinion withdrawn from publication by order of the court,* No. S036051, 1994 Cal. LEXIS 558 (Cal. Sup. Ct. Feb. 3, 1994). The argument was adopted by an Alaska trial court in Brause v. Bureau of Vital Statistics, 1998 WL 88743 (Alaska Super. 1998), but the decision was overruled later that year by an amendment to the state constitution. See Alaska Const., art. I, § 25. The argument was accepted by one judge of the Vermont Supreme Court, see Baker v. State, 744 A.2d 864, 904–7 (Vt. 1999) (Johnson, J., concurring in part and dissenting in part), but was rejected by the majority, see id. at 880 n.13 (majority opinion). One judge of the New Zealand Court of Appeal, that country's highest court, accepted the argument in Quilter v. Attorney-General, [1998] 1 NZLR 523, 535–36 (Thomas, J., dissenting), but none of the other four judges endorsed his argument. The United Nations Human Rights Committee declared that the prohibition of sex discrimination in the International Covenant on Civil and Political Rights includes sexual orientation, but it did not state its reasoning. Toonen v. Australia, para. 8.7, U.N. Doc. CCPR/C/50/D/488 (1992), reprinted in 1 Int'l Hum. Rts. Rep. 97, 105 (1994).

9. See Singer v. Hara, 55 P.2d 1187 (Wash. App. 1974); Smith v. Liberty Mut. Ins. Co., 395 F. Supp. 1098, 1099 n.2 (N.D. Ga. 1975), aff'd, 569 F.2d 325, 327 (5th Cir. 1978); DeSantis v. Pacific Tel. & Tel. Co., 608 F.2d 327, 331 (9th Cir. 1979); State v. Walsh, 713 S.W.2d 508, 510 (Mo. 1986); Phillips v. Wisconsin Personnel Comm'n, 482 N.W.2d 121, 127–28 (Wis. Ct. App. 1992); Dean v. District of Columbia, 653 A.2d 307, 363 n.2 (D.C. 1995) (Steadman, J., concurring); Baker v. State, 744 A.2d 864, 880 n.13 (Vt. 1999); X and Y v. UK, 5 E.H.R.R. 601 (1983); R. v. Ministry of Defence, ex parte Smith (1995), [1996] Q.B. 517; Smith v. Gardner Merchant, [1998] 3 All ER 852; Grant v. South-West Trains, E.C.J. Case C-249/96, ECR I-621, 1998 ECJ CELEX LEXIS 3673 (1998); see also Valdes v. Lumbermen's Mut. Cas. Co., 507 F. Supp. 10 (S.D. Fla. 1980) (discrimination against lesbians may constitute actionable "sex-plus" discrimination, but employer can rebut charge by showing that it discriminates equally against gay men).

10. See Pace v. Alabama, 106 U.S. (16 Otto) 583, 585 (1883), quoted in Koppelman, Why Discrimination Against Lesbians and Gay Men Is Sex Discrimination at 209–10.

11. 379 U.S. 184 (1964).

12. Id. at 188.

13. Id. at 192.

14. Id. at 192–93.

15. A complex, but fundamentally misconceived, objection to this claim has been raised by John Gardner. See John Gardner, On the Ground of Her Sex(uality), 18 Oxford J. Leg. Stud. 167, 180 (1998). I describe and answer it in The Miscegenation Analogy in Europe, or Lisa Grant meets Adolf Hitler, in Legal Recognition of Same-Sex Partnerships: A Study of National, European and International Law 623–33 (Robert Wintemute and Mads Andenæs eds., 2001).

16. See Ark. Stat. Ann. § 5-14-122; Kan. Stat. Ann. § 21-3505; Mo. Ann. Stat. § 566.090.1(3); Mont. Code Ann. §§ 45-2-101(20), 45-5-505; Nev. Rev. Stat. Ann. § 201.190; 1989 Tenn. Acts ch. 591; Tex. Penal Code Ann. § 21.06. See also Schochet v. State, 580 A.2d 176, 184 (Md. 1990) (holding that facially gender-neutral sodomy statute does not apply to "consensual, noncommercial, heterosexual activity between adults in the privacy of the home," and expressly distinguishing cases involving homosexual activity); Post v. State, 715 P.2d 1105, 1109 (Okla. Crim. App. 1986) (invalidating facially gender-neutral sodomy statute in case of different-sex sodomy, but noting that "We do not reach the question of homosexuality since the application of the statute to such conduct is not an issue in this case."). Cf. Jones v. Commonwealth, 80 Va. 538, 542 (1885): "To be a negro is not a crime; to marry a white woman is not a crime; but to be a negro, and being a negro, to marry a white woman is a felony; therefore, it is essential to the crime that the accused shall be a negro—unless he is a negro he is guilty of no offense." See generally Koppelman, Note, The Miscegenation Analogy at 149–51.

17. David Orgon Coolidge, Same-Sex Marriage? Baehr v. Miike and the Meaning of Marriage, 38 S. Tex. L. Rev. 1, 82 (1997).

18. See United States v. Virginia, 518 U.S. 515 (1996); Mississippi Univ. for Women v. Hogan, 458 U.S. 718 (1982).

19. Mississippi Univ. for Women v. Hogan, 458 U.S. 718, 724 (1982); see also United States v. Virginia, 518 U.S. 515, 531 (1996) (quoting same).

20. United States v. Virginia, 518 U.S. at 533.

21. Wardle, A Critical Analysis at 84, quoting Michael M. v. Superior Court, 450 U.S. 464, 481 (1981) (Stewart, J., concurring).

22. 453 U.S. 57 (1981).

23. Id. at 78.

24. Id. at 94 (Marshall, J., dissenting).

25. Laurence Tribe, American Constitutional Law § 16-28 at 1573 (2d ed. 1988).

26. 450 U.S. 464 (1981).

27. Id. at 473.

28. Id. at 476, quoting Orr v. Orr, 440 U.S. 268, 283 (1979).

29. Id. at 469.

30. It is, I hope, unnecessary to dwell on the inappropriateness of relying on generalizations that are not even statistically accurate, such as the canard that gay people make worse parents than heterosexuals do. Lynn Wardle has offered the most sustained argument for that claim, see Lynn D. Wardle, The Potential Impact of Homosexual Parenting on Children, 1997 U. Ill. L. Rev. 601, but it has been systematically refuted in Carlos Ball and Janice Farrell Pea, Warring with Wardle: Morality, Social Science, and Gay and Lesbian Parents, 1998 U. Ill. L. Rev. 253, who show Wardle's work to be pervaded by sexist and heterosexist assumptions that lead him to systematically misinterpret the evidence on which he relies.

31. See, e.g., Singer v. Hara, 522 P.2d 1187, 1195 (Wash. Ct. App. 1974).

32. Thus, Justice Bradley's notorious concurrence in Bradwell v. Illinois, 83 U.S. 130 (1873), defended the exclusion of women from the practice of law on the grounds that "[t]he natural and proper timidity and delicacy which belongs to the female sex evidently unfits it for many of the occupations of civil life," that "[t]he harmony, not to say identity, of interest and views which belong, or should belong, to the family institution is repugnant to the idea of a woman adopting a distinct and independent career from that of her husband," and that "[i]t is true that many women are unmarried and not affected by any of the duties, complications, and incapacities arising out of the married state, but these are exceptions to the general rule." Id. at 141; see also id. at 141–42 ("the rules of civil society must be adapted to the general constitution of things, and cannot be based upon exceptional cases."). In recent Supreme Court opinions, Bradley's concurrence has repeatedly been cited as an instance of precisely the type of sexist stereotyping that the fourteenth amendment is now understood to prohibit. See Mississippi Univ. for Women v. Hogan, 458 U.S. 718, 725 n.10 (1982); Dothard v. Rawlinson, 433 U.S. 321, 344 n.2 (1977) (Marshall, J., concurring in part and dissenting in part); Frontiero v. Richardson, 411 U.S. 677, 684–85 (1973) (plurality opinion).

33. United States v. Virginia, 518 U.S. at 533.

34. Id. at 550.

35. Craig M. Bradley, The Right Not to Endorse Gay Rights: A Reply to Sunstein, 70 Ind. L.J. 29, 30 n.9 (1994); Wardle, A Critical Analysis at 85. The response to these claims that follows is heavily indebted to conversations with Mary Anne Case, Joseph Miller, Jim Speta, and Kim Yuracko.

36. United States v. Virginia, 518 U.S. 515, 550 n.19 (1996). This requirement was agreed by the parties, and so the issue of its constitutionality was not before the Court, but the Court's easy acceptance of it is nonetheless notable.

37. The Court did say that such classifications were permissible in three narrow circumstances: "Sex classifications may be used to compensate women 'for particular economic disabilities [they have] suffered,' to 'promot[e] equal employment opportunity,' to advance full development of the talent and capacities of our Nation's people." Id. at 533, citations omitted. A footnote at the end of the quoted

sentence made it clear that the last category was intended to allow evidence that single-sex schools may help to dissipate traditional gender classifications. It is not clear how single-sex toilets could fit into any of these categories, but they all seem to allow some accommodation of women's needs, which single-sex toilets arguably do. It is, however, hard to imagine how any burden on homosexual conduct could be shoehorned into any of these categories.

38. To the extent that this is not the case, so that, for instance, lines outside women's rest rooms are burdensomely longer than those outside men's rest rooms, then heightened scrutiny will and should be harder to satisfy.

39. See Richard A. Wasserstrom, Racism, Sexism, and Preferential Treatment: An Approach to the Topics, 24 UCLA L. Rev. 523, 592-94 (1977).

40. As, in fact, the military's policy has. See Janet E. Halley, Don't: A Reader's Guide to the Military's Anti-Gay Policy (1999); Andrew Koppelman, Gaze in the Military: A Response to Professor Woodruff, 64 UMKC L. Rev. 179 (1995).

41. See Jay Alan Sekulow and John Tuskey, Sex and Sodomy and Apples and Oranges—Does the Constitution Require States to Grant a Right to Do the Impossible, 12 BYU J. Pub. L. 309 (1998); David Orgon Coolidge, Same-Sex Marriage? *Baehr v. Miike* and the Meaning of Marriage, 38 S. Tex. L. Rev. 1 (1997); John Finnis, The Good of Marriage and the Morality of Sexual Relations: Some Philosophical and Historical Observations, 42 Am. J. Juris. 97, 102 n.17 (1997).

42. 417 U.S. 484 (1974).

43. Id. at 496 n.20.

44. Id.

45. Id. at 496-97.

46. See Wardle, A Critical Analysis passim.

47. General Electric Co. v. Gilbert, 429 U.S. 125 (1976), which rejected claims that pregnancy discrimination violated Title VII of the Civil Rights Act of 1964, was overruled when Congress amended Title VII in 1978. See 92 Stat. 2076. For a lengthy list of law review articles condemning *Geduldig*, see Sylvia Law, Rethinking Sex and the Constitution, 132 U. Pa. L. Rev. 955, 983 n.107 (1984).

48. See Gerard V. Bradley and Robert P. George, Marriage and the Liberal Imagination, 84 Geo. L.J. 301, 307 (1995).

49. See Andrew Koppelman, Is Marriage Inherently Heterosexual?, 42 Am. J. Juris. 51, 92-95 (1997).

50. Lemon v. Kurtzman, 403 U.S. 602, 612 (1971).

51. United States v. Virginia, 518 U.S. at 533.

52. See, e.g., Opinion of the Justices, 530 A.2d 21, 24 (N.H. 1987); Macauley v. Massachusetts Comm'n Against Discrimination, 397 N.E.2d 670 (Mass. 1979).

53. Caroline J. Lindberg, *Lisa Grant v. South-West Trains:* The Limited Utility of Sex Discrimination Arguments in Securing Lesbian and Gay Rights, 12 Temp. Int'l & Comp. L.J. 403, 421 (1998); see also Danielle Kie Hart, Same-Sex Marriage Revisited: Taking a Critical Look at *Baehr v. Lewin,* 9 Geo. Mason U. Civ. Rts. J. 1, 44-45 (1998/1999). A similar argument was used by the Court of Appeal in England, rejecting the sex discrimination argument, in Smith v. Gardner Merchant, [1998] 3 All ER 852.

54. See Francisco Valdes, Queers, Sissies, Dykes, and Tomboys: Deconstructing the Conflation of "Sex," "Gender," and "Sexual Orientation" in Euro-American Law and Society, 83 Cal. L. Rev. 1, 119-207, 308-14 (1995). The loophole appears to operate in sex-asymmetrical ways. Courts are far more tolerant of gender deviance by women than by men. "When individuals diverge from the gender

expectations for their sex—when a woman displays masculine characteristics or a man feminine ones—discrimination against her is now treated as sex discrimination while his behavior is generally viewed as a marker for homosexual orientation and may not receive protection from discrimination." Mary Anne C. Case, Disaggregating Gender from Sex and Sexual Orientation: The Effeminate Man in the Law and Feminist Jurisprudence, 105 Yale L.J. 1, 2 (1995). Case observes that this tendency may have the misogynistic implication that "feminine qualities, which women are disproportionately likely to display, may legitimately be devalued although masculine qualities may not." Id. at 47. On the other hand, none of the cases cited by Valdes or Case involve a defendant's attempt to justify discrimination against a masculine woman by alleging her lesbianism. It remains to be seen whether such a defense will mesmerize courts as effectively as the corresponding charge has done in cases involving effeminate men.

55. Gardner, On the Ground of Her Sex(uality) at 183.

56. Mary Anne Case, Unpacking Package Deals: Separate Spheres Are Not the Answer, 75 Denv. U. L. Rev. 1305, 1315 (1998).

57. For similar reasons, I disagree with Danielle Kie Hart, who criticizes the Hawaii Supreme Court for neglecting to endorse a complex social description of hetero-patriarchy in its decision in Baehr v. Lewin. See Hart, Same-Sex Marriage Revisited passim.

58. I have previously emphasized that the formal argument is a complete legal argument that in no way depends on controversial sociological claims about the connection between heterosexism and sexism. See Why Discrimination Against Lesbians and Gay Men Is Sex Discrimination at 220.

59. 429 U.S. 190 (1976).

60. I will not put scare quotes around this word, but use it with the same caveats set forth by Peggy Pascoe:

> Many scholars avoid using the word *miscegenation,* which dates to the 1860s, means race mixing, and has, to twentieth-century minds, embarrassingly biological connotations; they speak of laws against "interracial" or "cross-cultural" relationships. Contemporaries usually referred to "anti-miscegenation" laws. Neither alternative seems satisfactory, since the first avoids naming the ugliness that was so much a part of the laws and the second implies that "miscegenation" was a distinct racial phenomenon rather than a categorization imposed on certain relationships. I retain the term *miscegenation* when speaking of the laws and court cases that relied on the concept, but not when speaking of people or particular relationships.

Peggy Pascoe, Miscegenation Law, Court Cases, and Ideologies of "Race" in Twentieth-Century America, 83 J. Am. Hist. 44, 48 n.11 (1996) italics in original).

61. 388 U.S. 1 (1967).

62. Id. at 7, 11. Arguments that rely on this passage in *Loving* include Wardle, A Critical Analysis at 77–78, and Richard F. Duncan, From *Loving* to *Romer:* Homosexual Marriage and Moral Discernment, 12 BYU J. Pub. L. 239, 241–42 (1998).

63. Perhaps one ought also to count Hunter v. Underwood, 471 U.S. 222 (1985), which invalidated a provision in the Alabama Constitution disenfranchising persons convicted of crimes involving moral turpitude because the law was motivated by desire to discriminate against blacks on account of race and had had a

racially discriminatory impact since its adoption. The Court quoted the opening address of the president of the constitutional convention, who stated that the convention's purpose was "to establish white supremacy in this State," and the Court noted that "this zeal for white supremacy ran rampant at the convention." Id. at 229. *Hunter* does not undertake the type of complex sociological inquiry that the *Loving* decision relies upon, because the *Hunter* Court could rely on a finite and known legislative history. In *Loving*, the only relationship to racism that was knowable was obvious from the context.

64. I have developed the claims made in this paragraph at much greater length in Why Discrimination Against Lesbians and Gay Men Is Sex Discrimination.

65. Christine M. Korsgaard, A Note on the Value of Gender-Identification, in Women, Culture, and Development: A Study of Human Capabilities 402–3 (Martha Nussbaum and Jonathan Glover eds., 1995).

66. See Toni M. Massaro, Gay Rights, Thick and Thin, 49 Stan. L. Rev. 45, 82 (1996); see also Roderick M. Hills, You Say You Want a Revolution? The Case Against Transformation of Culture Through Antidiscrimination Laws, 95 Mich. L. Rev. 1588, 1608–12 (1997).

67. Koppelman, Why Discrimination Against Lesbians and Gay Men Is Sex Discrimination at 255–57, footnotes omitted.

68. I have been educated in these matters by conversations with Iris Marion Young.

69. This kind of evidence is adduced at length in Koppelman, Why Discrimination Against Lesbians and Gay Men Is Sex Discrimination passim. The idea of function upon which I rely is described in detail in id. at 255–57 n.222.

70. Chief Justice Warren, writing for the Court, observed that the Supreme Court of Appeals of Virginia had held "that the State's legitimate purposes were 'to preserve the racial integrity of its citizens,' and to prevent 'the corruption of the blood,' 'a mongrel breed of citizens,' and 'the obliteration of racial pride,' obviously an endorsement of the doctrine of White Supremacy." Loving v. Virginia, 388 U.S. 1, 7 (1967), quoting Naim v. Naim, 87 S.E.2d 749, 756 (Va. 1955). On this evidence, he concluded that "the racial classifications must stand on their own justification, as measures designed to maintain White Supremacy," id. at 11, and that the purpose of the statute thus "violates the central meaning of the Equal Protection Clause." Id. at 12. Statements of this sort had, however, often been claimed to involve an evenhanded desire to preserve the integrity of all races—a purpose that the *Loving* court deemed impermissible, though it did not explain why. See id. at 11–12 n.11.

71. Valdes, Queers, Sissies at 253.

72. See Hills, You Say You Want a Revolution? at 1608–12; Wardle, A Critical Analysis at 83–88. Valdes acknowledges the distinction while insisting that it is not possible for law to remedy sex discrimination while leaving the sexual orientation loophole unclosed. See Valdes, Queers, Sissies at 204.

73. Charles H. Stember, Sexual Racism: The Emotional Barrier to an Integrated Society 206 (1976); quoted in Koppelman, Why Discrimination Against Lesbians and Gay Men Is Sex Discrimination at 232.

74. The proposition may be testable at particular sites within the culture, by intensively studying individuals or small groups.

75. Cheshire Calhoun, Separating Lesbian Theory from Feminist Theory, 104 Ethics 558, 562 (1994).

76. I endorse without reservation Calhoun's argument that "it is a mistake for feminists to assume that work to end gender subordination will have as much payoff for lesbians as it would for heterosexual women." Calhoun, Separating Lesbian Theory at 562.

77. George Dent is likewise correct that one can (and many do) defend heterosexual privilege without assuming that women ought to be subordinated. See George W. Dent Jr., The Defense of Traditional Marriage, 15 J.L. & Pol. 581, 608–14 (1999). Dent appears to think that the existence of such nonsexist motives proves that there is no link between heterosexism and sexism. Social causation is simply more complicated than this. If a sex-based classification could not be deemed sexist unless it were motivated by nothing but sexism, then few if any such classifications would be invalid.

78. Gardner, On the Ground of Her Sex(uality) at 183.

79. Eskridge, The Case for Same-Sex Marriage at 172; see also Eskridge, Gaylaw at 220 (similar comment).

80. Hart, Same-Sex Marriage Revisited at 11.

81. Wardle, A Critical Analysis at 39, 87.

82. John Finnis, The Rights and Wrongs of Abortion, in The Rights and Wrongs of Abortion 103 (Marshall Cohen et al. eds., 1974).

83. For a collection of horror stories from not very long ago, see Rhonda R. Rivera, Our Straight-Laced Judges: The Legal Position of Homosexual Persons in the United States, 30 Hastings L.J. 799 (1979).

84. This point was clarified in conversation with Douglas Baird and Eric Posner.

85. Abraham Lincoln, Speech on the Kansas-Nebraska Act at Peoria, Illinois, Oct. 16, 1854, in Abraham Lincoln: Speeches and Writings, 1832–58, at 316 (Don E. Fehrenbacher ed., 1989).

86. Here is Lincoln's statement in context:

> I think I would not hold one in slavery, at any rate; yet the point is not clear enough for me to denounce people upon. What next? Free them, and make them politically and socially, our equals? My own feelings will not admit of this; and if mine would, we well know that those of the great mass of white people will not. Whether this feeling accords with justice and sound judgment, is not the sole question, if indeed, it is any part of it. A universal feeling, whether well or ill-founded, can not be safely disregarded. We can not, then, make them equals.

Id. The passage invites comparison with Rep. Sonny Bono's very forthright speech on behalf of the Defense of Marriage Act:

> I think we go beyond the Constitution here. I think we go beyond all these brilliant interpretations here, and I think we have hit feelings, and we've hit what people can handle and what they can't handle, and it's that simple. And no matter how you justify what you say legally or whether it represents the Constitution, I think it breaks down to whether you're able to handle something or whether you're not able to handle something. I don't love my daughter any less because she's gay, and I don't dislike Barney [Frank, with whom Bono was debating] any more because he's gay. . . . I simply can't handle it yet, Barney. . . . I don't want to justify it because I can't. You just go as far as you can go. . . .

Transcript of Mark-Up Record of the Defense of Marriage Act, House Judiciary Committee, June 12, 1996, in Same-Sex Marriage, Pro and Con: A Reader 222–24 (Andrew Sullivan ed., 1997).

CHAPTER FOUR

1. See introduction, note 7. The most sophisticated defenders of this view, the new natural law theorists whom I consider at the conclusion of this chapter, would not put it this way. They would not regard "homosexuality" as a morally significant category, but rather would say that sex belongs in marriage and is (at a minimum) morally problematic outside of marriage. The category of marriage is central to their view, and the homosexual/heterosexual distinction is incidental, since their view also condemns heterosexual conduct when it occurs outside of marriage. Most Americans' condemnation of homosexual conduct has a different basis, however. One study found that 64.8 percent of respondents agreed with the statement that "same-gender sex is always wrong," while only 19.7 percent of the same sample thought that "premarital sex is always wrong." Robert T. Michael et al., Sex in America: A Definitive Survey 234 (1994). Evidently, most of those who condemn homosexual conduct do so on the basis of something other than its nonmarital character. (This study's numbers are already somewhat out of date, since attitudes are changing so quickly. More recent data indicate that exactly half of Americans think that "homosexuality should be considered an acceptable lifestyle." See Gallup News Service, Some Change Over Time in American Attitudes Towards Homosexuality, but Negativity Remains (March 1, 1999), available at http://www.gallup.com/poll/releases/pr990301b.asp.)

2. These developments are described in detail in the epilogue.

3. See generally Gregory M. Herek, Myths About Sexual Orientation: A Lawyer's Guide to Social Science Research, 1 L. & Sexuality 133 (1991).

4. Summa Theologiae, II-II Q. 154, 12, trans. Mortimer Downing, in Homosexuality and Ethics 46–47 (Edward Batchelor Jr. ed., 1980); for a similar view, see Bowers v. Hardwick, 478 U.S. 186, 197 (1986) (Burger, C.J., concurring) (quoting William Blackstone). I offer further evidence for this reading of Aquinas in Is Marriage Inherently Heterosexual?, 42 Am. J. Juris. 51, 70–77 (1997). John Finnis argues that I have misinterpreted Aquinas, and that this passage is concerned, "not with why unnatural vice is wrong . . . but only with the comparative gravity of types of act already assumed to be wrong." John M. Finnis, The Good of Marriage and the Morality of Sexual Relations: Some Philosophical and Historical Observations, 42 Am. J. Juris. 97, 113 (1997). It is beyond my competence to challenge Finnis's novel interpretation of Aquinas. (But see Jean Porter, Reason, Nature, and the End of Human Life: A Consideration of John Finnis's Aquinas, 80 J. Religion 476, 478–80 (2000).) I can note, however, that even if all his evidence is accepted, there is a considerable gap in Aquinas's argument as Finnis presents it. Finnis acknowledges that his own argument "goes beyond, while following the trajectory of Aquinas." Id. at 122 n.105. Finnis cites no passage in Aquinas that states that (as Finnis thinks) marriage is contrary to the good of integrity, nor does he offer any passage explaining Aquinas's claim that extramarital sex is contrary to the good of marriage. He argues that the admittedly "puzzling and unsatisfying" aspects of Aquinas's argument can be clarified by recognizing Aquinas's claims about "the necessity and goodness of the institution of marriage as the only acceptable framework for the generation and, ordinarily, the care of children." Id. at 126. But these claims do not entail anything about the value or

disvalue of nonmarital sex acts so long as those acts do not risk the production of unwanted children. Elsewhere, Finnis notes that "Aquinas' account would be much clarified by some sorting out of different ways in which one's choosing and acting are contrary to practical reasonableness, not least in relation to sex and marriage; but such a clarification seems not to have been offered until recently." John Finnis, Aquinas: Moral, Political, and Legal Theory 149–50 (1998), citing the work of Germain Grisez, whom I consider below; see also The Good of Marriage at 99, 113.

The upshot is that both Finnis and I are compelled to guess at what reasoning might have led Aquinas to the conclusion stated in the text. Even if Finnis is right, the (mis?)interpretation of Aquinas's argument I describe here is exceedingly common and needs to be addressed. But I remain uncertain whether he is right. Finnis interprets Aquinas as endorsing the same sexual ethic that Finnis propounds in his own writings, but Finnis does not endorse the proposition that consensual sodomy is worse than rape. That proposition seems hard to defend absent the religious interpretation that I propose.

5. David Hume, An Enquiry Concerning Human Understanding, in Enquiries Concerning Human Understanding and the Principles of Morals (L. A. Selby-Bigge ed., 3d ed. 1975), 142. See generally David Hume, Dialogues Concerning Natural Religion (Norman Kemp Smith ed., 1947).

6. There are, of course, also arguments against homosexual conduct that rely on religious revelation, but they are beyond the scope of this book. I assume here that the fact that conduct is condemned by religious dogma is not, without more, sufficient justification for a law penalizing that conduct.

7. Germain Grisez, The Way of the Lord Jesus, vol. 1: Christian Moral Principles 105 (1983). In fairness, it must be acknowledged that the defenders of homosexual conduct also sometimes fall prey to the naturalistic fallacy, arguing that, because homosexual sexual appetite is usually innate, it cannot be pathological. By this logic, Tay-Sachs disease and cystic fibrosis cannot be pathological, either.

8. Job 38:4, Douay version.

9. William N. Eskridge Jr., Gaylaw: Challenging the Apartheid of the Closet 144 (1999), quoting Reva Siegel, "The Rule of Love": Wife Beating as Prerogative and Privacy, 105 Yale L.J. 2117 (1996).

10. I will assume in this discussion that the only reason that we are interested in knowing whether homosexuality is a disease is because diseases are bad things that society has an interest in preventing. The question whether gays fit definitions of disease which bear no necessary relationship to human interests and concerns, such as "disease is any condition that prevents the organism from surviving and reproducing in a statistically typical way," seems beside the point. Interested readers should consult Michael Ruse, Homosexuality: A Philosophical Inquiry 203–35 (1988).

11. Jonathan Katz, Gay American History 132 (1976).

12. American Psychiatric Association, Diagnostic and Statistical Manual, Mental Disorders (DSM-I) 38 (1952), quoted in Ronald Bayer, Homosexuality and American Psychiatry: The Politics of Diagnosis 40 (1987).

13. These views are described in Bayer, Homosexuality and American Psychiatry at 28–38.

14. Id. at 41.

15. Evelyn Hooker, The Adjustment of the Male Overt Homosexual, 21 J. Projective Techniques 18 (1957). Hooker's work is discussed in Bayer, Homosexuality

and American Psychiatry at 49–53. See also Sylvia A. Law, Homosexuality and the Social Meaning of Gender, 1988 Wis. L. Rev. 187, 212–14, and citations therein.

16. See Letitia Anne Peplau, Lesbian and Gay Relationships, in Homosexuality: Research Implications for Public Policy (John C. Gonsiorek and James D. Weinrich eds., 1991); Andrew Koppelman, Three Arguments for Gay Rights, 95 Mich. L. Rev. 1636, 1664–66 (1997). More recent presentations of the disease view are reviewed and critiqued in David B. Cruz, Controlling Desires: Sexual Orientation Conversion and the Limits of Knowledge and Law, 72 S. Cal. L. Rev. 1297, 1311–33 (1999).

17. Norman Podhoretz, How the Gay-Rights Movement Won, Commentary, November 1996, at 40.

18. Alan P. Bell and Martin S. Weinberg, Homosexualities: A Study of Diversity Among Men and Women 308 (1978). Among the black males surveyed, 33 percent had had 500 or more partners, and 19 percent had 1,000 or more partners. Id. No aggregate figures, not broken down by race, were reported. These figures are cited to support conclusions much like Podhoretz's in George Dent, The Defense of Traditional Marriage, 15 J.L. & Pol. 581, 642 n.304 (1999), and Thomas E. Schmidt, Straight and Narrow? Compassion and Clarity in the Homosexuality Debate 105–6 (1995).

19. Bell and Weinberg's study "did not use probability samples and therefore could not be used to estimate population rates." Edward O. Laumann, John H. Gagnon, Robert T. Michael, and Stuart Michaels, The Social Organization of Sexuality: Sexual Practices in the United States 36 (1994). Rather, their respondents were recruited from "public advertising, bars, personal contacts, gay baths, organizations, mailing lists, and public places." Bell and Weinberg, Homosexualities at 30. There can be no confidence that persons recruited from such sources were representative even of San Francisco. Most studies of gay people have similar problems of sample selection.

20. Laumann et al., The Social Organization of Sexuality at 314, 316.

21. All these figures appear in a table in id. at 315.

22. Philip Blumstein and Pepper Schwartz, American Couples: Money, Work, Sex 272, 274 (1983).

23. Letitia Anne Peplau and Susan D. Cochran, A Relational Perspective on Homosexuality, in Homosexuality/Heterosexuality: Concepts of Sexual Orientation (David McWhirter, Stephanie Sanders, and June Machover Reinisch eds., 1990) 339.

24. Id. at 332.

25. See id. at 332–34, and sources cited.

26. See Lawrence A. Kurdek, Relationship Outcomes and Their Predictors: Longitudinal Evidence from Heterosexual Married, Gay Cohabiting, and Lesbian Cohabiting Couples, 60 J. Marriage & Fam. 553 (1998).

27. Grisez, whose work is the fountainhead of the new natural law theory, is a theologian as well as a philosopher; his most important work, The Way of the Lord Jesus, "is constructed primarily as a textbook in fundamental moral theology for students in Catholic seminaries." Grisez, The Way, vol. 1, at xxix. However, he also thinks that the principles of natural law are accessible to reason without recourse to revelation. Id. at 175. His argument about homosexuality appears to be capable of being detached from its theological context and sources, and offered as having independent philosophical value. It is so offered by Finnis, George, Bradley, and Lee. It is not clear to what extent Grisez himself approves of the detaching of these

reflections, nor is it certain that, were he to present the argument in its detached form, he would do so in the way that these other writers have.

28. Stephen Macedo, Homosexuality and the Conservative Mind, 84 Geo. L.J. 261, 276 (1995).

29. The following discussion is a compressed and revised version of Is Marriage Inherently Heterosexual?, 42 Am. J. Juris. 51 (1997).

30. A number of people have suggested to me in conversation that the NNL theorists are blind followers of Church teaching. I do not believe this and consider it unfair to the NNL theorists. Edward Vacek, who is a strong critic of NNL theory, acknowledges that the thought of Germain Grisez, the leader of the NNL theorists, has often preceded developments in papal teaching (notably with respect to contraception) and that Grisez has distanced himself from Church teachings with which he disagrees. Edward C. Vacek, Contraception Again—A Conclusion in Search of Convincing Arguments: One Proportionalist's [Mis?]understanding of a Text, in Natural Law and Moral Inquiry: Ethics, Metaphysics, and Politics in the Work of Germain Grisez (Robert P. George ed., 1998) 77 n.8.

31. NNL does not deny that such couples can achieve real goods, but claims that such goods are unrelated to their sexual activity and that all such couples would be better off if they repented and ceased to engage in any sexual activity with one another.

32. See introduction, note 7.

33. Germain Grisez, Joseph Boyle, and John Finnis, Practical Principles, Moral Truth, and Ultimate Ends, 32 Am. J. Juris. 99, 103 (1987).

34. Id. at 107–8.

35. Robert P. George, Recent Criticism of Natural Law Theory, 55 U. Chi. L. Rev. 1371, 1390–94 (1988).

36. Grisez et al., Practical Principles at 110.

37. John Finnis, Moral Absolutes: Tradition, Revision, and Truth 54–55 (1991). The incommensurability of basic goods, Finnis observes, "is compounded by a further incommensurability; for the basic human goods are not abstract entities but aspects of the *being* of persons each of whom is distinct from and no mere means to the well-being of any other person." John Finnis, Fundamentals of Ethics 89 (1983).

38. Finnis, Moral Absolutes at 54.

39. Id. at 87.

40. Grisez, The Way, vol. 1, at 124.

41. Patrick Lee and Robert P. George, What Sex Can Be: Self-Alienation, Illusion, or One-Flesh Union, 42 Am. J. Juris. 135, 139 (1997).

42. Germain Grisez, The Way of Lord Jesus, vol. 2: Living a Christian Life 556 (1993). The other NNL theorists have adopted the same view. See, e.g., John Finnis, Law, Morality, and "Sexual Orientation," 69 Notre Dame L. Rev. 1049, 1064–65 (1994).

43. Grisez, The Way, vol. 2, at 568 n.43. The arguments here rely heavily on religious authority, raising some doubt whether the same conclusion can be reached by reason alone.

44. Id. at 580.

45. See id. at 574–80. I cannot summarize here Grisez's argument for this proposition, which is in any case tangential to his principal claims about homosexuality.

46. Id. at 570.

47. Lee and George, What Sex Can Be at 144.

48. Id. at 146.

49. Id.

50. Grisez, The Way, vol. 2, at 633. Finnis (The Good of Marriage, 119) justly reproves me for ignoring this passage, which he concedes is "elliptical" and which I confess made no sense to me when I first read it. His response to my earlier critique has greatly clarified the argument.

51. Grisez, The Way, vol. 2, at 650.

52. Finnis, The Good of Marriage at 119.

53. Id. at 122.

54. Id. at 123. See also Finnis, Aquinas at 154.

55. Grisez, The Way, vol. 2, at 650–51.

56. See Martha C. Nussbaum, Platonic Love and Colorado Law: The Relevance of Ancient Greek Norms to Modern Sexual Controversies, 80 Va. L. Rev. 1515 (1994); Ronald R. Garet, Deposing Finnis, 4 S. Cal. Interdisc. L.J. 605, 628 (1995); Stephen Macedo, Homosexuality and the Conservative Mind, 84 Geo. L.J. 261 (1995); Paul J. Weithman, A Propos of Professor Perry: A Plea for Philosophy in Sexual Ethics, 9 Notre Dame J.L. Ethics & Pub. Pol'y 75, 87 (1995); Carlos A. Ball, Moral Foundations for a Discourse on Same-Sex Marriage: Looking Beyond Political Liberalism, 85 Geo. L.J. 1871, 1912–18 (1997); Nicholas Bamforth, Sexuality, Morals, and Justice: A Theory of Lesbian and Gay Rights Law 148–74 (1997); Michael J. Perry, Religion in Politics: Constitutional and Moral Perspectives 86 (1997); Paul Weithman, Natural Law, Morality, and Sexual Complementarity, in Sex, Preference, and Family: Essays on Law and Nature 228–29 (David M. Estlund and Martha C. Nussbaum eds., 1997); Mary Becker, Women, Morality, and Sexual Orientation, 8 UCLA Women's L.J. 165 (1998).

57. Finnis, Moral Absolutes at 86.

58. It is unclear whether NNL would deny that permanent sexual abstinence by married persons impairs their well-being.

59. See Charles Larmore, Patterns of Moral Complexity 134–39 (1987). The NNL theorists appear to be divided as to whether their moral theory makes sense without this theological underpinning. Finnis places great weight on faith in providence in Moral Absolutes at 9–20, and indicates that Aquinas cannot do without faith in his answer to this question, see Finnis, Aquinas at 315–19, but Grisez suggests that the theory makes sense even without such faith, and that "a generous and reasonable love of human goods will lead one to act in a way compatible with this ideal." See The Way, vol. 1, at 186.

60. Grisez, The Way, vol. 1, at 139.

61. Lee and George, What Sex Can Be at 155.

62. Id.

63. See Finnis, Fundamentals of Ethics at 37–42.

64. This point is argued well in Roger Scruton, Sexual Desire: A Moral Philosophy of the Erotic (1986). "In the case of sexual pleasure, the knowledge that it is an unwanted hand that touches me at once extinguishes my pleasure. The pleasure could not be taken as confirming the hitherto unacknowledged sexual virtues of some previously rejected person. Jacob did not, for example, discover attractions in Leah that he had previously overlooked: his pleasure in her was really pleasure in Rachel, whom he wrongly thought to be the recipient of his embraces (Genesis 29:25). . . ." Id. at 21–22. The intentionality of homosexual conduct does not appear to differ in any necessary way from that described here.

65. Lee and George, What Sex Can Be at 146.

66. See Shere Hite, The Hite Report: A Nationwide Study on Female Sexuality 139–48 (1976), and sources cited therein.

67. The use of the ideas of intention and side-effect in the ways that NNL suggests would produce strange results in this context. George and Bradley argue that an elderly married couple who no longer experience any pleasure in their acts of intercourse might still have reason occasionally to do so, in order to actualize their unity. Marriage and the Liberal Imagination at 310. In *their* case, it is clear that they are aiming precisely at that bodily unity, not at pleasure. But what then are we to think of a younger married couple who have intercourse when and only when it gives them pleasure to do so? For *this* couple—and I will bet that most married couples fit the description just given—pleasure is not an unintended (albeit welcome) side effect of their intercourse; it is precisely what they are aiming at. Is their intercourse morally licit or not?

The answer to this question is obscure. Finnis's sympathetic account of Aquinas's sexual ethics declares that "there is nothing wrong at all with our welcoming assent to such pleasure in the marital act, nor in our being motivated towards such an act by the prospect of giving and sharing in that delight as token of our marital commitment." Aquinas at 147; accord The Good of Marriage at 102. Moreover, it is appropriate for spouses to refrain from intercourse when there is some reason to abstain, "e.g. when either of them is disinclined or unwell." Id. at 109 n.47; Aquinas at 151 n.86. On the other hand, it is morally illicit for a spouse to desire intercourse "*simply* for the pleasure of it," Aquinas at 148, even if the desiring person is (for appropriate reasons) wholly unwilling to have sex with anyone other than the spouse. Id. at 149. What is morally wrong is an attitude in which "one is not interested in or concerned with anything about one's spouse other than what one would be concerned with in a prostitute or a gigolo." The Good of Marriage at 103. Some pretty fine line-drawing seems to be called for here. I do not know how one could tell whether the young married couple is engaging in sex for the sake of the marital act (in which case the act is innocent) or for the sake of pleasure (in which case it is evil). Probably the couple themselves will not know. It is possible that NNL has defined the good of marriage in so rigorous and exclusive a way that there are no, or almost no, clear instances of it in the world. The elderly married couple in Bradley and George's hypothetical struck me as an anomalous case when they first raised it, but it now appears that it is the only type of couple whose worthiness can be absolutely certain, either to others or to themselves.

68. Finnis, Moral Absolutes at 86.

69. Finnis, Law, Morality, and "Sexual Orientation" at 1066.

70. Id.

71. Lee and George, What Sex Can Be at 150.

72. Finnis, Law, Morality, and "Sexual Orientation" at 1066 n.46.

73. Finnis ignores this distinction when he writes that Stephen Macedo and I "absurdly think that *most of the time* . . . the couple's genitals are not reproductive organs—except in the sense that a dead man's *dead* heart 'is still a heart'!" The Good of Marriage at 127. The claim *would* be absurd as a taxonomic matter, but it is not absurd if it refers to the power of the organs. An organ either has reproductive power or it does not.

74. Id. at 129.

75. Id.

76. Id. at 131. Finnis, in his sympathetic account of Aquinas, argues that the cultural tendency that deems morally benign the sexual behaviors that he condemns "must, and manifestly does, damage and impede wider common goods, by wounding the marital commitment to children in their conception, bringing to birth, nurture, and education to the maturity, freedom, and virtue on which the political community depends." Aquinas at 152; see also The Good of Marriage at 125. This claim, about the bad consequences of rival views, depends on dubious claims about social causation, and seems less central to NNL's condemnation of homosexuality than the claims that I have examined in the text.

77. It is incautious of Finnis to seek Plato as an ally for his sexual ethics, since Plato understood this social variability and seriously entertained the possibility of abolishing marriage altogether and raising children communally. See Plato, The Republic, Book V.

78. Finnis knows that same-sex couples do raise children: "Of course, two, three, four, five, or any number of persons of the same sex can band together to raise a child or children. That may, in some circumstances, be a praiseworthy commitment. It has nothing to do with marriage." The Good of Marriage at 132. But he states (evidently reporting Aquinas's views with approval) that "the nurture without which no one survives cannot be more perceptively, lovingly, and fittingly provided than by a virtuous and capable mother and father." Aquinas at 243. He acknowledges that there is no evidence that children are harmed by being raised by same-sex couples, but indicates that such evidence is unnecessary, since such harm can be inferred from "reflective and morally-sensitive common sense." The Good of Marriage at 101 n.15. A good recent overview of the evidence (for those who do happen to be interested in it) is Judith Stacey and Timothy J. Biblarz, (How) Does the Sexual Orientation of Parents Matter?, 66 Am. Soc. Rev. 159 (2001).

79. See id. at 118. Finnis doubts that many such people exist, because surveys of their sexual experiences show that most gay people "are fully capable of heterosexual arousal and sex acts including marital intercourse." Id. at 124 n.108. Evidently the good of marriage as NNL understands it can be realized even if (as seems the case for many gay people) the person having sex is not sexually aroused by his opposite-sex spouse, is secretly fantasizing about having sex with a person of the same sex, and is able to perform sexually only by entertaining such a fantasy. In some ways, NNL's ideal of marriage seems impossibly stringent, see supra note 67, but on other ways it is remarkably undemanding.

80. One could, however, reject that claim while still accepting NNL's claim that nonmarital (or perhaps nonreproductive?) sex violates the good of integrity. If the pursuit of pleasure damages integrity, the integrity that is damaged is that of an actual person in the world, who is made worse off by that damage.

81. Robert P. George, Recent Criticism of Natural Law Theory, 55 U. Chi. L. Rev. 1371, 1392 (1988).

82. Id. at 1388–89.

83. See Lee and George, What Sex Can Be at 135; Gerard V. Bradley and Robert P. George, Marriage and the Liberal Imagination, 84 Geo. L. J. 301, 308 (1995). But see Koppelman, Is Marriage Inherently Heterosexual? at 62–63 n.55.

84. Lee and George, What Sex Can Be at 156.

85. Among sexually active Americans, 69 percent sometimes use contraception. Fifty-three percent of women and 47 percent of men always use contraception. Laumann et al., The Social Organization of Sexuality at 450. Sixty-three percent

of men and 43 percent of women sometimes masturbate. Seventy percent of men and 65 percent of women sometimes give or receive oral sex. Id. at 533–34. "It is estimated that about one-fifth of American women of reproductive age have had an abortion. Approximately 1.5 to 1.6 million abortions are performed in the United States annually. . . ." Barbara Hinkson Craig and David M. O'Brien, Abortion and American Politics 251 (1993). More than 80 percent of Americans believe that a woman should be able to have an abortion when she is pregnant as a result of a rape—a case in which, according to NNL, abortion is clearly impermissible. Id. at 253. The overwhelming majority of American Catholics believe that contraception is not morally wrong. See Andrew Greeley, Sex: The Catholic Experience 52, 55 (1994). Fewer Catholics (18 percent in 1988) than Protestants (34 percent the same year) think that premarital sex is always wrong. Andrew M. Greeley, The Catholic Myth: The Behavior and Beliefs of American Catholics 97 (1990).

86. Finnis, The Good of Marriage at 127.

87. Id. at 133.

88. Alasdair MacIntyre, After Virtue: A Study in Moral Theory 187 (2d ed. 1984).

89. Id. at 188.

90. Id. at 190.

91. Finnis, The Good of Marriage at 130. Finnis charges me with inconsistency for quoting with approval Sidney Callahan's claim that same-sex acts are valuable when engaged in "with a faithful partner," see id. at 129, but I nowhere say that this exhausts the set of valuable sex acts. My claim is merely that, to the extent that there are valuable monogamous relationships, it is morally irrelevant whether those relationships are homosexual or heterosexual.

92. MacIntyre, After Virtue at 191.

93. I thus plead guilty to Finnis's charge that I "have no principled moral case to offer against (prudent and moderate) promiscuity, indeed the getting of orgasmic sexual pleasure in whatever friendly touch or welcoming orifice (human or other-wise) one may opportunely find it in." The Good of Marriage at 133. If I condemn some sexual practices, my rejection will be too dependent on consequentialist judgments to be "principled" in the sense that Finnis intends.

CHAPTER FIVE

1. Developments in Vermont are described in detail in the epilogue.

2. Same-Sex Dutch Couples Gain Marriage and Adoption Rights, N.Y. Times, Dec. 20, 2000, at A8.

3. Kinney v. Commonwealth, 71 Va. (30 Gratt.) 858, 869, 32 Am. Rep. 690, 699 (1878).

4. The Vermont Civil Union statute states that it "does not bestow the status of civil marriage" on same-sex couples. An Act Relating to Civil Unions, H. 847, 1999 Gen. Assembly, Adjourned Sess. § 1(10) (Vt. 2000).

5. See Barbara J. Cox, Same-Sex Marriage and the Public Policy Exception in Choice-of-Law: Does It Really Exist?, 16 Quinnipiac L. Rev. 61 (1996).

6. The jurisdictions that have marriage evasion statutes are Arizona, Connecti-cut, the District of Columbia, Georgia, Illinois, Maine, Massachusetts, Mississippi, North Dakota, Vermont, Virginia, West Virginia, Wisconsin, and Wyoming. See Homer H. Clark Jr., The Law of Domestic Relations in the United States § 2.9, at 87 & n.52 (2d ed., student ed. 1988). On the other hand, in a number of other

states there are statutes validating all foreign marriages valid where celebrated, with no public policy exception. See id. at n.54.

7. The question whether (absent a clear statutory directive) any particular state has a strong public policy against same-sex marriage is beyond the scope of this chapter. See generally Barbara J. Cox, Same-Sex Marriage and Choice-of-Law: If We Marry in Hawaii, Are We Still Married When We Return Home?, 1994 Wis. L. Rev. 1033, 1066–82, 1100; Cox, Same-Sex Marriage and the Public Policy Exception.

8. For a list of thirty state statutes to this effect, see William N. Eskridge Jr., Gaylaw: Challenging the Apartheid of the Closet 362–71 (1999). The texts of twenty-four of these are collected in Andrew Koppelman, Same-Sex Marriage and Public Policy: The Miscegenation Precedents, 16 Quinnipiac L. Rev. 105, 134–51 (1996). Since Eskridge's book was published, California, Colorado, Nebraska, and West Virginia have enacted similar laws. See Cal. Fam. Code § 308.5 (2001); Colo. Rev. Stat. § 14-2-104 (2000); Neb. Const. art. 1, § 29 (2001); W. Va. Code § 48-1-18a (2000). Up-to-date lists of bills that have either passed or failed are available on the Web sites of the Lambda Legal Defense and Education Fund, http://www.lambdalegal.org, and the National Gay and Lesbian Task Force, http://www.ngltf.org. For the federal statute, see the Defense of Marriage Act, which is discussed at length in chapter 6.

9. This formulation appears in two executive orders that were issued in Alabama and Mississippi, both of which were subsequently superseded by statutes to the same effect. See Miss. Gov. Exec. Order No. 770 (Aug. 22, 1996) (declaring that same-sex marriage in another state "shall not be recognized as a valid marriage, shall produce no civil effects nor confer any of the benefits, burdens or obligations of marriage"); Ala. Gov. Exec. Order No. 24 (Aug. 29, 1996) (containing identical language, with the added observation that "God's law prohibits members of the same sex from having sexual relations with each other").

10. For purposes of this hypothetical, I am presuming that the child has been conceived by artificial insemination, and that State A's law would follow the rule, universal among all the states that have addressed the issue, that a child conceived by artificial insemination with the consent of the non-child-bearing spouse is to be treated as the legitimate child of both spouses, without any need for adoption or other proceedings. See Clark, Law of Domestic Relations, § 4.1, at 153–54. An obvious consequence of the universal rule is that, in order for the spouse of the biological mother to assert parental rights in a legal proceeding, he or she must plead the existence of the marriage.

11. John Rawls, Political Liberalism 4 (1993).

12. Many liberal political theorists have endorsed federalist solutions to intractable disagreements about how communities ought to govern themselves. See, e.g., Bruce A. Ackerman, Social Justice in the Liberal State 190–95 (1980); Robert Nozick, Anarchy, State, and Utopia 320–23 (1974). Michael McConnell has argued that an innovation as radical as same-sex marriage is particularly well suited to a federalist response:

> For those who believe in a prudent approach to social change, based on experience rather than abstract theorizing, the proposed statute [the Defense of Marriage Act] has the advantage of allowing this rather dramatic departure from past practice to be tested before it is imposed everywhere. While

powerful arguments have been made in support of same-sex marriage, the arguments on the other side are not inconsequential. Same-sex marriage has never been tried, and the effects on family, on children, on adoption, on divorce, on adultery rates, and on social mores in general are very difficult to predict. Whatever one's view on the merits of the social question, the advantages of using the "laboratories of democracy" provided by our decentralized, 50-state system, to test the results, before moving to a new national definition of marriage, should be apparent.

The Defense of Marriage Act: Hearing on S. 1740 Before the Senate Comm. on the Judiciary, 104th Cong. 57 (1996) (Letter from Michael McConnell, Professor, the University of Chicago Law School, to Sen. Orrin G. Hatch, July 10, 1996) [hereinafter McConnell Letter]. Incidentally, the claim that same-sex marriage "has never been tried" is historically inaccurate. See William N. Eskridge Jr., The Case for Same-Sex Marriage: From Sexual Liberty to Civilized Commitment 15–50 (1996); William N. Eskridge Jr., A History of Same-Sex Marriage, 79 Va. L. Rev. 1419 (1993) (both citing recognition of same-sex unions in ancient Egypt and Mesopotamia, classical Greece, pre-Christian Rome, and Native American, African, and Asian cultures). The modern tendency toward nonrecognition is hardly a consequence of the shared ancient wisdom of humankind. Militarily useful munitions were first developed in countries that interpreted their religious traditions as condemning homosexuality. They had no scruples about imposing their mores on the rest of the world. These are mere accidents of history, devoid of moral significance.

This position presupposes that no fundamental liberty or equality right is being violated by any region's laws. If such rights are being violated, a federalist solution is inappropriate. Diversity of this sort is intolerable. The most profound moral disagreement in American history for which a federalist solution was attempted was, of course, that concerning slavery.

13. Here I set aside the question of what marks the outer boundaries of "decent and tolerable" regimes. For a preliminary exploration of the question of what cultural forms are indecent and intolerable, see Andrew Koppelman, Antidiscrimination Law and Social Equality 57–76 (1996). This chapter stipulates that neither a law that permits same-sex marriage nor a law that forbids same-sex marriage is so morally odious that it ought not be permitted to exist.

14. See 1 Chester G. Vernier, American Family Laws § 44, at 204–9 (1931) (compiling statutes). For earlier surveys to the same effect, see Note, Intermarriage with Negroes: A Survey of State Statutes, 36 Yale L.J. 858 (1927); 1 F. J. Stimson, American Statute Law 667–69 (1886).

15. See Andrew Koppelman, Same-Sex Marriage, Choice of Law, and Public Policy, 76 Tex. L. Rev. 921, 992–1001 (1998).

16. See pp. 108–14 below.

17. This is the price of avoiding irrelevance. Imagine you were a lawyer in 1910 who believed that Plessy v. Ferguson, 163 U.S. 537 (1896), which held that the Fourteenth Amendment permits a law requiring racial segregation, was wrongly decided. In order to be able to converse with other lawyers about arguments that had any hope of being adopted in court, you would have to relax that assumption. Even if your view of the law were the one that ultimately would prevail, as in fact it did, that fact would be irrelevant to your immediate situation.

18. Russell J. Weintraub, Commentary on the Conflict of Laws 1.1, at 1 (3d ed. 1986).

19. Id. at 81.

20. Loucks v. Standard Oil Co., 120 N.E. 198, 202 (N.Y. 1918).

21. See Bradford Elec. Light Co. v. Clapper, 286 U.S. 145, 160 (1932), overruled in part by Crider v. Zurich Ins. Co., 380 U.S. 39 (1965).

22. Larry Kramer, Same-Sex Marriage, Conflict of Laws, and the Unconstitutional Public Policy Exception, 106 Yale L.J. 1965, 1974 (1997).

23. Friedrich K. Juenger, Choice of Law and Multistate Justice 79 (1993).

24. John K. Beach, Uniform Interstate Enforcement of Vested Rights, 27 Yale L.J. 656, 662 (1918).

25. Monrad G. Paulsen and Michael I. Sovern, "Public Policy" in the Conflict of Laws, 56 Colum. L. Rev. 969, 981 (1956).

26. Greenwood v. Curtis, 6 Mass. (6 Tyng) 358, 378 (1810).

27. See Holzer v. Deutsche Reichsbahn-Gesellschaft, 14 N.E.2d 798, 800 (N.Y. 1938) (per curiam).

28. Williams v. North Carolina, 317 U.S. 287, 298 (1942).

29. Douglas Laycock, Equal Citizens of Equal and Territorial States: The Constitutional Foundations of Choice of Law, 92 Colum. L. Rev. 249, 313 (1992).

30. See id. at 310–11.

31. Id. at 337.

32. Estin v. Estin, 334 U.S. 541, 553 (1948) (Jackson, J., dissenting).

33. William M. Richman and William L. Reynolds, Understanding Conflict of Laws § 116(a), at 362 (2d ed. 1993). For an illustrative survey of twentieth-century efforts to codify American law, see Koppelman, Same-Sex Marriage, Choice of Law, and Public Policy at 944–46.

34. There is also a handful of cases voiding marriages, valid where celebrated, on grounds of insanity. See, e.g., Beddow v. Beddow, 257 S.W.2d 45 (Ky. 1952); First Nat'l Bank v. North Dakota Workmen's Compensation Bureau, 68 N.W.2d 661 (N.D. 1955).

35. 2 Albert A. Ehrenzweig & Erik Jayme, Private International Law 166 (1973).

36. See State v. Brown, 23 N.E. 747, 750 (Ohio 1890).

37. Deborah M. Henson, Will Same-Sex Marriages Be Recognized in Sister States? Full Faith and Credit and Due Process Limitations on States' Choice of Law Regarding the Status and Incidents of Homosexual Marriages Following Hawaii's Baehr v. Lewin, 32 U. Louisville J. Fam. L. 551, 573 (1993–94).

38. See Loving v. Virginia, 388 U.S. 1 (1967).

39. See Peggy Pascoe, Miscegenation Law, Court Cases, and Ideologies of "Race" in Twentieth-Century America, 83 J. Am. Hist. 49 (1996).

40. See Andrew Koppelman, Why Discrimination Against Lesbians and Gay Men Is Sex Discrimination, 69 N.Y.U. L. Rev. 197, 220–34 (1994).

41. Peggy Pascoe, Race, Gender, and Intercultural Relations: The Case of Interracial Marriage, 12 Frontiers 5, 6 (1991).

42. Kinney v. Commonwealth, 71 Va. (30 Gratt.) 858, 869 (1878). Similar statements by leading legal authorities in the Southern courts are ubiquitous. See, e.g., Pace v. State, 69 Ala. 231, 232 (1881) ("Its result may be the amalgamation of the two races, producing a mongrel population and a degraded civilization, the prevention of which is dictated by a sound public policy affecting the highest interests of society and government."); Green v. State, 58 Ala. 190, 195 (1877) ("And surely

there can not be any tyranny or injustice in requiring both [races] alike, to form this union with those of their own race only, whom God hath joined together by indelible peculiarities, which declare that He has made the two races distinct."); State v. Gibson, 36 Ind. 389, 404 (1871) ("The natural law, which forbids their intermarriage and that amalgamation which leads to a corruption of races, is as clearly divine as that which imparted to them different natures.") (quoting West Chester & Philadelphia R.R. v. Miles, 55 Pa. 209, 213 (1867)); Pennegar v. State, 10 S.W. 305 (Tenn. 1889) (referring to "the very pronounced convictions of the people of this State as to the demoralization and debauchery involved in such alliances"); Naim v. Naim, 87 S.E.2d 749, 756 (Va. 1955) (arguing that the state's legitimate purposes in prohibiting miscegenation are "to preserve the racial integrity of its citizens" and to prevent "the corruption of the blood," "a mongrel breed of citizens," and "the obliteration of racial pride"); see also W. C. Rodgers, A Treatise on the Law of Domestic Relations 49 (1899) (describing the purpose of miscegenation laws as "to keep pure and unmixed the blood of the two races, to the end that the paramount excellence of the one may not be lowered by an admixture with the other").

43. See Williams v. State, 125 So. 690 (Ala. Ct. App. 1930).

44. 16 Mass. 157 (1819).

45. Id. at 160.

46. Id. at 160–61.

47. See Joseph Story, Commentaries on the Conflict of Laws 206–7 (Melville M. Bigelow ed., 8th ed. 1883).

48. See id. at 225–26 (discussing sources which argue that *Medway* was not based on sound principles of law).

49. See id. at 225 (citing an 1836 Massachusetts statute, which survives as Mass. Gen. Laws Ann. ch. 207, § 10 (West 1987)).

50. Story, Commentaries on the Conflict of Laws at 215.

51. See 1906 La. Acts 180.

52. Tex. Penal Code Ann. art. 326 (Vernon 1879) (emphasis added).

53. 76 N.C. 242 (1877).

54. Id. at 243.

55. Id. at 246.

56. Id.

57. Id. at 245.

58. Id. at 247.

59. Id.

60. Id. at 249 (Reade, J., dissenting).

61. Id. at 250.

62. Id.

63. 66 Tenn. (7 Baxter) 9, 10–11 (1872).

64. The reported *Bell* case does not state the parties' domicile, but the same court later described the case as one "where the parties were domiciled in Mississippi at the time of the marriage." Pennegar v. State, 10 S.W. 305, 307 (Tenn. 1889).

65. *Bell*, 66 Tenn. at 11.

66. 14 F. Cas. 602 (C.C.E.D. Va. 1879) (No. 7825).

67. Id. at 603.

68. Id.

69. Id. at 608.

70. Id. at 606.

71. Id.

72. Scott v. Epperson, 284 P. 19, 21 (Okla. 1930).

73. Id. at 21. These cases are likely to be highly relevant to the adjudication of the legal status of the small number of same-sex couples who were legally married before the recent wave of lawmaking. These couples typically were opposite-sex couples at the time of their marriage, and one of them thereafter underwent sexual reassignment surgery. Such reassignment surgery has never been held to render void or voidable a previously valid marriage, and the new statutes should not be construed to deprive these couples of their previously existing marital rights. See generally Phyllis Randolph Frye and Alyson Dodi Meiselman, Same-Sex Marriages Have Existed Legally in the United States for a Long Time Now, 64 Albany L. Rev. 1031 (2001). Nor, if any state legalizes same-sex marriage and then reverses this decision, should same-sex marriages celebrated in the interim be adversely affected by the reversal. The only precedent for such invalidation of which I am aware is the Nuremberg laws of Nazi Germany, which nullified some existing marriages between Aryans and Jews. See Richard Lawrence Miller, Nazi Justiz: Law of the Holocaust 149 (1995); Ingo Muller, Hitler's Justice: The Courts of the Third Reich 96 (1991); S. W. D. Rowson, Some Private International Law Problems Arising Out of European Racial Legislation, 1933–1945, 10 Modern L. Rev. 345, 346 (1947). Courts should not lightly presume that lawmakers intended to follow this example.

74. See Succession of Caballero v. Executor, 24 La. Ann. 573, 575 (1872); Whittington v. McCaskill, 61 So. 236, 237 (Fla. 1913); Miller v. Lucks, 36 So. 2d 140, 142 (Miss. 1948).

75. Willis L. M. Reese, Marriage in American Conflict of Laws, 26 Int'l & Comp. L.Q. 952, 955 (1977) (citing Restatement (Second) of Conflict of Laws § 283 cmt. j (1971)).

76. For this reason, I will make no reference to limitations on states' discretion based on due process or equal protection. The trouble is not that these arguments are unpersuasive, but that, if they are persuasive enough to rely upon in legal argument, the conflicts issue disappears.

77. Richman and Reynolds, Understanding Conflict of Laws § 116, at 362–63.

78. Me. Rev. Stat. Ann. tit. 19-A, § 701 (West 1964). Pertinent language from other statutes is collected in the article from which this chapter is adapted. See Koppelman, Same-Sex Marriage, Choice of Law, and Public Policy at 965–70 nn.160–77.

79. See supra note 14.

80. See p. 114 above.

81. See State v. Fenn, 92 P. 417, 419 (Wash. 1907) ("If the statute should be construed to avoid marriages contracted in other states by citizens of other states who never owed allegiance to our laws, it is the most drastic piece of legislation to be found on the statute books of any of our states. . . . [A] statute declaring marriages void, regardless of where contracted and regardless of the domicile of the parties, would be an anomaly and so far reaching in its consequences that a court would feel constrained to limit its operation, if any other construction were permissible.").

82. The clearest exception is Neb. Const. art. 1, § 29 (2001), which provides that "[t]he uniting of two persons of the same sex in a civil union, domestic partnership, or other similar same-sex relationship shall not be valid or recognized in Nebraska."

83. See p. 105 above.

84. See p. 106 above.

85. Mark P. Gergen, Equality and the Conflict of Laws, 73 Iowa L. Rev. 893, 902 (1988). Gergen goes on to note that neither order is required by the Constitution, and that no clear line can be maintained between them. See id. at 908–9.

86. 20 N.Y. 562 (1860).

87. "The fastest and most direct route at that time was to go first by boat from Virginia to New York and then by steamboat directly to New Orleans. Therewas no direct steamship service between any Virginia or Maryland port and the Gulf coast, and the overland route was difficult, costly, and time-consuming." Paul Finkelman, An Imperfect Union: Slavery, Federalism, and Comity 296 (1981). Further details about the *Lemmon* case may be found in id. at 296–310.

88. *Lemmon*, 20 N.Y. at 630 (Wright, J., concurring) (emphasis in original).

89. See Finkelman, An Imperfect Union at 313–38. Unpublished notes in the papers of Chief Justice Roger B. Taney indicate that when the war broke out, he may already have been preparing to write an opinion vindicating the "obligation of all to respect the institution of slavery." Id. at 338 n.76.

90. Restatement (Second) of Conflict of Laws § 283(2) (1971).

91. See Cox, Same-Sex Marriage at 1096.

92. Laycock, Equal Citizens at 323.

93. Eugene Scoles et al., Conflict of Laws § 13.3, at 434 (2001).

94. Id. § 13.2, at 433.

95. See pp. 108–14 above.

96. See State v. Bell, 66 Tenn. (7 Baxter) 9 (1872).

97. Herbert F. Goodrich, Public Policy in the Conflict of Laws, 36 W. Va. L.Q. 156, 266 (1930); see also Yarborough v. Yarborough, 290 U.S. 202, 218 n.10 (1933) (Stone, J., dissenting) (interpreting *Bell* as holding that "[w]ithout denying the validity of a marriage in another state, the privileges flowing from marriage may be subject to the local law").

98. Cox, Same-Sex Marriage at 1063 n.168; see id. at 1092–93.

99. See Henson, Will Same-Sex Marriages Be Recognized in Sister States? 564–66, 581–83.

100. Reese, Marriage in American Conflict of Laws at 954.

101. 1 All E.R. 342 (C.A. 1946).

102. Id. at 344.

103. Id.

104. Id. at 347.

105. Id.

106. Such a rule would not ignore the interests of this person's same-sex spouse, who would still be entitled to sue for divorce in the state of previous domicile and to secure a judgment for marital property or alimony. See Estin v. Estin, 334 U.S. 541 (1948). Perhaps it would also be possible for the spouse to make a property or contract claim in the deserting spouse's new domicile without pleading the existence of the marriage.

107. The constitutional right to marital privacy might bar a sodomy prosecution against a couple who were married pursuant to any state's laws. See Lovisi v. Slayton, 539 F.2d 349, 351 (4th Cir.) (en banc), cert. denied, 429 U.S. 977 (1976); Cotner v. Henry, 394 F.2d 873, 875 (7th Cir.), cert. denied, 393 U.S. 847 (1968);

Griswold v. Connecticut, 381 U.S. 479 (1965). To the extent that married couples as such have constitutional rights, the existence of the marriage is a federal constitutional question that states may not resolve by legislative fiat.

108. On the value of state action that seeks to alter the social status of unfairly stigmatized groups, see generally Koppelman, Antidiscrimination Law and Social Equality.

109. On Southern states' persistent refusal to give comity to free blacks, see Finkelman, An Imperfect Union at 109.

110. Does this symbolic harm to the institution of compulsory heterosexuality constitute a significant enough interest to outweigh, in all cases, the couples' interests in having their marriages recognized? All that can be said in response to this question is that similar symbolic stakes were involved in the polygamy, incest, and miscegenation cases, and in none of them did symbolism invariably outweigh the considerations supporting recognition of marriage. Perhaps the balance should be struck differently here, but an argument would have to be made why this case is different from the others.

CHAPTER SIX

1. The bill passed the House by a vote of 342 to 67 on July 12, 1996. 142 Cong. Rec. H7505–6. It passed the Senate by a vote of 85 to 14 on September 10, 1996. 142 Cong. Rec. S10129.

2. The president signed the bill at 12:50 A.M. on September 21, 1996. Peter Baker, President Quietly Signs Law Aimed at Gay Marriages, Washington Post, Sept. 22, 1996, at A21.

3. DOMA by its terms does not apply to Vermont civil unions, since such unions are not called "marriages" and are expressly distinguished from marriages by Vermont law. See chapter 5, note 4.

4. Pub. L. No. 104-199, 110 Stat. 2419, 1 U.S.C. § 7.

5. See 11 U.S.C. § 523(a)(5).

6. See 5 U.S.C. § 8901.

7. See 5 U.S.C. § 8701(d)(1)(A).

8. See 5 U.S.C. §§ 8101–8151.

9. See 17 U.S.C. § 304.

10. See 12 U.S.C. § 1701j-3(d).

11. See 29 U.S.C. § 2612(a)(1)(C).

12. See 42 U.S.C. §§ 401–433.

13. Since this chapter was first written, the General Accounting Office has compiled a much more extensive list of affected federal benefits. See U.S. General Accounting Office, Defense of Marriage Act (Jan. 31, 1997).

14. See Loving v. Virginia, 388 U.S. 1 (1967).

15. Romer v. Evans, 517 U.S. 620, 633 (1996).

16. Id.

17. Id. at 635.

18. See Wolfson and Michael F. Melcher, The Supreme Court's Decision in *Romer v. Evans* and Its Implications for the Defense of Marriage Act, 16 Quinnipiac L. Rev. 217, 219 (1996); Mark Strasser, Legally Wed: Same-Sex Marriage and the Constitution 139, 152 (1997); Scott Ruskay-Kidd, The Defense of Marriage Act and the Overextension of Congressional Authority, 97 Colum. L. Rev. 1435, 1444 (1997).

19. House Comm. on the Judiciary, Report to Accompany Defense of Marriage Act, H.R. Rep. No. 104-664 (hereinafter House Report), at 29 (1996), *reprinted in* 1996 U.S.C.C.A.N. 2905, 2934.

20. House Report at 29; Sen. Comm. on the Judiciary, Hearing on Defense of Marriage Act, 104th Cong., July 11, 1996 (S. Hrg. 104-533, Serial No. J-104-90, hereinafter Senate Hearing), at 27 (statement of Professor Lynn D. Wardle).

21. Wardle statement, in Senate Hearing at 27 n.4.

22. Prepared statement of Senator Don Nickles, one of the original sponsors of DOMA, in Senate Hearing at 18.

23. *Romer,* 517 U.S. at 635.

24. See Daniel R. Ortiz, The Myth of Intent in Equal Protection, 41 Stan. L. Rev. 1105 (1989).

25. 517 U.S. at 633.

26. Id., quoting Louisville Gas & Elec. Co. v. Coleman, 277 U.S. 32, 37–38 (1928).

27. Pub. L. No. 104-199, 110 Stat. 2419, 28 U.S.C. § 1738C.

28. U.S. Const art. IV, § 1.

29. It is unclear from the legislative history whether Congress intended to influence states' deliberations on whether to recognize same-sex marriages. The House Judiciary Committee report says repeatedly that each state will remain free to decide this policy issue for itself. See, e.g., House Report at 23–24. The report also indicates, however, that the legislation will provide "assistance" to those states that have no declared public policy against recognition of same-sex marriage. See id. at 10 n.33.

30. See Sun Oil v. Wortman, 486 U.S. 717, 729–30 n.3 (1988).

31. International Shoe Co. v. State of Washington, Office of Unemployment Compensation and Placement, 326 U.S. 310, 316 (1945) (quoting Milliken v. Meyer, 311 U.S. 457, 463 (1940)).

32. Phillips Petroleum Co. v. Shutts, 472 U.S. 797, 818 (1985) (quoting Allstate Ins. Co. v. Hague, 449 U.S. 302, 313 (1981)).

33. The *Phillips Petroleum* case cited above illustrates the difference between the two tests: jurisdiction over the parties was upheld, but the forum was not permitted to apply its law to some of the transactions at issue in the suit. It is also possible for application of a given state's law to be justified, but for that state to lack jurisdiction over all the parties. Hanson v. Denckla, 357 U.S. 235, 253–54 (1958).

34. Although I would love to take credit for devising these, both were suggested in conversation by Mark Gergen. I have filled in some details.

35. See Grace v. MacArthur, 170 F. Supp. 442 (E.D. Ark. 1959) (upholding service when made aboard a non-stop airline flight over, but not touching down within, the forum state). See also Ga. Code Ann. § 9-11-4(f) ("All process may be served anywhere within the territorial limits of the state"); Burnham v. Superior Court, 495 U.S. 604 (1990) (upholding constitutionality of jurisdiction over any party who is served with process while voluntarily present in forum state). "Generally . . . transient physical presence without more has been sufficient for judicial jurisdiction." Russell J. Weintraub, Commentary on the Conflict of Laws 150 (3d ed. 1986).

36. See Ga. Code Ann. § 19-3-3.1 (Supp. 1997).

37. This is a big "if." These are heuristic hypotheticals, and I do not mean to insult the courts of Georgia by implying that they would cooperate with these

disgusting stratagems. In other contexts, Georgia courts have not applied the public policy exception to ordinary choice of law principles when adjudicating transactions that occurred entirely outside of that state. See John Bernard Corr, Modern Choice of Law and Public Policy: The Emperor Has the Same Old Clothes, 39 U. Miami L. Rev. 647, 664–66 (1985) (collecting cases).

38. DOMA is a proviso to the full faith and credit statute, which provides generally that each state's "Acts, records and judicial proceedings . . . shall have the same full faith and credit in every court within the United States . . . as they have by law or usage in the courts of such State, Territory, or Possession from which they are taken." 28 U.S.C. § 1738(a). To the extent that DOMA is inapplicable, this statute remains in force.

39. See INS v. Cardoza-Fonseca, 480 U.S. 421, 452–53 (1987) (Scalia, J., concurring) ("Judges interpret laws rather than reconstruct legislators' intentions. Where the language of those laws is clear, we are not free to replace it with an unenacted legislative intent.").

40. Evan Wolfson, Winning and Keeping Equal Marriage Rights: What Will Follow Victory in Baehr v. Lewin?, Feb. 16, 1996, at 4, cited in House Report at 7–9, and in Wardle statement, Senate Hearing at 31–32. Wolfson's memo is reprinted in House Comm. on the Judiciary, Hearing on Defense of Marriage Act, 104th Cong., May 15, 1996 (Serial No. 69), at 14–31.

41. The Supreme Court has held that the Full Faith and Credit Clause requires the recognition of a sister-state money judgment even if the underlying cause of action could not have been brought in the forum. Baker v. General Motors, 522 U.S. 222, 232–33 (1998); Fauntleroy v. Lum, 210 U.S. 230 (1908).

42. Eugene F. Scoles and Peter F. Hay, Conflict of Laws 950 (2d ed. 1992).

43. See supra note 38.

44. Defense of Marriage Act, 28 U.S.C. § 1738C.

45. I assume, for purposes of this hypothetical, that the new forum has sufficiently significant contacts with the underlying transaction that its application of its own law does not violate due process. See text accompanying notes 30–39 supra.

46. This conclusion follows from the rule "that the last judgment—of several and possibly inconsistent judgments—is the one entitled to Full Faith and Credit in subsequent litigation even if such a last judgment itself erroneously failed to accord Full Faith and Credit to an earlier judgment." Eugene F. Scoles and Peter F. Hay, Conflict of Laws 950 (2d ed. 1992). The strategy described in the text is made possible by the interaction of that rule with DOMA, under which each of the later courts in the series would not misconstrue its obligations under the Full Faith and Credit Clause, but rather would recognize that Congress had authoritatively declared that the earlier judgments were not entitled (at least as a matter of supreme federal law) to full faith and credit.

47. The Romer Court, Janet Halley pertinently observes, did not attribute overt animosity to the voters of Colorado, but rather "a kind of blithe insouciance about the range of their action." Janet E. Halley, Romer v. Hardwick, 68 Colo. L. Rev. 429, 451 (1997).

48. Habib A. Balian, Note, 'Til Death Do Us Part: Granting Full Faith and Credit to Marital Status, 68 S. Cal. L. Rev. 397 (1995); Deborah M. Henson, Will Same-Sex Marriages Be Recognized in Sister States? Full Faith and Credit and Due Process Limitations on States' Choice of Law Regarding the Status and Incidents of

Homosexual Marriages Following Hawaii's *Baehr v. Lewin,* 32 U. Louisville J. Fam. L. 551, 588 (1993–94). This stratagem has been proposed before, as a way of thwarting the Southern states' nonrecognition of interracial marriages, but it does not appear ever to have been tried. See Albert A. Ehrenzweig, Miscegenation in the Conflict of Laws: Law and Reason Versus the Restatement Second, 45 Cornell L.Q. 659, 662 (1960).

49. House Report at 30.

50. Id.

51. See Restatement (Second) of Judgments § 76, cmts. a and c (1982).

52. Even if a court wanted to accept the invitation that DOMA proffers, it is doubtful whether Congress has the power to change the law in this way. The statute's questionable authority reinforces my conclusion that DOMA is a slapdash, ill-considered law that can only be explained by hostility toward a politically unpopular group. See Andrew Koppelman, Dumb and DOMA: Why the Defense of Marriage Act Is Unconstitutional, 83 Iowa L. Rev. 1, 18–24 (1997).

53. The House Judiciary Committee report included a section on *Romer,* but it was primarily devoted to denouncing the opinion rather than extracting a principle from it and showing that principle's inapplicability to DOMA. See House Report at 30–32.

54. *Romer,* 517 U.S. at 633.

55. Statement of Senator Orrin Hatch, Chairman, in Senate Hearing at 2.

56. *Romer,* 517 U.S. at 633.

57. See chapter 5.

58. *Romer,* 517 U.S. at 635.

59. Id.

60. Id. at 632.

61. On the usefulness of declaratory law that does not change underlying legal reality, see Sanford Levinson, How Many Times Has the Constitution Been Amended? (A) *26; (B) 26; (C) 27;* (D) 27: Accounting for Constitutional Change, in Responding to Imperfection: The Theory and Practice of Constitutional Amendment 13 (Sanford Levinson ed., 1995).

62. See Maurice J. Holland, The Modest Usefulness of DOMA Section 2, 32 Creighton L. Rev. 395 (1998).

63. See, e.g., United States v. Seeger, 380 U.S. 163 (1965); Welsh v. United States, 398 U.S. 333 (1970).

64. 481 U.S. 739 (1987).

65. *Romer,* 517 U.S. at 644 (Scalia, J., dissenting).

66. 481 U.S. at 745.

67. Michael C. Dorf, Facial Challenges to State and Federal Statutes, 46 Stan. L. Rev. 235, 239 (1994) (emphasis in original).

68. Richard F. Duncan, Wigstock and the Kulturkampf: Supreme Court Storytelling, the Culture War, and *Romer v. Evans,* 72 Notre Dame L. Rev. 345, 353 (1997), quoting Dorf, Facial Challenges at 279.

69. Romer v. Evans, U.S. Supreme Court Official Transcript, 1995 WL 605822 (U.S. Oral Arg. Oct. 10, 1995).

70. Ohio v. Akron Center for Reproductive Health, 497 U.S. 502, 514 (1990), quoted in Duncan, Wigstock at 354.

71. See chapter 1, which defends at greater length the interpretation of *Romer* offered here.

72. See Richard F. Duncan and Gary L. Young, Homosexual Rights and Citizen Initiatives: Is Constitutionalism Unconstitutional?, 9 Notre Dame J. Law, Ethics & Pub. Pol'y 93, 126–30 (1995).

73. *Romer*, 517 U.S. at 632.

74. Id. at 635.

75. Id.

76. Dorf, Facial Challenges at 279 n.192.

77. See Norman J. Singer, Sutherland's Statutory Construction § 44.04–44.08, at 501–22 (5th ed. 1993).

78. See pp. 127–30 above.

79. 508 U.S. 520 (1993).

80. John Hart Ely, Democracy and Distrust: A Theory of Judicial Review 243 n.11 (1980).

81. See id. at 250 n.64.

EPILOGUE

1. Baker v. State, 744 A.2d 864 (1999).

2. See H. 847, 1999 Gen. Assembly, Adjourned Sess. (Vt. 2000) (to be codified in scattered sections of Vt. Stat. Ann. tits. 4, 8, 14–15, 18, 32–33), available at http://www.leg.state.vt.us/docs/2000/bills/house/H-847.HTM.

3. *Baker*, 744 A.2d at 887.

4. Id. at 898 (Johnson, J., concurring in part and dissenting in part).

5. Id. at 888 (majority opinion).

6. Id.

7. Id. at 904 n.7 (Johnson, J., concurring in part and dissenting in part).

8. 323 U.S. 214 (1944).

9. Congress has lately declared, and the Court has since agreed, that "a grave injustice was done" by the forced relocation and internment, which "were carried out without adequate security reasons . . . and were motivated largely by racial prejudice, wartime hysteria, and a failure of political leadership." Pub. L. No. 100-383, § 2(a), 102 Stat. 903–4; quoted with approval in Adarand Constructors, Inc. v. Pena, 515 U.S. 200, 215 n.236 (1995). See generally Peter Irons, Justice at War: The Story of the Japanese American Internment Cases (1983); Morton Grodzins, Americans Betrayed: Politics and the Japanese Evacuation (1949). Reparations have been paid, and official apologies made, to the survivors of the internment.

10. See *Korematsu*, 323 U.S. at 244–48 (Jackson, J., dissenting).

11. *Baker*, 744 A.2d at 901 (Johnson, J., concurring in part and dissenting in part).

12. The classic presentation of this view of the judicial role is Robert G. McCloskey, The American Supreme Court (1960).

13. Prigg v. Pennsylvania, 41 U.S. (16 Pet.) 536 (1842). See Paul Finkelman, Sorting Out *Prigg v. Pennsylvania*, 24 Rutgers L.J. 605 (1993).

14. Dred Scott v. Sandford, 60 U.S. (19 How.) 393 (1857).

15. Bradwell v. Illinois, 83 U.S. (16 Wall.) 130 (1873); Minor v. Happersett, 88 U.S. (21 Wall.) 162 (1875).

16. Plessy v. Ferguson, 163 U.S. 537 (1896).

17. 410 U.S. 113 (1973).

18. 60 U.S. (19 How.) 393 (1857).

19. Richard A. Posner, Should There Be Homosexual Marriage? And If So, Who Should Decide?, 95 Mich. L. Rev. 1578, 1585 (1997).

20. Id..

21. The talismanic significance of the word "marriage," signifying the outer limit of what voters will concede to gays, suggests that the views of the new natural lawyers, considered in chapter 4, are not idiosyncratic. But see chapter 4, note 1.

22. Vt. Const. ch. 1, art. 7.

23. *Baker,* 744 A.2d at 876.

24. Id. at 873.

25. See id. at 889–97 (Dooley, J., concurring).

26. Adkins v. Children's Hospital, 261 U.S. 525 (1923); Lochner v. New York, 198 U.S. 45 (1905); Hammer v. Dagenhart, 247 U.S. 251 (1918).

27. *Baker,* 744 A.2d at 889.

28. Id. at 905 (Johnson, J., concurring in part and dissenting in part).

29. Id. at 880 n.13 (majority opinion).

30. Id. at 906 n.10 (Johnson, J., concurring in part and dissenting in part). The flaws in the argument that Amestoy made are described in greater detail in chapter 3.

31. The same is true of the indeterminate right to privacy, which I consider in detail in chapter 2.

32. 347 U.S. 483 (1954).

33. See Richard Kluger, Simple Justice 595 (1976).

34. Lucas A. Powe Jr., The Warren Court and American Politics 72 (2000).

35. Amestoy denied the analogy by noting that when the Supreme Court did strike down the laws against interracial marriage in 1967, "the high court had little difficulty in looking behind the superficial neutrality of Virginia's anti-miscegenation statute to hold that its real purpose was to maintain the pernicious doctrine of white supremacy." *Baker,* 744 A.2d at 880 n.13. Traditional marriage laws, on the other hand, were not adopted in order to discriminate against women. All this mischaracterizes the law and suppresses the relevant history. As I noted in chapter 3, the Supreme Court had already, in the 1964 case of *McLaughlin v. Florida,* 379 U.S. 184 (1964), invalidated a law against interracial cohabitation because the law was racially discriminatory. *McLaughlin* said nothing about white supremacy; the fact of racial classification was enough to invalidate the law. In order to hold that the marriage laws were "facially gender-neutral," Amestoy had to pretend that *McLaughlin* did not exist.

36. Baehr v. Miike, 994 P.2d 566 (Haw. 1999). The published version omits the opinion, which is available at http://www.state.hi.us/jud/20371.htm.

37. Pub. L. No. 104-199, 110 Stat. 2419, 1 U.S.C. § 7, 28 U.S.C. § 1738C.

38. See Haw. Const. art. I, § 23.

39. See Gerald N. Rosenberg, The Hollow Hope: Can Courts Bring About Social Change? (1991).

40. See John Gaventa, Power and Powerlessness: Quiescence and Rebellion in an Appalachian Valley 13–25 (1980).

41. Up-to-date lists of bills that have either passed or failed are available on the Web sites of the Lambda Legal Defense and Education Fund, http://www.lambdalegal.org, and the National Gay and Lesbian Task Force, http://www.ngltf.org.

42. See Christy Harvey, Optimism Outduels Pessimism, Wall St. J., Sept. 16, 1999, at A10.

43. See Rosenberg, The Hollow Hope at 107–56, 228–46.

44. I here follow Rosenberg's definition of significant social reform: "those specific social reforms that affect large groups of people such as blacks, or workers, or women, or partisans of a particular religious persuasion; in other words, *policy change with nationwide impact*." Id. at 4 (emphasis in original).

45. See Howard Schuman, Charlotte Steeh, Lawrence Bobo, and Maria Krysan, Racial Attitudes in America: Trends and Interpretations 106 (rev. ed. 1997).

46. See George H. Gallup, The Gallup Poll: Public Opinion, 1935–1971, vol. 3, at 2168 (1972).

47. All these figures are drawn from Schuman et al., Racial Attitudes at 106–7.

48. Associated Press, Interracial Marriage Ban to End, The Herald (Rock Hill, S.C.), Nov. 4, 1998, at 9A, 1998 WL 7646273; Opinion: Controversial Amendments, The Herald (Rock Hill, S.C.), Nov. 5, 1998, at 11A, 1998 WL 7646279.

49. See Derrick Bell, Race, Racism, and American Law § 1.9, at 64 (3d ed. 1992).

50. For a recent compilation of such claims, which have been made by Justice Ruth Bader Ginsburg, among others, see Neal Devins, Shaping Constitutional Values: Elected Government, the Supreme Court, and the Abortion Debate 1–4 (1996).

51. See Jennifer Gerarda Brown, Competitive Federalism and the Legislative Incentives to Recognize Same-Sex Marriage, 68 S. Cal. L. Rev. 745, 780–97 (1995).

52. Mississippi Univ. for Women v. Hogan, 458 U.S. 718, 724 (1982) (quoting Kirchberg v. Feenstra, 450 U.S. 455, 461 (1981)), quoted in United States v. Virginia, 518 U.S. 515, 531 (1996).

53. Alexander Bickel, The Least Dangerous Branch 174 (2d ed. 1986).

54. Id. at 69. The parallels between the prudential problem presented by interracial marriage and that presented by gay rights are thoughtfully elaborated in Marc Spindelman, Reorienting *Bowers v. Hardwick*, 79 N.C. L. Rev. 359 (2001).

INDEX

abortion: *Planned Parenthood of Southeastern Pennsylvania v. Casey,* 38; right of privacy and right to, 35, 38; right to bodily integrity and right to, 168n. 103; *Roe v. Wade,* 49, 144, 151; and women's right to be free from burden of motherhood, 52
Ackerman, Bruce, 39, 47, 48
Adkins v. Children's Hospital (1923), 196n. 26
adoption, gays prohibited from, 1
Alaska, 72, 142
Allied Stores v. Bowers (1959), 159n. 83
Allport, Gordon, 22
Allstate Ins. Co. v. Hague (1981), 192n. 32
Amar, Akhil, 28
Amendment 2 (Colorado). *See* Colorado Amendment 2
American Psychiatric Association, 76
Amestoy, Jeffrey, 141–42, 143, 145, 146–47, 148–49, 196n. 34
antidiscrimination laws, 1, 17–19

Baehr v. Lewin (Haw. 1993), 133, 162n. 145, 170n. 8, 174n. 57
Baehr v. Miike (Haw. 1999), 149–52
Baindail v. Baindail (C.A. 1946), 123
Baker, Lynn, 6
Baker v. General Motors (1998), 193n. 41
Baker v. State (Vt. 1999), 53, 141–42, 145–49, 171n. 9
Balkin, Jack, 67, 69
Ball, Carlos, 172n. 30
basic goods, 80–81; dialectical defense required for, 89–90; versus human well-being, 84–85; as incommensurable, 81, 180n. 37; integrity as, 81–82; marriage as, 82–83, 86–93
Beach, John K., 104
Beddow v. Beddow (Ky. 1952), 187n. 34
Bell, Alan P., 77, 179nn. 18, 19

ben-Shalom v. Marsh (7th Cir. 1989), 162n. 145
Berger, Peter, 166n. 84
Bickel, Alexander, 11, 153–54
Bill of Rights, 36
Black, Charles, 20, 29
Black, Hugo, 36, 143
Blackmun, Harry, 44–45, 48, 51
blacks: Americans' feelings toward, 22; gays compared with, 2; Lincoln on Americans' feelings against, 71, 176n. 85; *NAACP v. Alabama,* 37. See also *Brown v. Board of Education;* race; slavery
blanket nonrecognition: of interracial marriage, 100; of polygamous marriages, 123; of same-sex marriage, 95, 97–98, 100, 102, 117
Blumstein, Philip, 78
Boddie v. Connecticut (1971), 163n. 4
Bolling v. Sharpe (1954), 40–41
Bono, Sonny, 176n. 85
Bork, Robert, 38–42, 44, 164n. 37
Bowers v. Hardwick (1986), 35–52; assessment of, 49–52; and authoritarian tendency in privacy cases, 50; Blackmun's position, 44–45, 48, 51; Burger's position, 177n. 4; discrimination against gays reinforced by, 6, 7, 17, 35; homosexuality not an issue in, 51; reconciling *Romer v. Evans* with, 29–32; on state's legitimate interest in prohibiting homosexual conduct, 6, 7, 17, 31, 35; White's position, 48, 51
Boy Scouts of America v. Dale (2000), 28–29, 161n. 140
Bradford Elec. Light Co. v. Clapper (1932), 187n. 21
Bradley, Gerard V., 43, 80, 166n. 66, 182n. 67
Bradley, Joseph P., 172n. 32